# United We Fall

*Ending America's Love Affair
with the Political Center*

Phil Neisser

 PRAEGER

Westport, Connecticut
London

**Library of Congress Cataloging-in-Publication Data**

Neisser, Philip T., 1957–
    United we fall : ending America's love affair with the political center / Phil Neisser.
        p.   cm.
    Includes bibliographical references and index.
    ISBN: 978–0–313–35885–2 (alk. paper)
    1. Consensus (Social sciences)—United States.   2. Political participation—United
States.   3. Communication in politics—United States.   I. Title.
    JC328.2.N46   2008
    324.0973—dc22          2008016467

British Library Cataloguing in Publication Data is available.

Library of Congress Catalog Card Number: 2008016467
ISBN: 978–0–313–35885–2

First published in 2008

Praeger Publishers, 88 Post Road West, Westport, CT 06881
An imprint of Greenwood Publishing Group, Inc.
www.praeger.com

Printed in the United States of America

The paper used in this book complies with the
Permanent Paper Standard issued by the National
Information Standards Organization (Z39.48–1984).

10 9 8 7 6 5 4 3 2 1

# Contents

# Preface

On a Sunday in June 2007, I came across an essay in *The New York Times* called "Home Alone" by Erica Goode. The subject was a just-released study reporting lower levels of social trust and public interaction in cities and towns marked by higher levels of ethnic and racial diversity. Residents in relatively diverse locales were found to have, on average, "less confidence in local government and less confidence in their own ability to exert political influence," and they also "rated their happiness as generally lower."[1] Apparently, some people respond to new diversity by becoming more careful and less trusting and by keeping within the lines drawn by home, car, job, and television.

Robert Putnam, the author of the study, was surprised by these results, as were other scholars. Why, they wondered, would discomfort in the face of new diversity "translate into social isolation and a weakening of social bonds"?[2] One hypothesis is that humans experience stress and fatigue when around others they consider "different," and this leads them to back away. Another possibility is that the cause of the isolation is some yet-to-be-guessed-at aspect of places that happen also to be more diverse, rather than the diversity itself. Putnam wants to know more, to resolve the puzzle, in part because he's not ready to give up on integration and diversity. And in this regard he has hope, despite the troubling news, because "what people perceive as unfamiliar . . . can and does change over time," because the "others" who cause discomfort today, may not do so tomorrow.[3] Citing this observation, Goode manages to end her essay on a positive note.

Like Putnam, I have not lost hope when it comes to the dream of vibrant, diverse communities, but I nonetheless found Goode's essay a little exasperating, especially its expressions of surprise and mystery. "Of course people withdraw in such situations," I said to no one in particular. I had this reaction because earlier on that very same morning I had been trying (unsuccessfully) to make progress writing about the same subject. More exactly, I was trying to make sense of the fact that, while American culture lauds free speech and free choice, it does not likewise celebrate disagreement, at least not if one understands the latter as a process, as an activity, rather than simply as a state of affairs. Second and as a result, most Americans have little or no practice engaging across borders, be they of economic class, geographical location, political philosophy, race, or age. Armed with this perspective, it seems to me obvious that many Americans might find new levels of diversity intimidating.

To expect otherwise is to expect people to have internalized an ethic of generosity towards the new and apparently different. This is both desirable and possible, but it doesn't happen automatically. The German philosopher Hegel was right to claim that all human points of view have reason to them, even the worst and most harmful, but it's hard to grasp this at a gut level unless one has engaged in some sustained conversation with people who seemed to be impossibly different. The mere presence of many sorts of people shopping in the same store, or driving to work on the same road, will not by itself create vibrant, cross-border communities. If that's the goal, then encounters of depth—which sometimes include clashes of perspective and understanding—need to be common practice.

So it was that, upon reflection, I became less than pleased by Goode's optimistic conclusion. More needs to be said to convince doubters that increased integration is a viable goal. One such doubter is David Brooks, who published an opinion piece on the subject in *The New York Times* just a few weeks after Goode's essay appeared.[4] Bemoaning the "waning dream of integration," Brooks concludes that maybe it's just "not in the cards." After all, he says, "dozens of social science experiments have made clear [that] if you separate people into different groups—they will quickly begin discriminating against others they deem unlike themselves... [because] what they really want to do is live... with people like themselves."

Personally, I don't believe Brooks is right about what people "really want," and I find support in the fact that there are (as reported in the chapters ahead) also plenty of "social science experiments" that show that something as simple as a good, honest conversation, without agreement at the end, can undermine demonization and reduce discrimination. Such conversations can, in fact, make people *want* to be around people who are *not* like themselves. Putnam is right, in other words, that the content of the categories of insider and outsider, along with the salience of labels ("black," "white," "Muslim," "American," and the like), can and does change over time. On the other hand (and here's where Brooks has a point), they do not change automatically, and they do not always change for the better. To improve the world or even just to keep it from becoming a lot worse, "we the people" need to step beyond home, car, job, and television and make disagreement a bigger part of our lives. This doesn't mean one must feel affection for one's opponents, and it doesn't mean becoming relativist or otherwise shying away from principle. What it does mean is finding ways to peacefully learn about others, seeking out those who seem most distant or most wrong, in order to make an effort to see their humanity and to share one's own.

All in all, Erica Goode's essay was a big help to me. After I read it, I began writing more clearly. My faith in my project was rekindled. People need to speak out in favor of disagreement, I told myself. More exactly, people need to defend disagreement both as intrinsically valuable and as worth the time and trouble it sometimes requires. So I pushed ahead, and this book is the result.

Chapters 1 through 3 describe today's impoverished disagreement landscape and explain how the United States made its way, over time, into that condition. Chapters 4 and 5 address three key obstacles to better, more productive forms of disagreement: the excessive caution of the mass media, conspiracy thinking about power, and the myth that unity makes a nation stronger. Chapter 6 situates the idea of disagreement democracy among various theories of "deliberative democracy" offered elsewhere and then responds to critics, both real and conceivable. Chapter 7 argues in favor of a different brand of "multiculturalism," one not defined by tolerance so much as by impassioned, civil, cross-border engagement, where people generously consider the views of their fiercest opponents. Chapter 8 addresses disagreement practice by providing guiding principles and representative examples and also by making the case for further applications. Specifically, it argues that a pro-disagreement ethic needs to be incorporated into civic education programming at the college level, used to transform discussions about race-related issues, and brought into the ways people think about and combat terrorism.

Chapter 9, the conclusion, takes note of a dilemma. How can people combine community with the freedom to make up their own minds? The pressures of conformity are tremendous. It's not easy to live interdependently with others and still have thoughts that are truly one's own. It's not easy to walk the line between generosity of spirit, on one side, and political and ethical conviction, on the other. Doing so requires epistemological humility, also known as a self-questioning spirit. To put it another way, doing so calls for a pro-disagreement sensibility, and that means having faith in what one stands for while also having faith in the higher truth that one's opponents always have something worthwhile to say. The good news is that such dual faith is possible. The challenging news is that it will suffer or even wither without the support of widespread disagreement practices. People can be both interdependent and free but only if they argue with each other, listen to each other, and celebrate that process.

# Acknowledgments

My commitment to disagreement has many roots, some of them personal. When I was a teenager, maybe fourteen or fifteen, I wrote to President Nixon, criticizing the war in Vietnam. In response I got a letter thanking me for my support, an embossed booklet about the presidency, and an invitation to join the Nixon fan club. That didn't seem to me like the right way to respond to my remarks. Then there was my teenage friend Warren. His family argued a lot and at high volume, and at first this made me uncomfortable. Eventually, however, I figured out that they were conversing, not fighting, and they loved it. Argument, I realized, can be okay. I learned a similar lesson on the basketball courts down the street. Some kids (mostly white, mostly struggling, mostly middle-class) were uncomfortable or threatened when others (mostly Hispanic, mostly from poorer families) talked trash or otherwise argued loudly. At first I was one of the white kids who didn't get it. As at Warren's house, I felt threatened by the volume and—at a less conscious level—by the mysteries of class and race. But I soon came to see style and fun where I had seen danger, and I even grew fond of border crossing.

My mother's rules for her four kids were also a good influence. She was dedicated to politeness, not for its own sake but because other people's feelings mattered. At our dinner table the rules were "no politics" and "talk about something of general interest." In part this meant "don't take up the entire meal talking about sports with your brother," but it also sent the message that paying attention to others goes a long way. This wasn't always easy at my house for reasons I won't go into, but by the time I was in high school I had another home of sorts where I could practice being with others—my friend Adam's house. His family exposed me to a world of ideas and good influences and to Buddhism, jazz, philosophy, and more.

And, like my mother, they believed in discussion and learning. They carried me across many borders.

I also came to disagreement by reading. Works by Nietzsche turned me toward the idea of a community as a place of multiplicity. Professor David Brown gave me a new appreciation of critical thinking when I was an undergraduate at State University of New York (SUNY) at Potsdam. In a class at Georgetown in 1979 a pair of graduate students made a presentation about gender that pointed me in a similar direction. James V. Schall, a Jesuit priest and professor also at Georgetown University, was calm and welcoming in the face of disagreement, and I took note. And William E. Connolly, while professing at University of Massachusetts Amherst, helped me move towards the acceptance of human uncertainty, even regarding basic questions of life and truth.

I also am in debt to SUNY Potsdam, where I teach in the Department of Politics. My immediate colleagues, like the college in general, have provided me with a supportive community marked by dedication, attention to students, and intellectual ferment. I especially owe thanks to Jackie Rush, secretary and office manager extraordinaire, and Richard Del Guidice, who helped teach me to write thirty years ago and who still, in his "retirement," gives his all both for students and the college. This book would have been much harder without each of them. Two students helped as well: Natalia Detko did some reformatting when time was running out, and Danny Smith read two chapters and made several helpful comments.

Scholars and friends elsewhere have likewise lent me a hand. Sandy Hinchman, Ethan J. Leib, and John Hart each gave me a needed thumbs-up at a key time. Peter Muhlberger provided detailed feedback on several chapters. John Kenneth White deepened my understanding of American politics and encouraged me. Four health practitioners helped me gather strength and energy: Jeff Chen, Dorine Forand, John Liscio, and Shelby Connelly. And I am deeply in debt to three intellectual partners and friends of many years standing, each of them dedicated to thinking and understanding and each sharing whatever they have with others. One of them is Peter Silsbee, a novelist and fellow musician who reads history and political theory while on the way to his public opinion job, feeds me one must-read book after another, and sometimes talks politics with me for hours at a time. Many ideas in this book grew from those conversations. Another is Sandy Schram, who supported me in my undergraduate days as a teacher and later became a coauthor and scholarly collaborator. Sandy opened doors for me, and today he's both a good friend and a political and intellectual inspiration.

Then there's Eudora Watson, with whom I am lucky to share home. Every day Eudora—an intense and challenging conversationalist, a beacon of good character, and a pleasure to be around—is an inspiration. As it happens, she is also a writer and has painstakingly edited every one of these pages.

I have also benefited from the editorial advice and support of two editors: Hilary Claggett, who now works at Potomac press and believed in my project from the start, and Robert Hutchinson, who works at Praeger. Together, they helped make *United We Fall* a reality.

Finally, I offer thanks to fellow musicians Dan Caldwell and Doug Schatz. As a drummer, I'm in awe of their chords and melodies. More to the point, I'm in their debt for the spiritual sustenance they provided while I was writing this book. Working with Doug and Dan is easy; they're a veritable breath of fresh air, even when we disagree (which is rare).

# CHAPTER 1

# Disagreement Today

How is it possible for there to exist over time a just and stable society of free and equal citizens, who remain profoundly divided by reasonable religious, philosophical, and moral doctrines?[1]

—John Rawls

In November 2003, on a street in Boston, a group of assembled spectators were witness to a mix of tradition and change. The occasion was the annual Veterans Day Parade. As in years past, a host of representatives from local military organizations marched by in proper fashion. On this occasion, however, they were followed by a scattered group of fifty or so members of the local Veterans for Peace chapter. They hoisted a banner saying, "Honor Veterans, Abolish War," and they chanted in critique of U.S. intervention in Iraq. One newspaper reported "quiet applause from many people lining the streets" and also noted that "while every other entry was announced as it passed the review stand, the loudspeaker was silent as the protestors passed by."[2]

Probably many of the spectators were unsure about how to respond. On the one hand, criticism of the nation's foreign policy was on display right in the middle of a public celebration of a national holiday; on the other hand, there was no official recognition of its presence. Was applause appropriate? It's hard to say. The silence from the review stand may have been the result of similar uncertainty on the part of the Parade organizers. How does one celebrate the contributions of veterans when some of them want to introduce a discordant, less-than-celebratory note? What is patriotism exactly, and are the veterans for peace patriots? Does one honor them on Veterans Day, and if so how? It seems that in Boston an uneasy compromise was forged. People decided to agree to disagree, even about something as absolute as war and peace, but they also agreed not to talk about it. Radical disagreement was permitted to enter public space but only as a fact silently on display, not as engagement, with each side listening to and acknowledging the other.

Consider another story. In February 2003, a U.S. attack on Iraq seemed imminent, and members of Alternatives to War (ATW)—a group to which I belonged at the time—met each week across from the post office in Canton, New York, in order to hold up signs or otherwise stand up against the looming military action. On that particular cloudy and cold Friday evening in Canton, there was a surprise: a Support Our Troops group also showed up, with signs and flags, to rally on the opposite corner. A couple of ATW stalwarts made a personal decision to cross the street and initiate conversation. They were polite, asking if anyone would like to talk, and they were just as politely rebuffed. Only one person responded, saying, "We don't want to talk to you; I didn't come here to talk to anyone."

I found this reaction understandable. The street crossers were, after all, transgressing an accepted boundary; they were challenging the common idea of protest as people making statements, and leaving it at that. Also, some might have thought it pointless to talk to the other side, not knowing what good would come of it and knowing that it could cause trouble. I myself was tempted to join the would-be talkers—for I knew they had good points to make—but I hesitated for long enough to miss my chance. I didn't want conflict; I didn't want to violate unspoken norms of civility, and I didn't want to be rejected, so my feet didn't move fast enough.

Looking back at that day, both at the brief cross-border exchange and at the entire event, it seems impressively civil. True, a few people did yell something negative-sounding from their cars as they drove by, but most who responded did so with a honk or a wave. No one was assaulted; nothing was thrown at anyone, and all in all everyone was quite polite. Indeed, most people paid no attention to what was going on—an attitude that was more or less mirrored by the minimal coverage the press afforded the weekly protests. (Though they did make the local news on that occasion, I think because there were two groups rather than one.)

The degree and style of the civility on display in Canton and Boston was, when looked at from a historical perspective, a tremendous achievement. Humanity could, however, do better still. Clearly protests now function for some as nothing more than entertaining displays, and for others they simply go unnoticed. And, generally speaking, people go to great lengths to keep disagreement at a safe distance.

To get personal one more time, I think of my relationship with my former in-laws. I'm no longer married to their daughter, but still friends. This is because we like each other, but another reason is that we (my in-laws and I) have always done well at avoiding certain topics. When politics comes up in conversation we don't exactly run away screaming, but we know better than to stick with it for long. I'm a college professor, from the city, and left-leaning (on most issues); they're small town locals, right-leaning, and working in the "real world." So there's a certain amount of being careful. None of us wants to feel judged or looked down upon, and we certainly don't want conflict. It's too bad in a way, as we're actually very interested in the same things, such as the economic struggles of so many hard-working people, the dilemmas that confront those who work in the schools (trying to educate children well amidst misplaced rules and inadequate resources), and the general uncertainty of the future. But we don't seem to have enough common language or an agreed-upon method to talk about these topics. It's like we're within inches of the finish line but cannot step over it. We seem well positioned to step away from disagreement as a mere state of affairs to disagreement as an activity, but we either don't know how to begin or don't see why we should bother.

We—humans in general, not just me and my in-laws—should bother. We should step towards disagreement and regard it as a worthwhile activity rather than as a mere fact to be accepted or decried. We should bring disagreement further into our lives, both in public and in private, and put it to use. There is a temptation to go in the opposite direction; the many daunting problems of the world—violence, incivility, exploitation, environmental degradation, terrorism, and the like—might seem to call for more unity and moderation. What they actually demand, however, is a turn towards the celebration of disagreement. They demand a focus on the truly problematic aspect of "polarization," the "polar" (frozen) part. The problem, in other words, is the failure to talk and listen rather than the existence of deeply opposed views. Differing philosophies and religions, the clash between radicals, liberals, and conservatives, the fact of bias and political passion, all are potentially positive; all are sources of ideas and energy; and all can be sources of community as well.

When humans succeed in going beyond tolerance and the ritual celebration of "difference" to build disagreement practice into their communities, what they stand to discover is a dance of argument and listening. They stand to discover the safety and satisfaction that can come from being at odds while remaining engaged. They stand to discover new levels of generosity, without thereby becoming the same or losing sight of principle. And their societies stand to get better public policy, along with less alienation and less violence. These results are not guaranteed, but one can improve the odds by taking advantage of the many well-developed techniques of discussion, disagreement, and conflict resolution and also by inventing new ones. Moreover, the current trajectory of humanity poses plenty of threats of its own. The best answer is to turn, both in theory and practice, towards disagreement.

## POLITICAL SEGREGATION, UNITY, AND FREEDOM

The one way people deal with the potential discomfort of disagreement is to carve out life amongst the like-minded. Or, conversely, they call for more unity, for less distance between the points of view to which they are exposed. David Brooks, in a 2004 *New York Times* op-ed column, takes the latter position. Like me, he's concerned about "political segregation," but he frames the issue as one of ideology, as if the problem is that people's views are too "extreme." Education, he points out, is not an answer; higher education seems, in fact, to make people more ideological. "The more you crack the books, the more likely it is you'll shoot off to the right or left."[3] Brooks attributes this to a New Age focus on the self, abetted by the technology of the information age. The new generation is "into self-validation," and its fancy devices—accessed more by those who are more educated—cater to this desire by hooking them up to resources which help them better validate opinions they already have. Modern technology also lets more people choose where they want to live, so they can gravitate towards the similar-minded. "Once you've joined a side, the information age makes it easier for you to surround yourself with people like yourself." And so people self-segregate along dividing lines of cultural aesthetics and political values. "The political result is that Republican places become more Republican and Democratic places become more Democratic."

Brooks has a point to make but fails to distinguish between having a strong opinion that others disagree with and being accusatory when it comes to the intentions and motivations of one's opponents. (It's no accident that the word "ideology," which carries both the connotations, is commonly used by political scientists to refer to any relatively coherent set of interlocking political views.) Brooks also follows many political analysts in exaggerating the enclave effect, thanks to his assumption that a neighborhood which is rated as "solidly" for one party or the other is, in fact, politically homogeneous. What such a classification really means is simply that pollsters can reliably predict ahead of time which candidate will get the most votes in an election, even if the margin of victory is just 5 percent. Similarly, the electoral college method of selecting presidents encourages the perception that winning most of the states is equivalent to a "landslide" even if each state is rather evenly divided. (Perhaps, then, U.S. voters would be less polarized if social science couldn't predict outcomes so well and voters—not knowing in advance of an election how "divided" they were and who was going to win in their district—were thereby encouraged to listen more to others and to argue more.)

I agree with Brooks that people don't mix enough across philosophical borders. He also is correct to hint at the fact that many people are overenamored of "education" per se, assuming that the acquisition of facts, skills, and degrees somehow makes people more objective and open-minded. Education is valuable. Facts are needed. But the reality is that people can all too easily use facts and education to keep their minds shut tight to rationalize all the more brilliantly. In fact, one is most likely to become wise, and more likely also to be happy, if one tries to grasp (not agree with) multiple points of view rather than facts in and of themselves. Indeed, as John Stuart Mill argued years ago, facts come most clearly into view, and are most useful, when "biased" and passionately held perspectives genuinely collide in cross-border conversations between interested parties. It's all the better if the people behind the differing ideas thereby get to know one another.

Few people get this sort of political education. Brooks is thus on target when, at the end of his essay, he mentions an ambitious national service program as one way the nation might respond to today's political segregation. A fully enforced national service requirement has the potential to create mutual understanding and social bonding between currently separated classes and ethnic groups. But people need to do more than just mix as they perform shared tasks. They need to make an explicit effort to talk; they need to focus on disagreement itself. And Brooks is way off the mark in grasping the source of the divide as excessive "shooting off" to one side or another, as if "the middle" were necessarily the right place to be or the only way people could talk productively and live side by side voluntarily was if they mostly agreed with each other.

In making this error, Brooks echoes the almost daily chorus of voices that call for an end to "partisanship." What's needed, one hears over and over, is more bipartisanship. Unfortunately, this idea often functions, in practice, to support the same negative politics that people are upset about; the appeals for unity become nothing more than another weapon for low-ball accusers. I don't mean to suggest that the problem is hypocrisy or manipulative intent. Most politicians who post vicious campaign ads think they have no choice—and for good reason. They know that they are themselves vulnerable to such attack, and they want to stay in office, often because they believe in public service and think they have something to offer in that regard. They therefore hold their noses and "do what it takes."

If what people want are good policies and democracy, they are better off celebrating division than calling for bipartisanship. I confess to being a bit circular here, as by my lights full democracy is by definition the spirited clash of opposed points of view, extremes included, where that clash helps to form public opinion and shape public policy. But the argument is not merely circular; the point is that values widely recognized as democratic—the inclusive sharing of decision making across the adult population and giving those who are ruled the final say over how they are ruled—are best served by the cultivation of an ongoing politics of fervent, nonviolent argument and struggle.

But, one might ask, isn't being a member of a political party, or taking a firm political position and sticking to it, a negative, something intransigent, a refusal to compromise? Isn't being nearer the political center more sensible than being at one extreme or another? Isn't a nation most truly a nation when it is united? This book uses history, along with stories of the present, to answer, "No," to each of these questions and to argue that, on the contrary, humans need to move decisively, in both words and action, towards more disagreement rather than less.

I do not mean to merely repeat the old saw that party squabbles are a price that must be paid for freedom. The claim is, much more ambitiously, that the clash of deeply opposed, partisan ideas is itself a blessing; that disagreement, when deployed in the right context, is a valuable, life-enhancing activity; and that personal engagement in nonviolent argument is a central aspect of a well-lived life. This, I believe, is the best way to understand Aristotle's famous claim that humans are political animals.

In the final analysis, this book is an argument about freedom. To be free one must live in a community where disagreement is alive and well. To say this is to grant a degree of validity to the classic idea of freedom as the absence of interference, but it's also to challenge it in some ways. One problem with the classic view is that any person who is "left alone" didn't come to be a grown-up all on their own, so one's freedom as a grown-up is always dependent on, or limited by, support systems and historically given identities. And, to go further, even among adults there is—and can be—no such thing as being entirely alone, if it means being dependent on no one and nothing else. The vision is not coherent; it doesn't add up. Each person is connected to other people, for both good and ill; everyone comes to be as part of something bigger; there is always a "we" in culture, family, and history before any given "I" comes into existence.

Granted, it is possible for people to be left alone if it means that they make many decisions on their own and that much about their lives is up to them. Such "freedom" will, however, only provide them with meaningful autonomy if they also possess independence of mind and are exposed to relevant information, and these conditions require disagreement to flourish. Another way to make this point is by bringing up the underlying issue of government power. The idea of freedom as the absence of interference arose, after all, as a means to counter the threat of excess government power. As such, it's a powerful and valuable idea. On the other hand it tends to backfire as a strategy if the "freedom" it calls for is taken to mean total independence, including freedom from political engagement and argument. To actually keep government power appropriately in check people need something else: meaningful autonomy. They need to be engaged in disagreement. And to go further, extensive disagreement does more than protect against excessive government power. It also stands to improve government and to support government power when it's the appropriate, useful kind.

## DISAGREEMENT VERSUS THE ARGUMENT CULTURE

But what is disagreement? When books and essays defend some ideas as better than others, academics often call it "argument," whether anyone disagrees with it or not. The ideas being defended are also called "arguments" even if they just sit on the page unread. The idea is that the very act of defending a claim is an implicit entry into a conversation—a way of staking one's claim against other claims made elsewhere or which could be made. Argument in this case has a mostly positive connotation; it refers to an exchange of reasons and is thus potentially of use in the search for meaning, useful knowledge, or truth. On the other hand, the word argument also means a "fight," a heated, angry exchange where little to zero listening goes on and plenty of aggression is in play.

This semantic confusion is just one reason that this book calls for "disagreement" rather than "argument." Disagreement (as I use the word) is akin to academic argument in that it's an exchange of ideas or of people otherwise making themselves heard, where differences of some kind are apparent. On the other hand, it's unlike academic argument in that it necessarily includes more than one view in the same room (or conversation space) at the same time. It's an encounter. This means that, as in a fight, the talk will sometimes get heated. If it becomes obvious that people are so angry that clear listening cannot take place or if the situation becomes dangerous, then it's time to take a break, start over, or quit, at least when it comes to that issue, with those people, at that time. Nonetheless, the world needs more disagreement. Difficult words sometimes need to be said, emotions included. With practice—and with the help of a pro-disagreement ethic—people can get better at it.

Those who remember books from 1998 might ask how this argument connects to that made by Deborah Tannen in *The Argument Culture: Stopping America's War on Words*. Tannen treats arguments and fights as more or less the same thing and concludes that the United States now features too much of each. This argument culture, she says, "urges us to approach the world—and the people in it—in an adversarial frame of mind. It rests on the assumption that opposition is the best way to get anything done."[4] This culture at work appears in angry shouting matches on political talk shows and in public policy titles like the "war" on poverty, and the results are woeful. People have a knee-jerk tendency—an "automatic response"—to pick fights,[5] for one, and public discourse has been sullied: "If public discourse provides entertainment first and foremost—and if entertainment is first and foremost watching fights—then citizens do not get the information they need to make meaningful use of their right to vote."[6] The alternative, says Tannen, is "dialogue," a form of talking where "there is opposition, yes, but no head-on collision."[7] Instead of thinking that "every issue has two sides—no more, no less," people, Tannen writes, need to recognize that "often the truth is in the complex middle, not the oversimplified extremes."[8]

This book makes a very different claim. Yes, people often find argument entertaining, but that doesn't mean they value argument as a personal activity, much less that they consider disagreement to be a good thing. The fact that people often lose their temper is likewise not a sign that they like doing so or think of it as a way to get things done. True, people do often reduce multisided arguments to two sides, but that's no reason to suppose that the best, or most "complex," argument is in the middle somewhere. Sometimes the middle is the oversimplified position. The best part of Tannen's argument is her critique of the culture of winning and losing. Americans do indeed often look at political differences as if they were gladiators and consider winning—rather than learning or problem solving—to be the goal of argument. The question, however, is why. This book makes the case that one reason is opposition to disagreement. Many people enter into disagreement with the idea that there shouldn't be any. Rather than assuming that "opposition is the best way to get anything done," they imagine unity to be the solution.

## FREE SPEECH, ABSOLUTISM, AND ENCOUNTER

But, one might ask, isn't disagreement a cause of the proliferation of terrorism and other cycles of violence? No. People hate and kill for many different reasons— self-righteousness, fear, the thrill of duty, the identity they gain by joining the struggle, the belief that people they love are under attack, for example—but in any case some sort of demonization or abstraction of the "enemy" is always more truly the cause than any actual level of philosophical or religious difference between one side and the other. In other words, it is almost never the degree of difference between any two sides that in itself brings people to violence. The problem comes when people dwell in disagreement instead of engaging each other in disagreement and instead of participating in the inherently humanizing process of face-to-face dialogue and argument. And the problem comes when people use declarations of disagreement to create a group, to gain membership or status in a group, to police a group, to get press for a group, and thus, when all is said and done, to suppress and oppose disagreement. The antidote, then, is more disagreement, not less.

Granted, there are ways of looking at the world that are fundamentally at odds. And some views are clearly dangerous, even wrong. This does not mean, however, that standing up for more unity, or that avoiding and discouraging disagreement, is the best response. If two people are fundamentally at odds, appealing to them to make nice will not bring them towards unity. It won't help to accuse anyone of believing his or her ideas too much. What can, and sometimes does, help is if those involved engage in philosophical and political confrontation across their apparently impassible borders. Participants in such talk always stand a chance of learning, over time, whatever positive facts about each other are there to learn. There are always at least a few such facts, and they always have the potential to change people's perspectives for the better. Regular cross-border encounter can, moreover, teach people (over time) to bring interpretive generosity to confrontations and arguments, and this can in turn increase the odds that positive learning will take place in the future.

The long-standing dictum "United We Stand" should, then, be rejected in favor of the proposition that a nation can be strongest precisely when it features division, provided, that is, that people are nonviolently engaged across their lines of difference. And this requires in turn that they develop the frame of mind whereby they look forward to repeatedly climbing whichever walls of difference seem highest and then doing so all over again. This is the attitude Camus imagined for Sisyphus, who according to myth was doomed to push a rock up a hill for eternity, only to have it roll back down over and over. "The struggle to reach the top is itself enough to fulfill the heart of man. One must believe that Sisyphus is happy."[9]

But, one might ask, isn't the United States already a disagreement leader because of its provision of free speech? Don't Americans deserve to be the envy of the world when it comes to disagreement? Yes and no. The U.S. Constitution features the First Amendment and a tradition to go with it, and this is worth being proud of. Citizens publicly argue about issues of importance. Presidential hopefuls debate on television, and many citizens watch. On the other hand, the debate contestants are constrained by rules that don't allow for direct dialogue, whether between each other or with the audience. Most Americans are not very experienced—indeed, many are not even interested—in talking to people with whom they disagree. More than a few go so far as to deem their political opponents as unpatriotic simply by virtue of their views.[10] And, finally, politicians are continually at risk of being labeled "divisive," and so often go to great pains to extol unity and avoid difficult questions and controversial ideas.

What these failings reveal is a tendency to understand free speech as a legal system to be proud of rather than as a call to live a certain sort of life. This notion of free speech is passive; it supports complacency and separation rather than a healthy marketplace of ideas. It suggests that having the right to speak is enough, when in fact it is also necessary that people actually speak and listen to each other across borders of difference. Finally, the passive free speech idea also supports the lazy notion that all ideas are equal, that what each person thinks is true is "true for them." The problem is if that's true, it's too easy to conclude there's no point in talking at all or, alternatively, to end up engaging each other in ways that are mushy and unchallenging.

Fortunately, ideas are not mere feelings or subjective inclinations. They include beliefs about what the world is and how it got to be that way. Thus when people talk, think, and listen to each other—at least in settings that are not patronizing, overly sculpted by a particular agenda, or controlled by fear or excessive politeness—they often grow in wisdom and knowledge, especially about the people they are talking to. Moreover, the forms of polarization currently afoot in American politics and in the world at large are not, when one gets right down to it, indicative of unbridgeable philosophical chasms. Nor are they due to conspiracies of the powerful. Instead they are mostly the result of the faulty ways people think about and practice disagreement itself. Where do these "faulty ways" come from? In the chapters that follow many sources are identified and discussed:

- The role played by contradictory policies implemented by Democrats in the 1950s and 1960s, which helped to give government a bad name and create wedges of polarizing misunderstanding.
- Demonizing rhetorical strategies used by Republicans in the 1970s and 1980s to win their way back into the political majority.
- The Cold War, with its emphasis on absolutes of good and evil and its endorsement of unity as essential for national security.
- Stark geographical separations wrought by suburbanization and other geographical and economic shifts.
- The mass media focus on sensation, the "story," and the bottom line, along with its concern to avoid criticism by appearing "objective."
- The sway of various antidialogue philosophies, including excessive individualism, absolutisms of all stripes, simplistic views of power, and the myth that political decisions can be based strictly on objective, undisputed information.
- The fact that many people fear disagreement or at the least find it uncomfortable.
- The reality that Americans are often too overworked, stressed, or isolated to connect to anyone outside their immediate circle.
- A lack of trust in the abilities of "ordinary" people to do anything more than register their dissatisfaction by means of a vote every few years.

While the obstacles are many, there's also reason for optimism. One positive reality is that ordinary citizens are, it turns out, just as capable as experts and elites when it comes to reaching wise conclusions about public issues. What such citizens need is to be properly included and respected in challenging cross-border, public conversations, with enough time to get beneath the surface and access to competing sources of information. Such discussions should not aim at agreement. What they should do, and will do if well-constructed and well-facilitated, is shed a new and humanizing light on the issues which divide the participants, bringing them to the realization that they have a great deal in common. Liberals, for example, might learn that conservatives are not especially greedy, heartless, sexist, or racist. Conservatives, conversely, might discover that liberals are not, as a rule, immoral, relativist, soft, or without self-control. Can people hold such discussions? I demonstrate throughout this book that they can, recounting stories of the world's nascent, largely under-the-radar dialogue movement. In so doing I compare the discussions that are well designed with those that are poorly designed or downright bogus. The latter category includes events that preach to the converted, "debates" that only provide room for fundamentally similar perspectives, and gatherings that tacitly guide participants toward one preconceived "right" answer.

Even if people have the ability to disagree well or to learn how to do so, do they want to? Will they? There is no doubt that disagreement is not especially popular, but why is this? Manipulative discussion settings are one reason. Then there are the antidisagreement philosophies and perspectives I mentioned. Included in this category are any claims that there are certain truths so patently true, and so deserving of reverence, that they are not, and should never be, open to discussion. A word often used for such perspectives is "fundamentalist," but I prefer "absolutist" because I have met too many people who identify themselves as fundamentalists and yet are remarkably ready to listen to anyone and everyone. On the one hand, they have certain firm beliefs: God exists, sacred texts reveal the literal word of that God, these texts are resolutely clear in their meaning, and all people are obligated to live by them. On the other hand, this does not mean that they won't listen to, and respect, the firm views of others. Absolutism, on the other hand, is a variant of fundamentalism whereby the belief is that there is simply no conversation to be had—other than attempts at conversion— with those who are outside the fold. Absolutism can and does appear in almost all philosophical and religious camps. What makes a belief system absolutist is, again, its opposition to disagreement; in fact one might say that an absolutist is anyone who is too in love with his or her own certainty, who carries it as a flag to mark his or her high level of commitment and principle.

Absolutism is, like fundamentalism, deeply attractive to many people. This is easy to understand, given that the world's political and economic systems are increasingly built around pursuits—expanded consumption, increased choice, and winning—that have an inherently competitive element and are spiritually inadequate. In this context, absolutism provides core values of meaning and con-nectedness and for that reason deserves respect and consideration. I nonetheless by means of this book respectfully ask all people—myself included—to give their absolutisms up as best they can, to disregard their love of certainty and take the plunge into disagreement. My arguments boil down to two basic points. First, there are other, more effective ways to achieve the values of meaning and connectedness. Second, absolutism is immoral, thanks to its inherent hubris and negative judgments of others. It fails to honor the fact that every human, as part of nature, has inherent worth. And, as a kind of declaration of war, absolutism typically leads to actual war and then depends on war to sustain itself. It is ultimately destructive.

To say that many Americans shy away from disagreement is of course not to say they're absolutist. Many are influenced instead by the very antiabsolutist principle that each individual is due what Alan Wolfe calls "moral freedom,"[11] meaning that no one has the right to tell anyone else what to think. Another very basic, also nonabsolutist, reason people hesitate to engage in public argument is uncertainty and anxiety about what will happen. One could "lose" and look like a fool. One could be manipulated. Those concerned about the latter might be worried about the bias of others or might simply lack confidence in their power to sort out good argument from bad—perhaps believing there's really no difference between the two—and thus assume that any argumentative space is potentially dangerous, a place where people easily get confused or "brainwashed."

There are additional reasons—closer to absolutism but not there yet—that lead people to oppose or avoid disagreement. It can be unsettling, leaving one feeling rootless and unconnected. It might be unnecessary, if, as many believe, truth is found only in measurable facts which cannot be disputed. Finally, some see disagreement as akin to, or as supportive of, an immoral version of relativism—as giving succor to the dangerous notion that all opinions are equal, that there is no moral truth and no such thing as right and wrong.

These are legitimate concerns. On the other had, the pro-disagreement position has answers to offer. For one, while there's no denying that the regular practice of talk and argument means hard work and occasional discomfort, there's no reason for participants to fear humiliation as an outcome, provided that the conversation is well conducted. Good dialogue design and skilled facilitation can do a lot to make a discussion safer and easier. Also, some initial disagreement problems will fade if and when a disagreement tradition is established in a given community. Even absolutists may discover, over time, that granting consideration to other opinions is not a denial of truth, will not put an end to community, and is not the opposite of unity. This is because disagreement is not truly about winning and losing; it's about peacefully including and considering. Its ultimate values are respect and respectful truth seeking.

True, the expression of political difference has been known to bring with it a host of ills, from imperious moralizing and the end of friendships to war, murder, and other forms of violence. But these problems almost always stem from an opposition to disunity as such, or from hatreds and misunderstandings bred by failures to properly communicate rather than from disagreement in and of itself. To cite a famous example, the peaceful, nonviolent protests of the Civil Rights Movement cannot be fairly said to have been the cause of the violent responses that often followed—though many did cast such blame at the time. The problem, as Martin Luther King, Jr., pointed out on more than one occasion, was that some were so deeply threatened by any real discussion of the issues at stake that they felt they could not allow the protests to take place. Likewise, the ethnic murders that took place during the Bosnian War of the 1990s were not the result of a fundamental opposition of belief between Serbs, Croatians, and Muslim. Those groups had, in fact, lived together successfully for centuries. The problem was instead the notion—as deployed by leaders and then cemented in the hearts and minds of those who proceeded to kill in its name—that order and morality require ethnic and cultural unity and that the presence of certain groups constituted a mortal threat to others.

My name for healthy disagreement practice is "cross-border, public conversation." Talk is "cross-border" when the participants come from several groups of people or when all participants see themselves as somehow different from at least some of the others in a significant way. It is "public" when it is widely publicized and potentially accessible to all or at least to many. Finally talk is "conversation" (rather than, say, negotiation, debate, a hearing, entertainment, news analysis, or a political meeting) when no policy decision is made as a direct result (though this can come later and as a result), when the participants speak for themselves rather than as representatives or experts, and when the main goal is not to resolve an issue so much as to change intergroup dynamics, form opinions anew, and increase understanding.

Cross-border, public conversation is inherently democratic, community-building, and antitotalitarian. Such talk, engaged in regularly, helps participants to see issues from multiple points of view and does so without asking them to give in to the nonthinking of mere tolerance. People who take part in such conversations are more likely to face the difficult issues politicians love to avoid, thereby pushing—and enabling—politicians to do better. A regularized disagreement practice in the United States would cultivate respect for humanity, as participants observed themselves and others making sense, being civil, and in general doing a good job under pressure. It would thus support the moral freedom so many believe in, as the talkers decided things for themselves in the face of (and with the help of) opposition.

## A GLIMPSE AT TODAY'S DIALOGUE MOVEMENT

The disagreement work being done today in the United States is tentative, overshadowed by polarization, and not without problems. Nonetheless, a sizable—and increasing—number of citizens are disagreeing in public and feeling good about the experience. They are swallowing enough of their fear and distrust to take part in civic encounters which cross over borders of difference, allowing for venting, listening, learning, and bridge building. One such encounter began in December 1994, after a man shot and killed two people at two women's clinics, both in the Boston neighborhood of Brookline. In response, three pro-life and three pro-choice activists were asked, by local politicians and other leaders, to meet and talk, and they reluctantly agreed. Their main goal was to defuse the situation, but one of the participants—Frances Hogan, the President of Women Affirming Life—spoke of another aim, which was simply "to sit with people with whom . . . [she] had such a profound disagreement and talk at a very deep level." She and her fellow activists had, she explained, "always thought of the people on the other side as kind of icons in a movement and had never really seen them as human beings on a kind of personal level."[12] And one of those people on the other side—Nicki Nichols Gamble, the Director of the Center for Reproductive Law and Policy—likewise came to the meetings hoping "that through a conversation" they "might reduce the lack of civility in the dialogue and rhetoric and . . . diminish the violence and hatred that was occurring between the two sides."[13]

The dialogue was far from easy. The six women spent weeks just to decide what sort of talk was acceptable. Progress came when rules were established about terminology. Thus the "pro-choice" group was asked to refrain from calling abortion a "medical procedure," while the "pro-life" women had to try to call their opponents "pro-choice," since that was their self-chosen appellation. Slowly, progress was made; trust was established. And so, while the initial plan had been to meet four times, the gatherings continued for no less than seven years, and in the end each of the participants spoke of the experience as highly worthwhile. Some even said it was life changing. Did anyone change her mind about abortion? No. Instead the central benefit, according to all involved, was improved understanding, both of themselves and their opponents. As Gamble put it:

> I think most of us on issues in which there are major divisions tend to talk primarily with those with whom we agree . . . one of the enormous values of this kind of dialogue is . . . you can not only learn to understand at a much deeper level the opposing point of view, but you've learned to articulate your own view that much more clearly and effectively.[14]

This idea was echoed by Reverend Anne Fowler, of the Religious Coalition for Reproductive Choice, who discovered "hopefulness that people . . . [could] tackle a very difficult, divisive, painful issue and be civilized and even friendly in the discussions."[15] And Madeline McComish, of Massachusetts Citizens for Life, said she gained respect for the people on the other side, without confusing this with respect for the pro-choice stance: "I do respect their belief, the fact that it's sincerely held and that they have goodwill, but the position itself, I cannot respect."[16]

Perhaps one reason McComish was able to see the good will of her opponents was that, as it turned out, she and they shared a good deal of common ground— concern for the poor, opposition to the death penalty, and belief in the validity of an active role for women in public life. But, it's important to note, McComish only found this out because she made the effort. As she puts it, "One thing I really learned . . . is to really listen when you're talking to an opponent, . . . and, if you don't understand, make sure you are really hearing what they say. I think

that . . . would just help you as a human being in all your relationships."[17] Gamble
seconded this notion: "I think the kind of conversation we had is the kind of
conversation I would like to have on every important topic with everyone who's
important in my life. And I think what we've learned is that it takes some effort
to do that."[18] This hard work, according to Gamble, paid off in ways that reached
beyond the personal lives of the women involved, as each brought her respect for
each other into groups they worked with and to the media. "I think," says Gamble,
"our commitment to speak civilly with one another really was manifested in the
way the media covered the issue."[19]

Another, more spontaneous encounter took place on September 11, 2001,
in the "Multipurpose Room" at SUNY Potsdam, where I work. One by one,
students, faculty, and staff took turns to rise and speak, groping to come to terms
with the tragic events of that day. There was no plan and no agenda, just a
public space and some gentle facilitation. People spoke in many different ways.
Some expressed anger. Some grieved. A few (students as much as professors,
and with more brevity) offered sophisticated political opinions and arguments.
What inspired me—we were all looking for some sort of inspiration where we
could find it—was the fact that virtually everyone was gentle and respectful,
even as they were profoundly upset and despite being deeply in disagreement in
many ways. No one can say what exactly the conversation accomplished—or will
eventually accomplish—but for me it was a profoundly antiterrorist experience,
as the participants showed each other that there are nonviolent ways to speak
and be heard across sharp boundaries of emotion and ideology.

A final, more light-hearted example: On November 21, 2002, students at
thousands of grade schools across the country participated in what was dubbed
"Mix It Up at Lunch Day." The students were asked to make it a point during
lunch to sit with, and talk to, students they had never sat with or talked to.[20] The
creators of Mix It Up Day were not trying to create philosophical discussions, nor
were they responding to a specific crisis, but their initiative nonetheless shared
key features with the events described above. In all three cases the following could
be observed:


- The participants had something specific to talk about or common experience to draw upon.
- An expectation of civility was communicated by the way the gatherings
  were put together.
- A plan was used which made it likely that all present would take part
  in the action while allowing each individual to retain some control over
  how much, and how, they got involved.
- The settings were small-scale and face-to-face.
- There was a good chance of interaction between people who were, in one
  way or another, different from each other, or who perceived each other
  as such. Thus potential existed for the clash, or encounter, of multiple
  points of view.

- There was some uncertainty about what would happen. The events were not prepackaged or overly controlled by an agenda or a rigid set of questions.
- There was no insistence on agreement. The activity of interaction was considered an end in itself. Thus difference and disagreement were not merely tolerated; they were celebrated.
- This celebration of difference in no way implied that all the points of view or arguments expressed were equally valid. No one was instructed to tone down what they had to say or to give equal credit to all points of view.

This list provides something of a template for the creation of cross-border, public talk likely to lead to what Daniel Yankelovich calls "the magic of dialogue."[21] Citing Martin Buber, the philosopher and theologian, Yankelovich explains that dialogue at its best is more than a discussion technique or a means of gathering information and ideas; it's a way to advance human understanding and build new relationships. "In dialogue, we penetrate behind the polite superficialities and defenses in which we habitually armor ourselves. We listen and respond to one another with an authenticity that forges a bond between us."[22] And, Yankelovich goes on to say, such transformative talk does not require highly specialized, esoteric knowledge. Instead, it's a "practical, everyday tool accessible to us all,"[23] requiring nothing more than the grasping of some basic skills and principles, a willingness to try, and a little practice.

Yankelovich usefully boils down successful dialogue into three key principles, which I summarize as follows:

1. Equality—the participants are free of coercion and meet as equals in the conversation.
2. Listening with empathy—new possibilities open because someone in the conversation sincerely expresses empathy for, or sympathetic understanding of, someone on "the other side."
3. Bringing assumptions into the open—participants, thanks to the creation of a degree of trust, say risky things. They air some of their own assumptions and try to summarize those of others. They show respect and avoid reacting with emotional disdain.

Those who have read Yankelovich's book might notice that I have made his third principle somewhat less demanding than he does. While he says that "dialogue requires that participants be uninhibited," so that "others can respond to them without challenging them or reacting to them judgmentally,"[24] I expect dialogue to get heated on occasion, and I am also ready to call some conversations successful even if only some—rather than all—of the many assumptions at work in the room are brought into the open. It's important to make one's template for dialogue realistic and reasonable and keep it free from any fear of peaceful conflict.

## DISAGREEMENT FAILURE, DISAGREEMENT SUCCESS, AND DISAGREEMENT POTENTIAL

What about the flip side? Is there a template for disagreement failure? Not exactly, but there are typical causes, and these can likewise be derived from examples.

Consider the infamous event of March 3, 1991, when three white Los Angeles police officers, in the presence of eighteen fellow LAPD members, severely beat Rodney King, an unarmed black motorist, who had been chased and then pulled from his car. What the officers did not know was that the beating was being videotaped by an amateur cameraman, and upon the tape's release, four of the policemen were accused and brought to trial. Then, to the dismay of many, they were found not guilty. This led to destructive rioting in several cities, causing fifty-two deaths in Los Angeles alone. Events took a further twist when, during the Los Angeles uprising, four black men were videotaped beating a white truck driver. The driver was forgiving of his attackers, but they were nonetheless accused of assault, with bail amounts one hundred times those set for the four policemen. After a controversial trial in which the original (black) judge was removed from the bench for judicial misconduct, each of the defendants was found guilty. In the meantime, two of the four white police officers were recharged under federal law and convicted.

One reason one can call this set of events disagreement failure is that none of the eighteen officers who watched the beating stepped forward to say, "Stop!" Why? There is no way to completely plumb this question, but surely one contributing factor was the popular notion—without a doubt shared by at least some of the policemen that day—that agreement with one's group is part of being a loyal member. Even if some of the officers did not, as a matter of personal philosophy or intellectual commitment, buy into this idea, it does not mean they could, when push came to shove, act as their own ideas told them to. Other factors kick in; it's not easy to oppose one's comrades.

While one might argue that the pivotal factor when it comes to such behavior is strength of character, the fact is that social norms and customary practice mean a lot. Those with some experience saying, "No," in a setting of group action are much more likely to do so when under pressure, and many would have some such experience if disagreement were regularly encouraged and witnessed. Unfortunately, the opposite ideal is taught in myriad ways. Members of teams, especially those that are military or quasimilitary, are often lauded for backing up the actions of other members at all costs. In the world of sports (and sports consumption) such thinking is legion: hockey announcers frequently mention that a team isn't looking good if the players haven't been retaliating enough when one of their players is hit hard, and baseball announcers routinely glow about their team's future chances, or otherwise toss praise around, if and when every single player on the team rushes on the field to join a fight on behalf of a teammate.

A second reason to call the beating of King and its aftermath disagreement failure is because those events are connected to the near-absence—among most

Americans—of cross-border talk about race and issues thought by some to be connected to race. In a more pro-disagreement world, I imagine citizens arguing about the following:

- What causes crime, and what prevents it?
- How does the media shape the way people think about crime?
- What's behind cases of mishandled evidence in criminal cases?
- What are the right police policies when it comes to dealing with resistance by suspects?
- How should officers be trained so that they are likely to put the law above loyalty to their fellows?
- Is racial profiling ever just? When is the use of statistics about group behavior legitimate, and what dangers do they present?
- How does it feel to be black and be pulled over by the police? What goes through one's mind?
- How does it feel to be a white police officer who has pulled over a black, male driver? What goes through one's mind?

It's likely that America's failure to create sustained, face-to-face, mixed-race conversation about such questions had much to do with the actions of the police officers who pulled King over on that sad day in March. What's more certain is that the failure played a role both in the original acquittal and in the angry reactions to that verdict, as it contributed to the intense pressure put on the judge and jury to use the trial to "do something" about the race problem. Some people wanted the court to render a verdict that would support police officers around the country, and others wanted it to send a message about the prevalence and unacceptability of police brutality and racist police action and policy. Of course no court could come close to satisfying these contradictory demands, and to try to satisfy either would be to compromise the principles behind the rule of law. Courts, as forums designed to resolve questions of individual guilt regarding specific charges and to deal with problems of legal meaning, are well suited when it comes to the protection of individual rights and checking the power of the government—even though they often fall short of this ideal. They are not designed, however, to deal with social problems for which many groups share responsibility, that call for serious listening across borders, that require some degree of learning so as to create new possibilities, or that can best be resolved by means of gestures of generosity, empathy, apology, and the like. Many—maybe even most—social problems have these features. Certainly the race situation in America does.

Imagine an alternative scenario. Imagine that, once the attack on King happened and the video was out for all to see, Americans gathered, in a variety of groups, to talk. What might have been said? If honesty prevailed, at least a few people would surely have claimed that the tape depicted, not a case of obvious and ugly assault, but a drama in which officers of the law acted in the line of duty, the latter being a realm where judgments have to be made on the spot, where the work being done is inherently dangerous and of great societal importance, and where respect for authority is both all-important and dangerously in decline.

This claim would, however, certainly have been countered by stories told by those who experience the police in a very different way, as potential danger, as a force that can at any time suddenly step into their lives, randomly and capriciously, to commit injustice and to wreak havoc. To this group, lionizing the police in order to restore authority is wrongheaded times two: There isn't really anything to "restore," as there never was a time for them when the officers of the law successfully symbolized and defended a righteous order; and by their lights the respect that's most needed is not respect for the police but for law-abiding citizens, all of them. This means holding police to a high standard of conduct.

But if people were speaking their minds, the conversation would not have stopped there. At least some of the authority-conscious type would certainly have argued that the accused police officers were not likely to get a fair trial, thanks to the public outrage and the nation's history of racism. One argument, then, could be that the police officers must be acquitted, lest they be made into scapegoats for the racial crimes of millennia. This argument would, however, have to encounter the claim that what is badly needed is a guilty verdict, in order to say "No," both to racist history and to present-day practices of racist presumption.

What else might have happened? If the conversation went on for some time and if the facilitation were of high quality, then it's possible that the face-to-face quality of the dialogue would have worked some of its characteristic magic, bringing to the participants a new appreciation of their shared humanity. Maybe, for example, at least a few of the pro-acquittal group would have begun to see those on the other side of the issue as like them in that they play by the rules, want safe neighborhoods, and want to be treated fairly. Maybe they would have begun to realize that up to then they had been treating King as a symbol of disorder, when he was really a person, a single individual, who, because of the concatenation of a long history and a particular circumstance, got beaten nearly to death. And maybe their placement of the police in an iconic position, as pillars of order, would have been undermined or made less necessary to them, as they—those leaning toward acquittal—became somewhat less afraid of their counterparts and more willing to consider combining respect for officers of the law with mechanisms of accountability.

Conversely, those on the pro-conviction side might have eased up in their assessment (or their definition) of racism as the heart of the problem and come to more generous forms of disagreement. They might, for example, have decided that those who began the day defending the police officers were—possibly like the police itself—operating with mistaken ideas or thinking from a space of fear rather than simply acting out of hate or lack of concern for others.

If things got that far, any number of different conversations might have then begun. Perhaps the subject would have changed to fears felt jointly on both sides, whether they be fears of a general decline in authority, decline in order, or a safe future for one's children. Or perhaps participants would have begun to discuss the touchy subject of race and racism without moving into the usual stances of accusation and defense. Maybe in the process some would have moved away from a reflexive, all-or-nothing idea of racism (whether traditional or "reverse") to entertain more generous—but no less passionate—ideas about why people are so prone to categorize humanity into fixed, ranked groups. These notions might have included the idea that racism is essentially a way (an unfortunate, damaging way) by which people make sense of the world and therefore is something ultimately amenable—over time—to persuasion or at least to the kind of persuasion that comes from new personal experience.

Of course these are just my speculative visions. They are also biased, in that they reflect my personal hopes. And they are rooted in a particular, and contestable, interpretation of human nature, how ideas work, and where the idea of race comes from. Moreover, even if millions of Americans were to sit down, in thousands of small groups, to talk about race using just the right process, they might not go anywhere near the places I imagine, and without a doubt they would travel to spots I can't imagine, some good and some not so good. Such is the inherent risk, and the beauty, of human dialogue. The point, nonetheless, is this: there is every reason to believe that the overall result would be positive and that America would be different and better as a result.

Unfortunately, no such border-crossing, national conversation ever came to pass. What happened instead was a very public trial with too much at stake. What happened was disagreement failure. I hazard a definition: disagreement failure exists when ideas and experiences that are playing an important role in a given situation are not brought to the surface in cross-border, public conversations and when that omission leads to serious harm or injustice or to a failure to realize worthwhile goals that would otherwise be within reach.

This brings us back to Yankelovich's definition of dialogue, which can now be reconceptualized as "disagreement success." Cross-border, public talk is successful if there is equality in access for relevant points of view, cultivation of empathy across varied perspectives, and an airing of assumptions, such that ideas and experiences that are playing an important role in the situation are brought to the surface. What is emphatically not required is agreement.

It follows from these two notions that some situations possess disagreement potential, meaning the presence of points of view that would, if given voice and heard, address misunderstandings, deepen understandings, encourage humility, and give participants new strength of perspective. When is such potential present? To find out, disagree.

## WHAT'S TO COME

In the following pages, I make use of several strategies. I delve into U.S. history, making the case that recent decades have been marked—sometimes tragically— by key misunderstandings and missing perspectives. Along the way I show that while many deserve at least a share of the blame, that's beside the point; the important problems are bad ideas and problematic structural arrangements.

Another strategy I follow is to gently criticize and praise political viewpoints from across the American political spectrum. I myself have been labeled a leftist more than once and with some justification, but I also truly believe that many other points of view have good points to make. Many conservatives teach the importance of public talk about personal behavior, questions of ultimate truth, and the proper extent of government. They point out that these subjects should not be pushed aside in the name of tolerance, the right to privacy, or the right of free speech. Conversely, many liberals teach that people fail to honor their full human potential as rational agents if they declare that the truth on any subject has already been decreed and that the proper human role is basically one of obedience to those truths.

A third strategy I employ is to speculate about the learning that might take place on this or that issue if societies became more disagreement-friendly. I pay specific attention to terrorism and race in Chapter 8, for example. In each case the aim is to show that dialogue can help address difficult issues in concrete, practical ways.

Finally, I explain the basic principles that lie behind well-designed disagreement events and provide specific guidelines for creating productive cross-border discussions.

## CONCLUSION

Six principles of disagreement flow from this book:

### Value the Extreme

In this time of terrorist threat, it might seem wise to avoid extremes, but such ideas are not necessarily worse, or better, than middle-of-the-road ones. The real danger lies in the rejection of the realm of ideas as the proper forum for solving problems. Thus all concerns and grievances—including those articulated by terrorists—need to be invited into the realm of discussion so as to take them away from, and weaken, the sphere of violence.

### Challenge Manipulation by Diving into It

With so many images and ideas beamed at people all the time, with so much effort to sell them this or that, get them to believe something, or vote for someone, it's tempting to try to rely only on undisputed facts or give up on public discourse entirely, figuring that it's all just a "matter of opinion." But neither of these options can work. First, many important decisions necessarily involve questions of value and also must be made when the relevant facts are contestable. Second, public discourse is always already inside everyone's head in one way or another—it can't be avoided. The best bet, then, is to dive in and examine the views of the biased and passionate, one's own included. There's no need to be afraid of bias. People can learn how to weigh the claims of others and then decide for themselves. There is, in other words, a difference between being convinced and being manipulated and engaged disagreement can help people reside in the world of the former instead of the latter.

## Expect to Find Cross-Border Commonalities

The actual distance between any two sides is often not very great. And beneath even the most intense disagreement lies common ground. Thus more engagement in actual disagreement will often make people less angry and less accusing, helping them reach enough agreement to better address problems. It is best, then, to avoid assuming that one knows ahead of time where the agreements lie.

## Expect to Find Differences, Even within "Your" Group

Do not, to borrow a term from postmodern philosophy, "essentialize." Do not, in other words, assume that some are in "your" group by definition, as a matter of essence. All "women" do not have the same interests just because they are women. Neither do all men, all Israelis, or all Palestinians. One should avoid group thinking as best one can, without denying the need to form coalitions or otherwise get organized.

## Put Time in Now, and Save It Later

A move to more disagreement might seem impossibly time-consuming and inefficient, but in the long run investment in inclusive discussion pays off. The time and energy spent on the front end is repaid, with interest, when it's time to act (or refuse to act).

## Combine Certainty with Uncertainty

Acting on principle does not require absolute certainty. On the contrary, it requires the personal strength to have principles while also acknowledging that humans, as such, cannot indisputably prove the truth of even their deepest beliefs. Humility is thus the first virtue of political morality.

Inherent in these principles is the idea that it's time for people to seek nationality without seeking a unity of ideas, to be citizens of their respective nations by sharing in civil conversations with their fellow citizens rather than by hoping to come to the same conclusions. Just as family members can, by respectfully living together—listening to each other, showing care, and sharing tasks—constitute themselves as a community, so citizens can, by regularly meeting to engage in conversation, foster cross-border bonds without imposing a particular vision of the "politically correct" or sliding into moral relativism.

Fortunately, there are powerful elements in the American political tradition which support civil forms of contention and conversation. In fact, each of the major competing political philosophies in the United States—liberalism, conservatism, and libertarianism—provides ideas that point in a pro-discussion direction. Many liberals call for generosity in considering the problems of fellow humans, reminding people to walk in the shoes of the other. Many conservatives draw on the Biblical tradition to warn against hubris—"Judge not, lest ye be judged," for example—and thus point us to conversation. Finally, libertarians tell people in no uncertain terms that each of them bears some responsibility for her own condition. They remind each person not to leave the improvement of the world to others—especially not to the government.

It should, then, be no surprise that many Americans are taking to conversation, experimenting with new forms of dialogue, and producing remarkable displays of civility, eloquence, mutual education, and commitment. Despite the awesome reach and sophistication of today's governmental/corporate megastate and in opposition to the efforts of experts who try to predict and manage citizen behavior, these people are engaged in what Sheldon Wolin calls the "self-discovery of common concerns."[25] They are engaged in disagreement, which is to say they are engaged in democracy. They understand that despite the often-heard claim that a nation must "speak with one voice," disagreement is not weakening. On the contrary, it is probably safe to say that the gravest danger of our time lies in excess unity.

CHAPTER 2

# A Mixed
# Disagreement Legacy

I don't want you to believe anything I say; I only want you to try to see what makes
me believe it.[1]

—Oliver Wendell Holmes, Sr.

In 2001 a group of *New York Times* correspondents published a collection of essays
culled from their Pulitzer Prize-winning newspaper series on "How Race Is Lived
in America." One of the featured characters in the series is Rick G. Castaceda,
the owner of an engineering firm in Houston, Texas. Journalist Mireya Navarro
describes Castaceda as a Mexican-American entrepreneur who shares a long and
collaborative political and economic history with two other men: Richard W.
Lewis, an Anglo contractor, and Brian G. Smith, a black architect. According
to Navarro, the men feel deep respect for each other but are not close. Why? It
could be for any of the usual personal reasons; e.g., they're not compatible, too
busy, or too committed to others to make emotional room. And of course some
men do not get close to others easily. But what about race? This is the angle taken
by Navarro—and not without reason. Interestingly, however, Castaceda himself
points to another, alluringly simple possibility: "Most relationships outside the
family are superficial anyway."[2] With these words, Castaceda put his finger on a
crucial aspect of today's polarization; for the most part, when it comes to whom
they really get to know, people run in narrow circles. Personal relationships do not
often carry Americans across borders of neighborhood, background, and belief.

This reality poses a challenge when it comes to the creation of healthier forms
of disagreement, and this chapter and the next respond by selectively reviewing
U.S. history. The goal is to uncover some of the causes of the situation and also
bring attention to pro-disagreement resources from the past. I begin, however,
with a little conceptual groundwork: a consideration of the idea of "social capital."

The idea of social capital goes way back, with roots in the thought of Karl Marx and John Dewey, as well as Edward Bellamy and Emile Durkheim.[3] Robert Putnam popularized the idea recently in *Bowling Alone*, his best-selling book about its decline in the United States. Social capital is the degree of trust and reciprocity that makes people likely to step up to help others—whether strangers or their own group taken as a whole—without any expectation of a quid pro quo. Social capital likewise entails that many people know they could get such help from someone else if needed; they have a "confident expectation that someone else will do something... down the road"[4] for them. All other things being equal, more social capital means lower crime levels, higher happiness levels, lower suicide rates, and better economic performance.[5] It is "productive of future collective action or goods, in the manner of other forms of capital.[6]"

How do communities accumulate social capital? Not by accident and not simply because "it's part of the culture." It can only be formed over time as members of a group regularly engage in joint activities that create social networks of respect and when individuals thereby observe others contributing to the welfare of the group and earning praise and respect as a result. In the words of conceptual historian James Farr, these networks "of associations, activities, or relations... bind people together as a community via certain norms and psychological capacities, notably trust."[7]

Consider barn raisings in the American Midwest, common some 150 years ago. Neighbors would gather to help a local household get their new barn walls, joists, and beams up and in position, so the roof could be put on. Author Daniel Kemmis celebrates the border-crossing aspect of one such event in a heart-warming tale of "Albert and Lilly," neighbors who did not like each other one bit until they performed hard carpentry work side by side.

> In another time and place, Albert and Lilly would have had nothing to do with each other. But on those Montana plains, life was still harsh enough that they had no choice. Avoiding people you did not like was not an option. Everyone was needed by everyone else in one capacity or another.... [Now w]e have as little as possible to do with those whose "lifestyles" make us uncomfortable.[8]

Kemmis's idea is that on those Montana plains people's interdependence was manifest. It had a personal component. One could and did experience it directly by engaging in joint, necessary tasks and seeing one's neighbor chip in. This, says Kemmis, changed the participants for the better by expanding their notion of what counts as in their self-interest. On the other hand, warns Kemmis, people today lack such social capital building experiences. This is also Putnam's message, his version beginning with the observation that there has been a precipitous decline in bowling league membership in recent decades. Social capital is in big trouble, says Putnam, thanks to television, residential patterns, overwork, and consumerism.

Social capital is not, however, always altogether salutary. It depends on who counts as part of the group. Barn raisings, for example, seem to have created social capital among a rather homogenous lot. What about ex-slaves who in 1870 had no property or access to credit and were not included in Albert and Lilly's community? Did they have social capital to draw on? Some did, especially through church communities, but barn raisings and other forms of settler cooperation did not bring them into circles of trust with the wider population. Worse, these acts may at times have actively depended on excluding them, on defining them as "other," both outside the group and a negative point of comparison, as in "we" are better than "them."

Even when not exclusive, social capital can be elusive because of conditions. While the technology of barn building of 1870 made it possible for neighbors to witness their interdependence right before their eyes, many contemporary connections between people are more complex and less amenable to direct experience. Neighbors cannot gather to help each other make computer chips, for example. And much of the information people have about the rest of the world is acquired in impersonal, mediated ways that do little or nothing to build relationships. This makes it easier to define "we" in a narrow and divisive way, thereby missing the many similarities and mutual interests that cross group borders and instead telling or believing stories that build walls of negative judgment. This challenge has arrived, unfortunately, at the same time that such walls have become more dangerous then ever, when available technologies provide many individuals, groups, and territorial states with the capacity to do great harm to others, whether by means of war, hate crime, or terrorism.

What is needed, then, is what Putnam calls "bridging social capital," meaning a reservoir of trust that reaches across borders. Some of this "sociological superglue"[9] was created by a Wellesley College policy of the 1920s, whereby undergraduates were routinely treated the way Virginia Durr was treated when, upon her arrival at the school, she was told she had to sit at the dinner table with a black student for a month. By Durr's account, the meals that followed were transformative, as she came to realize that her tablemate was "intelligent and cultured," and this cast doubt on what she had been taught as a child in her "genteel (and racist) Alabama family." She took another big step away from racism years later when she joined the Women's Division of the Democratic National Committee where she worked closely with black women on voting rights issues. "Over time these working relationships led her to change dramatically her perspective on race and to look back on her earlier views with a sense of shame."[10]

Another story of transformation is that of C. P. Ellis, an uneducated white man who grew up in Durham, North Carolina, after World War II. Ellis, like thousands of others, worked seven days a week but never had enough money. His father had labored at a textile mill before he died at the age of forty-eight, probably from brown lung disease. Ellis tried to do better, eventually even managing to get a bank loan to buy a service station, but he had a heart attack just before he could finish paying it off. This, he says, is when he "began to get bitter." "I didn't know who to blame," he says. "I tried to find somebody. I began to blame it on black people."[11] So, just when the Civil Rights Movement began filling the streets with protest, Ellis joined the Ku Klux Klan, thinking of it as "the only organization in the world that would take care of white people." And Ellis did indeed feel taken care of when over 400 men applauded for him at his Klan initiation. He felt like somebody, bonded to others in a pledge to "uphold the purity of the white race" against the black enemy.

But, while Ellis quickly made his way into a position of leadership, the Klan couldn't hold on to him. His doubts began when he noticed how poor the blacks were, how just like him they were. He also noticed that the middle- and upper-class supporters of the Klan who patted him on the back at meetings did not want to be seen with him in public, and he suspected he was being used. Still, he soldiered on, even becoming involved in town politics in order to defend "Klan values." Then one day the president of the state AFL-CIO (American Federation of Labor-Congress of Industrial Organizations), looking to spend some HEW (Health, Education & Welfare) grant money, invited him to a meeting where people from "all walks of life" would talk in an effort "to solve racial problems in the school system." Ellis was plenty suspicious, but "tax money was being spent" so he went.

As it turned out, Ellis walked into a mixed-race group that welcomed him as had the Klan, further undermining his racist ideas and offering him an alternative community. For example, when he spoke up bluntly against black children in "his" schools, a black man named Howard Clements praised him as "the most honest man here tonight," and at the end of the meeting other blacks tried to shake his hand. And at the next meeting an African-American participant nominated him for the position of co-chair of the task force, the other nominee being Ann Atwater, a black civil rights activist who Ellis "had just hated with a purple passion" up to then.[12] He accepted the position—as he couldn't say no to being included and respected—and soon he was knocking on doors, trying to get poor white parents to come to interracial discussion sessions, while Atwater did the same in black neighborhoods. The two grew close, and Ellis went on to walk away from his old world into a life as an antiracist labor activist.

## THE BOURGEOIS PUBLIC SPHERE

The stories of Durr and Ellis should serve as reminders that U.S. history—like those of the Middle East, Bosnia, and other places—includes many examples of successful cross-border engagement that can teach or inspire us, even as we acknowledge the presence of forces that undermine social capital, forces that have brought us to the place where "most relationships outside the family are superficial." One element of the past worth remembering is the sphere of public conversation that rose up in Europe and the United States in the eighteenth and early nineteenth centuries, a sphere that was to a significant degree independent of ruling authorities. A key factor in the rise of revolutionary movements in France and the United States, this "bourgeois public sphere," to use Jürgen Habermas' phrase,[13] was composed of small town church meetings and town hall gatherings on the one hand and "lecture halls, museums, public parks, theaters, meeting houses, opera houses, coffee shops, and the like" on the other.[14] This collection of spaces, called "civil society" by some, found its growth enhanced both by the invention of the printing press and by economic developments that had begun to displace the household economy. Its theme was conversation. Speeches counted as entertainment but were also recognized as politics. Opinions were expressed, but opinions were also formed and transformed. In the prebellum United States, the well-chosen witticism was a step to recognition, even celebrity, and skill in conversation was highly prized. The various discussions brought people together who otherwise might have been strangers, and class lines were sometimes crossed.

While access to the bourgeois public sphere was no by means equal and many were excluded altogether—it was, for example, largely a zone of male performance—it is also true that its multiplicity supported the development of alternative (weaker) publics. "[T]he democratic expansion of publicness in the decades before the Civil War . . . created space in which women could organize on their own behalf."[15] Women were active players in urban salons, on prome-nades in holiday towns, and in church and charity groups. And multiple points of view appeared in the male-dominated public meetings; they "were rowdy . . . , festive . . . , and fiercely partisan."[16] In general the setting was one of "vigorous publicity and broad, active citizenship"[17] though "more rambunctious than ration-al in style of debate."[18]

On the other hand, the preindustrial U.S. public sphere featured many antidis-agreement aspects, thanks in part to its roots in the philosophy of republicanism. This worldview, inherited from Rousseau, Jefferson, and Christian and feudal ideas of obligation, held that to be a true citizen one had to be male, a believer in a provident universe created by the one omniscient God, ready to defend the nation as a soldier, an owner of property, and a husband.[19] This image of the citizen worked hand in hand with legitimized, legal violence to weaken and/or suppress the various fugitive, alternative publics. The overall result was to greatly narrow the range of topics, perspectives, and claims allowed entry into the official public realm. Social capital was accumulated but not of the bridging kind.

The bourgeois public sphere also failed to live up to its proclaimed ideals even within its own narrow province. Those famous New England town meetings, for example, were often not well attended. Or, rather, they were only well attended during the seventeenth century in those towns in which eligible voters were few in number, largely known to each other, living almost next door to the town hall, roused by the town crier if late, and fined for not going. Later, in the nineteenth century, in the many towns that did not impose fines, the turnout rates were about 30 percent, not much different than for town meetings held in the 1970s.[20]

What of the colonial newspaper, often thought of as a locus of fierce parti-sanship and high-powered political argument? According to Michael Schudson, most of the newspapers "scrupulously avoided controversy on almost all occa-sions up to the decade before the revolution . . . when the printers were dragged, sometimes kicking and screaming, into taking sides."[21] Another problem faced

by disagreement was that the press often had difficulty getting political information to publish, as much legislative business of the time was conducted in secret.
Reporters were not even allowed in Congress until 1800.

Consider also the oft-celebrated Lincoln/Douglas debate of 1858, when thousands of spectators gathered and the two men delivered lengthy, erudite, intellectually challenging speeches. This was an impressive rhetorical event compared to
what passes for on-the-campaign-trail wisdom today but was not normal politics
for its time.[22] The impending national crisis made for an unusually politicized
population. One can also safely surmise that many in the audience were not paying too much attention to the arguments made but instead came to cheer their
team on or just to join in the festivities of the day, taking in the ritual of it all.

## BREAKFASTS AND BOARDWALKS

Even if Lincoln and Douglas were putting on a show more than trying to convince,
they provided an occasion for people from many walks of life to mingle in a charged
atmosphere, a sort of border crossing that was highly valued at the time. Historian
Peter Gibian speaks of this period as home to the "culture of conversation" in
a book that tells the story of its star, Oliver Wendell Holmes, Sr. A physician,
novelist, celebrity, person of letters, and father of the Supreme Court justice with
the same name, Holmes spoke for many in his generation when he celebrated
"table talk" in a popular series of essays published in *The Atlantic Monthly*, later
collected in *The Autocrat of the Breakfast Table*.[23] By table talk he meant friendly
but spirited repartee treated as an end in itself, as potentially satisfying and
ennobling. Table talk was performance, a form of entertainment. Holmes, says
Gibian, had a "sense of life as an ongoing verbal performance," even engaging his
"young children in a conversational free-for-all at the dinner table—offering an
extra helping of marmalade as prize for the cleverest remark at each meal."[24]

For Holmes such banter was fun, but it was also the stuff of truth. Like William
James, his student at Harvard, and like the contemporary philosopher Richard
Rorty, Holmes believed that truth spoke in many voices, each version rooted
in a different sensibility, none capable of defeating the others with once-and-
for-all scientific certainty.[25] To Holmes, truth made multiple appearances, in a
sense existing in the space between propositions and questions, in that zone of
agreement, disagreement, and laughter that makes for a good conversation. He
thus in some ways anticipated the twentieth century work of Mikhail Bakhtin
who, like Holmes, loved the work of Rabelais and other Renaissance writers,
celebrating their depictions of the truthful space of the carnival laughter of late
medieval celebrations, with their freewheeling role-playing and their logic of
ambivalence.[26] Holmes saw conversation as carnival-like, as electrical. In a good
conversation one can take on roles, just as Holmes enjoyed speaking as many
characters in his breakfast table dialogues. And, in the words of one of these
characters, "conversation must have its partial truths, its embellished truths, its
exaggerated truths . . . One man who is a little too literal can spoil the talk of a
whole tableful of men of *esprit* [italics in original]."[27]

The culture of conversation was, as Gibian points out, an alternative to the "dogmatists and Truth-sayers" of the time, each of which sought "to sum up the world according to the fixed discourse of his or her church, institution, political party, or scientific discipline."[28] These included the competing fundamentalisms and scientisms of social Darwinism, utilitarianism, phrenology, Victorian sermons, and the religious revival of the "Third Great Awakening." Each of them pronounced some sort of monologic "final word" on reality (as Gibian puts it), while Holmes instead dished up "exploratory dialogues of edifying, anti-foundationalist philosophy."[29] Like the others, he was attempting to make moral sense of, to provide a stabilizing foundation amidst, the intense changes of civil war, industrialization, and urbanization, with their frightening trails of opportunity, new freedom, changed values, and destroyed lives. But the culture of conversation made sense of the world in a questioning way. It was pro-disagreement; the reassurance it could provide about the world came from acts of engagement, as well as from the community and freedom of persona that it brought. Yes, humans should pursue truth, said Holmes, but for him the truths humans can actually find lie in their pursuit, not in possession.

Meanwhile, an analogous approach to truth and identity was being acted out in the resort towns of Saratoga, Newport, and Coney Island. Jon Sterngrass' book on the subject paints a remarkable picture of Americans streaming to these "liminal" (on the border) places while on holiday. There they gazed at each other across lines of class and ethnicity; there they mixed and met in hotel rooms and on the boardwalks. Strangers connected; upper-class professionals shared rooms with tramps; men and women experimented with gender roles; people adopted playful vacation personalities: they upended the world as they knew it, knowing they could later return to safety.

> These public cities flowered in a society that supposedly revered the domestic hearth; they promoted a titillating culture of artificiality for people who claimed to detest hypocrisy, encouraged heterosexual leisure in an era dominated by the concept of a separate female sphere, and offered urbane pleasures for a nation with a strong antiurban streak.[30]

By the time the twentieth century arrived, however, these carnival-like zones of "promenading, flirting, and other non-commercial interactions" were mostly gone.[31] Leisure was more commercialized, more privatized, and more segregated by class. Many resorts specialized: Newport for the very rich, Coney Island for the working class. The society had turned to the notion that happiness came through consumption and through possession, rather than activity.

## THE RISE OF MODERN POLITICS

The trajectory of these resorts can help make sense of the political transformation that occurred around the same time. To some, the period from 1840–1900 was "the golden age of American political culture," as voter turnout rates of 80 percent were common.[32] But this is misleading, one reason being that during most of the nineteenth century the competitive political parties sought high levels of popular participation by moving "self-consciously away from ideological stances" and towards the promotion of ethnic and religious solidarity.[33]

> [M]id-nineteenth-century Americans were devoutly attached to political parties. They tended to live in "island communities" surrounded by other people like themselves. Ethnic and religious communities provided the basis for political allegiances and very often were closely connected to the ideological content of political parties. Political campaigns were, in a sense, more religious revivals and popular entertainments than the settings for rational-critical discussion.[34]

In other words, while political participation was high, for many voting was more like going to church on Sunday than taking part in a critical or partisan discussion. The media of the time, moreover, did little to facilitate or encourage cross-border political engagement. True, a wide range of views could be found by those citizens who went to the trouble of comparing newspapers, as many of the latter served as "information-promoting boosters of a particular political organization." But why would a devout party loyalist who lived in an "island community" do so? Few did. Other newspapers, moreover, were already more like the modern commercial version, understanding themselves as providers of information and thinking of "the good story" as whatever it is that sells or that sells advertising.[35] While an improvement in certain respects, this did not facilitate more partisan argument.

Urban political "machines" were an important part of this set of developments. Cities had grown rapidly, peopled by massive numbers of immigrants who moved into those island communities. The machines were local political systems that assimilated those immigrants, buying their votes with crumbs (for most) or with jobs or lucrative contracts (for some). Meanwhile the economy was transformed by mergers, other forms of corporate concentration, and the introduction of assembly-line manufacturing; an oligopoly-dominated, government-linked system similar to that of today was being born. For the first time in history, most people worked in large organizations—or in small companies that bought from or sold to large ones.[36]

One way to think of machine politics is as an inadequate response to a new social capital problem. More relationships were impersonal, whether among workers, among business magnates of different stripes, or between employees and employers. Many of the new elites, some of whom were incredibly rich, were intensely individualist, and thus America's limited version of feudalism, with its ideas of rank, deference, and noblesse oblige, lost ground both to social Darwinism and to the rhetoric of the rights and wisdom of the "common man." How, in this context, was bridging social capital to be built, or any sort of social capital for that matter? Political parties partially filled the vacuum by organizing political choices and democratizing the nation in some respects, but the parties also commercialized politics and discouraged cross-border talk. Ironically, then, America's highest levels of political participation came precisely at the time when America began its movement away from the antebellum culture of conversation.

While machine politics, consumer culture, and faith in reason as a way to end politics each contributed to the decline of the border-crossing resort promenades and witty breakfast tables of mid-century, that decline was also the result of the new power of an antidisagreement element that had been present from the earliest days of republic. This was the venerable contract idea of society, the theory that all social systems of rules and laws are artificial, that each human in a given society has, in effect, decided to voluntarily give up some of their natural freedom from rules, in order to obtain a crucial degree of protection from attacks to person and property that might be perpetrated by others. Societies, the thinking goes, can be, and at one time were, started from scratch by individuals.

I personally cannot make much sense of this idea. How can one conceive of "humans" at all except as members of some sort of group, be it a clan or nation? And, if humans did ever live in a presocial world, how could they at the same time also possess notions of "freedom," "right," "interest," or "property"? Such questions are best put aside here, however. The relevant point is not the validity of contract theory, whether taken as an account of the origins of the state or of its legitimate role; what is at issue is its effect as political culture. One problem on this score is that it easily supports the notion that one can always start again, from scratch. This idea has, in U.S. history, combined powerfully with the idea (and the reality, such as it was) of "the frontier" to foster the attitude that a moral life means making a pact with like-minded people or striking out "on one's own" rather than finding a way to make some common cause among different sorts. Thus it was not uncommon in the preindustrial west for people to head to an "unoccupied" (unoccupied by Europeans and their descendants) place in order to declare it a "town" and then make it so, sometimes getting rich in the process.[37]

Some praise the American emphasis on independence for breeding a sense of individual responsibility for one's actions and for offering the hope that can come from believing in personal power: to wit, no matter how bad things are, there is a way to begin again and do better. This is true as far as it goes, but individualism also acts to diminish the power people have to shape their lives by obscuring the forces they are up against, for example by hiding fundamental, constitutive connections between people and by rendering invisible the forces of history, class structure, and gender identity. In any case, the argument being made here sidesteps this debate to a degree, the point being that American individualism, whatever its merits, has in many ways been unsupportive of disagreement because it says loud and clear that each of us can choose our own communities, that we need not deal with alternative viewpoints or find ways to live morally among people of diverse faiths, philosophies, and sensibilities. We need not find ways to create bridging social capital.

## PROGRESSIVES TAKE THE STAGE

When the twentieth century dawned the rapidly industrializing United States reached a point of profound societal transformation. Harshly illuminated by the deep depression of the 1890s, the new world featured rank exploitation and amazing opportunities, fabulous opulence and tempting consumer pleasures, giant trusts and staggering personal fortunes, teeming cities and displaced farmers, and innumerable sweatshops. Thousands did not have enough to eat each day, many putting the few extra pennies they had into a family fund to bring relatives to join them in America. Others carried on in opulent mansions that rivaled the great castles of the absolute monarchs.

While this situation had arrived gradually, the turn of the century was when it came home to many as a crisis, as a scary sea change. What, they asked, counts as virtue in this newly commercial world? How much wealth is acceptable? What is appropriate personal behavior? What will become of my children? Which is my community? Who are those new and different people? How should we react? The answers to these questions were as intense as they were varied. Old, established Victorian individualism competed with antiurban agrarianism and nativist hostility to immigrants and cities. Some turned to millennial religion; others turned from the asceticism of their wealthy parents to conspicuous consumption. Some made careers as muckrakers, exposing corporate and political abuses, and others spoke up as anarchists, feminists, syndicalists, and Marxist socialists.

In the end the stars lined up, politically speaking, in favor of the middle-class reformers who became known as Progressives. They succeeded in getting anti-monopoly legislation passed, creating regulatory commissions, turning the national bureaucracy into a professional civil service, putting the polity on the road to direct primaries as the means of choosing political candidates, and passing initiative, referendum, and recall laws in many states. Like the more agrarian Populist movement represented by William Jennings Bryan and the Grange movement, Progressives sought to end destructive class conflict by drawing on the "common sense" of the "common person" and by limiting economic inequality. They did not, however, share the Populist distrust of large organizations and the city, instead seeing them as positives, as a potential foundation for a government/free enterprise partnership that was based on reason and enlightened public opinion. They imagined trained experts working in government agencies to implement the will of the people, who would in turn want what the experts knew was best in the first place. This partnership, they hoped, would bypass the ugly world of vote trading, secrecy, irrationality, and private gain. Capitalism would be unleashed from the tentacles of corruption, and America would enter an age of prosperity and fairness.

One way the various Progressive causes came together was in opposition to "special interests," in favor of "popular rather than the boss control of the community or district."[38] The way to get there, they believed, was to better educate the people, put trained experts in charge and insulate them from political influence, and let voters have more control over the legislative process. The idea that the people and the experts could simultaneously serve as the decision-makers did not seem contradictory because each group was understood to be inherently opposed to private gain and political corruption. Once special interests were out of the picture, the thinking went, the people and the experts would reach consensus, and the nation would enjoy social cohesion and efficiency.

One reason Progressives enjoyed political success in their call for a more regulated economic system was that some business leaders saw in those changes a potential for profit and predictability. Full-blown federal management of the economy, in partnership with big companies, would have to wait until the Great Depression had intensified the sense of crisis in the business class, but already by the 1890s numerous profitable firms had come to realize that intense labor strife and a depression every ten years or so was not good for the bottom line. Progressive reform efforts also benefited from the specter of, and repression of, more radical alternatives. Socialism was getting legs, and business and government reacted. Perhaps above all the Progressives gained adherents because their ideas were appealing; their "powerful blend of reworked domesticity, restrained pleasure, anti-individualism, association, and state power, managed to seem reassuring: it was an ideology of the center, in a society seemingly torn between . . . individualism and socialism."[39]

These are the words of historian Michael McGerr, who sums up the Progressives well when he says their call to "association" was rooted in a preoccupation with "Transforming Americans." Changing people (men in particular) could, they believed, create a new social harmony based on virtue and restraint. Thus, while they fought for antimonopoly regulation and worker protection, they also said no to socialism, seeing it as unrestrained, selfish, and materialistic. They had no quarrel with inequality in itself but did consider the ostentatious display of wealth to be a character flaw. They attacked Victorian gender roles and the sexual double standard. They tried to "ban liquor, eradicate prostitution, and limit divorce."[40] People, they thought, needed to be modest in their demands and demeanor and dutiful to the community, to embrace a "middle-class" sensibility, a kind of "golden mean" between socialism and individualism.[41] In the words of Walter Rauschenbusch, "New forms of association must be created. Our disorganized competitive life must pass into an organic cooperative life."[42]

The concern with association took many forms. Protestant ministers of the new Social Gospel called upon Christians to cross borders between classes, to join together with others and do good works. So it was that in 1889 Jane Addams moved with Ellen Starr into a house in a poor neighborhood and called it Hull House. At first they envisioned hosting poetry readings, so as to raise up workers culturally and spiritually, but quickly adapted, tossing aside patronizing attitudes and turning to practical neighborhood projects, like taking care of children while parents were at work, and finding ways that neighborhood residents could buy coal for less. Hull House soon grew into thirteen separate buildings, and other "settlement houses" sprang up around the country. A border-crossing movement, mostly of middle-class women, was afoot, and Addams was optimistic: "We are passing from an age of individualism to one of association."[43]

## URBAN DEMOCRACY, PROGRESSIVE-STYLE

The optimism many Progressives had when it came to achieving efficiency and objectivity through rational administration led them to conceptualize democracy in naïve ways. They thought, for example, that a society could insulate government regulators from politics simply by insulating them from political party control. Thus it was that they saw to it that the government commissions were run by boards whose members were appointed for lengthy, staggered terms, and their programs were administered by professional civil servants who had passed civil service exams and were hard to remove from office. In hindsight it is not hard to see that, while these changes were positive in abolishing the corrupt spoils system, politics was not thereby kept out of the bureaucracy. On the contrary, interest groups replaced parties to a large degree, in some ways making the decision-making process less democratic and less objective rather than more so.

Some Progressives danced to a more demanding tune. They knew faith, reason, ambiguity, and passion are inevitably intertwined. They understood that politics is a permanent feature of human life. Thus it was that Jane Addams, Frederic Howe, Charles Zueblin, Edward Ward, and Mary Parker Follett were committed to democratic deliberation. Like all Progressives, they emphasized education, but to them the ultimate form of schooling was political participation. John Dewey was a member of this group, arguing not only for better-funded, more accessible public schools that taught democratic values but also for "the improvement of the methods and conditions of debate, discussion, and persuasion."[44] Likewise, Glenn Frank declared that citizens needed to "break the audience habit."[45]

Frederic Howe became one of these democracy advocates after he moved from the small town where he grew up to the big city of Cleveland to practice law. There he joined Tom Johnson in the "city beautiful" movement. They planned city spaces—parks and buildings—that they thought would inspire citizens to good citizenship, cultivating public values. And while some city beautiful activists were elitist and antiurban, concerned with pacifying potentially dangerous masses, Howe and Johnson, following in the footsteps of Charles Zueblin in Chicago, embraced cities and the diverse people who lived in them. To them cities were exciting, providing the raw material needed to support a cosmopolitan participatory democracy. Johnson came to the movement after an 1883 "conversion experience" that transformed him from a stereotypical, wealthy, monopoly-owning businessman into the mayor of Cleveland and an advocate of initiative, referendum, recall, and municipal ownership of collective goods.[46] While he lost his battle for the city takeover of streetcars, he succeeded—and influenced Progressives around the country—with his creation of "tent meetings." These were Populist-style public gatherings that featured opposing speakers, heckling and cheering, and raucous question and answer sessions. A wide range of speakers were given the stage, even Emma Goldman, the controversial anarchist and feminist. Johnson created the meetings out of a passion for public involvement as the heart of democracy. To him "indifference" was the chief evil to be avoided. The common persons were capable of sound judgment and virtue as long they were involved. The "public opinion" formed by an active public would not err in the long run.[47]

Another innovation, the People's Forum, was a product of the People's Institute of New York, founded in 1897 by Charles Sprague Smith.[48] Forums in New York met often and for some twenty years. The biggest events were held at the Institute, but meetings were also held all around the city. While they began as rather academic affairs, modeled after the university extension program in Chicago crafted under the hand of Charles Zueblin, within a year they became overtly political. Controversial questions were addressed by one—or more than one—speaker, and members of the audience (as many as 1,000) asked questions. "Working-class immigrants formed the majority of the audience, and forums produced a lively color dynamic, with sharp questions interspersed with booing and heckling."[49] At the end of each forum those in the crowd voted on various resolutions, and these were often then sent on to politicians on the city council. The forums, moreover, did not shy away from tough issues. They tackled "municipal ownership, imperialism, and American foreign policy (with a majority voting against intervention in the Philippines), tenement housing, socialism, and other issues."[50]

By the time Howe joined the Institute in 1912, forums and other similar events were taking place in many cities. George Coleman had created the Ford Hall Forum in Boston. In Rochester, New York, professors were giving university extension lectures in the evening, workers were attending city-sponsored "lyceum" discussions much like the forums, unions were sponsoring a "Labor Lyceum," and the Women's Educational and Industrial Union was bringing political speakers to town. But Rochester's most ambitious conversation program, begun in 1907, was created by citizen groups, ranging from nativists to socialists, who succeeded in getting the Board of Education to open public schools (after hours) to community members and to provide funds. These became the "social centers." Unlike the People's Forums, social center discussions were controlled by the citizen audiences. They, not the organizers or the School Board, decided (by voting) what topics would be debated, how they would proceed, and what would be done with the results.[51] The only stipulation laid down by the Board was attendance. At least twenty-five citizens had to show up on a given evening or funding would be cut.[52]

Like the forums, social centers caught on around the country. By 1909 Charles Zueblin, Lincoln Steffens, and New York's Governor Charles Evans Hughes had each visited Rochester to see the centers and to praise them, and according to Lee Hammer, who wrote about the movement in 1913, "in 1912, 101 cities carried on some form of evening center work and used 338 school buildings for that purpose," and "ten states" had "amended their school laws during the past two years so as to provide for the maintenance of this work at public expense."[53] But by the time World War I arrived, the social centers movement was dead. Why? One reason was simple: the movement had opponents in high places. Some churches, for example, saw the social centers as sources of "anarchy" and as antireligious. And at least a few political elites were threatened by the citizen power that the centers created.

For example, Boss Aldridge, a Republican Party boss in Rochester, "hated" the debates, and Hiram Edgerton, the mayor of Rochester who eventually closed down the social centers, was, in Kevin Mattson's words, "essentially Aldridge's pawn."[54] Newspaper editors, moreover, often sided with Aldridge and Edgerton, rather than with forum participants, whom one described as "ignorant and unthinking." The controversy over the Rochester meetings came to a head in 1911 when the participants at No. 9 Social Center voted to invite a socialist speaker named Kendrick Shedd who criticized American nationalism, along with nationalism in general. Opponents of the centers attacked him, calling him unpatriotic and anti-American. The mayor forbade him from speaking in public schools or other public buildings, also ordering the removal of the Labor Lyceum from the city council building. Most importantly, this gave him the excuse he needed to shut down the centers.[55]

## ONE RIGHT ANSWER

While some Rochester social centers did manage to reopen, they no longer had public funding or the legitimacy those funds had brought. They had to rent school space and did not always have enough money. These problems lowered attendance, which the current leadership then drove down further when, in an attempt to avoid controversy, they set limits on the topics that could be discussed. This move, which took the heart out of the movement, would have not have happened, says Mattson, had the second generation of leaders possessed the same degree of commitment to participatory democracy as their predecessors. Thus while Edward Ward, the first director of the Rochester program, was "an enthusiastic apostle of democracy" who "became a national spokesman for the movement,"[56] Howard Weet, his successor, did not "trust the people to act responsibly or democratically."[57]

Mattson is also critical of the first generation of leaders but for different reasons. Their problem, he says, was a failure to live up to the vision they believed in. This, he goes on to say, was due to temptation; all of them had their own political goals and sometimes fell prey to their "role as a political activist."[58] Thus Mattson points to Howe's use of forums in New York City to defeat proposed subway contracts. As Howe tells it, "I organized a campaign for their rejection; they were a betrayal of the city's interests . . . . Meetings were held, the [People's] Institute took the lead in rejecting the contracts."[59] Similarly, says Mattson, Charles Sprague Smith and George Coleman sometimes "directed and steered their respective forums . . . losing sight of the freedom necessary for open deliberation."[60] And Ward, Smith, and Coleman are each said by Mattson to have at times been pulled away from principle by "their own goals and agendas."

Another problem for the movement was that it lacked institutional stability and legitimacy, compared to elected officials, government agencies, and courts, depending instead on the support of politicians. A securer status might have been won had the public discussions been somehow made part of the authoritative governing process, and so Mattson argues that the center advocates in New York should have put more energy into initiative and referendum legislation, which never passed in the state. Perhaps if forum and center audiences could have put resolutions on the ballot, they would have been less vulnerable to attack by opponents and shifting winds of public attention: "the deliberation carried out in social centers could have become politically effective and . . . social centers could have protected themselves."[61]

Ethan J. Leib, a contemporary advocate of deliberative democracy, offers a similar analysis, saying that the social centers were "never systematized and integrated into the separation of powers; they were always a site of mobilization or education, and never contributed systematically to forming and measuring a representative popular will. They were voluntary and not mandatory."[62] In Leib's view, participatory democracy cannot work well if it is voluntary. Discussions will too often degenerate into mere theaters for polarizing displays, and be inadequately attended as well. Ordinary people will not take the time to get deeply and responsibly involved in political discussions unless they feel a sense of duty and a decision hangs in the balance. This leads Leib to a provocative proposal: mandatory service for randomly selected citizens on deliberative "civic juries" that would be convened regularly to consider specific issues, deliberate for a specified period, and then make law. This "fourth branch of government" would be subject to checks and balances by the other branches.[63]

Leib's proposal is very important. Indeed I personally would love to see it happen. But I can't imagine people starting where he asks them to start, politically speaking. In other words, I cannot see the people, in our consumption-oriented, overworked, antidisagreement society supporting the kind of constitutional amendment that Leib calls for. What I do believe is that the people will go where he wants them to go (or somewhere better) if we start by creating a pro-disagreement movement of culture and practice, and this means that we have to think further about what was less than ideal in the Progressive experiment with participatory democracy. Mattson and Leib do not fully explain why it is that so many undemocratic "mistakes" were made. Yes, Howe was a political activist opposed to the subway contracts, and he chose to put that ahead of his democracy. There is nothing, however, *intrinsically* top-down or manipulative about being a "political activist." One could conceivably internalize a commitment to public disagreement into one's activism. True, Ward, Smith, and Coleman each had his own goals, but a person's "own" goals are not *necessarily* independent of, or at odds with, the goals of others. Indeed the goals, and even the interests, that people have and then bring to the political table come into being through a social, cultural process. How did the Progressives understand activism, their goals, and the sources of their goals? That's a big question, but part of the answer is that, in their view, they were following the shining star of reason, a font of clear knowledge about what was best for all, and this star told them what the people needed and even what sort of people we all should be. In the end, the Progressives had faith in one right answer to each question, and this is what allowed them to be too in love with their own answers, too ready to dictate to "the people."

Were the Progressives antipolitical, social control advocates, as some historians contend?[64] There is no denying that political participation, whether measured by voter turnout or by partisan membership, proceeded on its historic twentieth century decline just as the Progressive reforms began to change the political landscape. It is also true that the direct primary system championed by the Progressives ended up weakening political parties, and this contributed to the decline in voter turnout. There is, however, no evidence that such a result was intended, and in any case it had other causes, including the rise of a more consumer-oriented culture, the victory of the suffrage movement (which took that mobilizing issue off the table), the crackdown on dissent that began as a reaction to the victory of the Bolsheviks in Russia and persisted throughout much of the century, and above all the freeze on disagreement that was perpetrated in the name of the World War I cause.

It is, then, unfair to say that the Progressives really meant to control the masses, without any commitment to full democracy. But the social control historians nonetheless have a point, as many an act of social control was perpetrated or supported by those in the movement and not just by accident or error. Most Progressives made the theoretical mistake of believing that politics can and should be transcended by reason and expertise. Also most were so committed to ending social conflict that they let it trump their belief in cross-border interaction. And, finally, many Progressives wanted and expected democracy to build a certain sort of character and create a certain sort of government. They imagined democracy making people into dutiful, modest, earnest citizens while also fashioning an activist, rational state.

This interpretation makes sense of Mayor Johnson's attempt to block the referendum vote on his municipal ownership effort. He, like Howe, believed that "no conflict existed between democratic deliberation and the rule of experts."[65] And since Johnson was in his mind an expert on municipal ownership and in his expert view the people were about to make the wrong decision, why not conclude that they had not deliberated "properly" or "enough"? He stepped in, to guide and protect.

This interpretation makes sense also of the Progressives' defense of segregation. The thinking was, when people can't be transformed fast enough to create conflict-free association, let them be kept apart. Thus it was that many Progressives supported, or failed to stand against, the rise of Jim Crow racial segregation laws in the South. Thus it was also that the Progressive era saw witness to an increase in racial segregation in the North, the forcing of Native Americans onto reservations in the West, and the imposition of new restrictions on immigration. Jane Addams, Jacob Riis, and a few other Progressives knew better and spoke out against these developments, but they were in the minority.[66]

The notion that Progressives were too worried about conflict, too in love with Enlightenment reason, and too ready to change others also helps make sense of their almost unanimous endorsement of World War I. For some, the war promised a return to duty, away from the new "insipid" and indulgent consumer world. "We need trouble and stress!" said Ray Stannard Baker, a muckraker journalist.

To him the war was "the whirlwind" that "had to come" in order to reform all the people who were "All overdressed! All overeating! All overspending!"[67] Alexander Whiteside was similarly excited: "There is a wonderful chance in this country to weld the twenty-five or thirty races which compose our population into a strong, virile and intelligent people."[68] Harriet Stanton Blanch, on the other hand, welcomed the war for the employment opportunities it would create for women. And other Progressives saw the war as providing the means and rationale to create a truly activist, interventionist state. Even John Dewey, more radical than most about democracy, said the war would provide many "social possibilities," teaching "the supremacy of public need over private possessions."[69]

I cannot, then, conclude with Mattson that the Progressives truly offer us a "political and institutional alternative—a democratic public—to partisan loyalty."[70] Their idea of a democratic public was not pro-disagreement enough. Indeed I would not choose to state the alternatives quite as Mattson does, with "democratic public" juxtaposed to "partisan loyalty." By my lights this signals too much endorsement of the Progressive ambivalence about democratic politics; it says in effect that being loyal to a party is a form of corruption. In the eighteenth century Rousseau made a similar assertion, believing that the single true and rational answer—the "general will"—would always carry the day of public discussion if only the expression of "private wills" was kept out of the political process. This notion has often been criticized, and rightly, for its authoritarian potential. Shouldn't we also think twice about the way we—in true Progressive fashion—routinely use the phrase "special interests?" Let us instead say proudly that there is nothing wrong with having an interest—even one that's individual and self-regarding ("special") —and working politically on its behalf.

In sum, the optimistic outlook of Addams and other Progressives was, like the cultural revolution of the 1960s, powerful and transformative but also politically naïve, with aims both impossible and contradictory. Their radical, border-crossing democratic aims were, in the end, too accepting of the antipolitical animus inherited from the Enlightenment and too in love with the idea of reason as singular, unambiguous, and adequate to the world of political judgment. Thus, while they gestured toward a truly pro-disagreement society, they could not quite go there.

## DISAGREEMENT UNDER SIEGE

The entry of the United States into World War I dealt the final blow to the already fading urban democracy movement and brought to the fore the Progressive impulses toward character molding and big government. In short order, the nation had a draft, controls on prices and finance, nationalized railroads, and stepped-up labor/management regulation. It also was subject to an intense campaign to create "loyalty" and "patriotism," defined as support of the war effort. A host of new laws gave the government sweeping powers to control and punish dissent. The Sedition Act, for example, prohibited "uttering, printing, writing, or publishing any disloyal, profane, scurrilous, or abusive language about the United

States Government or the military."[71] Several prominent socialist labor leaders, including presidential candidate Eugene V. Debs, were sentenced to lengthy jail terms.

Many citizens joined in the fever to root out "disloyalty." People were sometimes forced to kiss the flag, tarred and feathered, or beaten. Members of the "American Protective League" "opened mail and bugged telephones" and also "detained over a thousand members of the IWW [the International Workers of the World, a relatively radical union], transported them out of town, and left them in the desert without food or water."[72] The word of the hour was unity, often spoke of as "manly" and "healthy" and contrasted with cowardice. McGerr cites a chilling sentence in an editorial in *The Washington Post*, written after a German-American was lynched in Collinsville, Illinois: "It spite of excesses such as lynching . . . [I]t is a healthful and wholesome awakening in the interior of the country."[73] And Edward Ward, one of the leaders of the movement for urban democracy, spoke, in 1915, about the campaign for military preparedness: "Under its unifying compression we may . . . develop a skeleton inside, instead of a shell outside, and become a vertebrate nation—liberated instead of enshackled—and as much more powerful than a people cowering behind mere external fortifications, as a man is than an oyster."[74]

Americans, while surely not oysters, were not unified by the war. Conservative voices invoked the nation's individualist tradition in speaking out against the wartime expansion of government powers. Many complained about the inflation and higher income taxes that came with war spending. Labor conflict intensified, with 2,600 strikes in 1919 alone. War industry expansion led to black migration to Northern cities, and anxious white workers unleashed brutal race riots in response. A renewed Ku Klux Klan led an anti-immigration campaign. And loyalty fever spilled over into hysterical anti-Bolshevism, an irrational fear of subversives everywhere. This was the moment of the nation's first red scare—a panic about Communist infiltration, accompanied by government repression of its critics, and one of the victims was Jane Addams. Only a few years after her reign as a national hero, she was branded a Bolshevik for her criticism of the war, her name first on the military's list of those who possessed "dangerous" sentiments.[75]

In the meantime, the Committee on Public Information (CPI), which was organized in 1917 and headed by George Creel, had put together a nationwide propaganda campaign, one goal of which was, as Mattson puts it, "to make the war seem local and democratic."[76] Towards this end, the CPI modeled "Community Councils of Defense" after the social centers, trading on the popularity of the latter. The Councils were local people meeting in public schools to discuss how the community could support the war effort, their job also being to communicate to others in their area just what the "national needs" were. Social center activists cooperated, as they were pleased by the attention, hoped to keep the centers idea alive, and were influenced by their own patriotic feelings. This was the final blow to the credibility of the centers as democratic, seeing as the goal of the Councils was to direct public opinion while making it "appear to be growing directly out of local neighborhoods."[77]

These antidemocratic developments were in keeping with postwar trends in elite opinion and social science, which Mattson describes well.[78] H. L. Mencken and Walter Lippman derided the ability of the common person and called for the management of public opinion by specialists, for example. And Edward Bernays went from government service into advertising, helping to bring the term "public relations" into common usage. These were the opening moves in the deployment of techniques commonplace today: pseudodialogues in which the people are "consulted" under highly managed conditions, and "grassroots" groups that are grassroots in name only.

World War I, then, brought out the antidisagreement aspect of the Progressive philosophy while smothering the movement itself along with its democratic experiments. Soon Republicans were back in the White House and another era of individualism and laissez-faire was underway. This was not, however, a return to the status quo ante. The government was bigger and more far-reaching. Disloyalty fever was still around, with the specter of Bolshevism and the Soviet Union there to fuel periodic red scares in the 1920s. And public opinion management had been sent onto its path to sophistication. The megastate of the Cold War period had not yet arrived, but America was well on its way.

## THE ADMINISTRATIVE MEGASTATE

Compared to other industrialized nations, the United States came late to full-fledged national government. The turning point was the Great Depression, with its demands for temporary relief, the propping up of consumer demand, protections against bank failure, oversight of labor/management conflict, and coordination of growth in the money supply. The Supreme Court eventually bowed to pressure and declared the necessary increases in federal power legitimate. The revolution towards activist pro-capitalist governance was further advanced by the intense administrative demands of World War II, and the Cold War then helped to justify the permanence of the new arrangements. The military was not downsized, as it had been after World War I, but instead became a vehicle by which the government could pump money into the economy. By the time Eisenhower was elected, the two major political parties had tacitly agreed to the basic framework: government would be responsible for economic performance, but the nation would remain capitalist. The central mechanism of the government regulation would be support and subsidy for the investor class, members of which would be given a role in the formulation and implementation of policy. A subsidiary role, the thinking went, would be played by a set of modest welfare programs and wage supports. So it was that Arthur Larson, an Eisenhower adviser, declared, in 1956, "Now we have as much government activity as necessary, but not enough to stifle the normal motivations of private enterprise."[79] So it was also that Karl Meyer, a liberal, complained in 1961 about the transformation of the New Deal commitment to labor and the downtrodden into what he called the "Smooth Deal," meaning the movement of the Democrats towards excessive compromise and elevation of image over substance.[80]

Grant McConnell mapped these developments in detail in his 1966 classic, *Private Power & American Democracy*, and Theodore Lowi followed his lead in 1969 when he published *The End of Liberalism*.[81] A longer title would have been more descriptive, as he actually describes the "end" of not one but three competing public philosophies: the limited-government individualism of the nineteenth century (which had long been on the defensive), the pro-planning collectivism of Progressives and New Dealers, and traditional social conservatism.[82] All had been eclipsed, says Lowi, by the new and dangerous animal called interest group liberalism. In this system policies are the result of behind-the-scenes bargaining among interest groups and government officials rather than a product of public debate, law making, and implementation. Powerful interests groups come to have a kind of property right in the state. The sovereignty that officially belongs to the public is, in other words, farmed out to the well-positioned, well-organized, and well-financed, by means of their inclusion in the work of government agencies and congressional committees. "Meaningful adversary proceedings" are displaced by "administrative, technical, and logrolling considerations."[83]

In Lowi's view the resulting system is both unaccountable and rigid. The only way for the government to do anything new is to add yet more government. Each addition tends to follow the same pattern, giving key interest groups a piece of the action while adopting the fiction (first for others and then as a matter of faith) that the resultant merging of the public and the private somehow counts as "self-government" and "local government."[84] This "ersatz public philosophy"[85] seeks to "solve the problems of public authority by defining them away."[86] The real action of power happens behind the scenes, accompanied by "a purely ritualistic public dialogue."[87]

*The End of Liberalism* was on the mark in many ways. A "government-group nexus"[88] was indeed firmly in power by the mid-1950s, and its growth has since continued apace, to the point where political theorist Sheldon Wolin could, in 1989, make sense of American government by using the terms "megastate" and "economic polity." Just as Lowi was right to speak of "self-government" as a fig leaf for farmed-out sovereignty, Wolin is right to sound the alarm about the way the term "privatization" functions to hide the merging of the state with the so-called private sector while also obscuring the coronation of expansion and efficiency as if they were given, prepolitical necessities, merely requiring proper administration.[89]

In the final analysis, however, Lowi does not do enough to explain the problem he glimpses. This is because he buys into the erroneous idea that the basic battle between political right and political wrong is waged between "special interests" on one side and "the people" on the other. To him the options of politics are a people free by virtue of being ruled by rational laws that they have chosen or free because they are not ruled at all; by his lights a people can never be free if special interests are in the saddle. This is, however, a classic mistake. The fact is that politics without interests—and without at least some carving up of whatever pie there is—doesn't make any sense. Moreover, "the people" are many individuals and groups and they have interests and beliefs worth organizing around. Some of those interests are pretty "special" without thereby being illegitimate. It is not helpful, then, to bemoan the loss of a phantom public that was free from the taint of private concerns. It makes more sense to try to imagine how to include many voices in government, without turning government into a bargaining center where the most powerful get to shop first. This is, of course, where publicly conducted disagreement, open to extremes, comes in.

It also makes sense to think of the post–World War II "second republic" (Lowi's term) as a difference in degree that became one in kind. The Cold War, Keynesianism, and the military-industrial complex fatefully came together and interest group liberalism was born, not out of a misguided attempt to represent interests but because of the collision between the nation's long-standing animus against politics and new structural realities that demanded more social coordination—of aggregate demand, health care research, energy provision, transportation, growth of the money supply, etc.

"Interest group liberalism" is, then, not really liberal at all, whether that term means commitment to the downtrodden, standing up for freedom, or defense of the minimal state. It is a form of the state based on fragmented, parceled out power and public-private cooperation, buttressed by a litigation and rights approach to questions of basic justice. State power is organized as a collection of somewhat coordinated bargaining policy centers, each dominated by its own set of interest groups, while the courts sit to one side as the place where—at times awkwardly and certainly inadequately—groups press those claims based on fundamental arguments about just deserts and proper government power. This is one of the reasons that Congress and the president did not respond to overwhelming public opinion in the postwar period and pass an antilynching law or put an end to school segregation. True, these failings were due to the power of the Southern states (and Southern elites) in the Democratic Coalition. But they were also due to the fact that those problems did not fit the modus operandi of the administrative megastate. Advocates for the rights of minorities usually had to see their day in court, a place where give-and-take, educational conversations are not allowed or appropriate and where the only remedies available are all-or-nothing decisions about rights. This fact alone goes far to explain the mixed record of the Civil Rights Movement. It did well on voting rights and de jure segregation in transportation and education but did poorly when it came to residential segregation and occupational discrimination.[90]

Rights-based claims also proliferated because they seemed nonpolitical and in part because in the era of the Cold War partisanship had once again become a bad word. Criticism of the system was shunted to the political margins or downright repressed. Service to the public was widely understood to mean being above party and politics. President Truman started a tradition when he eliminated all reference to his membership in a particular political party from his major speeches, instead equating himself with the nation by, using expressions like, "We must go forward."[91] Barry Goldwater, a man who prided himself on putting principle ahead of pragmatism, nonetheless declared, in a California speech while running for president in 1964, "I deplore those far-out partisans of principles that are trying to tear the American people apart."[92]

As I said, this was an attitude bred by the Cold War. The Soviet Union was for the most part understood as a total enemy, a kind of pure evil, and the opposite of everything American and everything good. Communism was seen as akin to a disease, not unlike that which afflicted the "pod people" in the 1956 film *The Body Snatchers* (remade in 1978). It was actively infiltrating the nation, stealing minds, and making people into comrades and dupes. In this context, national unity seemed an absolute priority, crucial to the survival of the "Free World" and even the human race.

The prevailing bias against bias was, however, also a creature of the megastate, as the process of bargaining among big players, while bringing home bacon to the right voters, cannot work well when it comes to dealing with multiple ideological stances, each of which offers some sort of societal vision. How, after all, can one divide up pieces of the pie among societal visions that each have an all-or-nothing aspect at their center—e.g., the notion of a socialist economy, a libertarian economy, a Christian kingdom, an Islamic republic, easy access to abortion, or no access to abortion? It's not possible. What competition among such dreams calls for is instead a process of encounter, opportunity to be heard, and inclusion even for the losers of the day—sending them the message that they belong.

## CONCLUSION

When it comes to disagreement, little in the American past deserves glorification, but there are traditions worth recovering and examples to learn from. Practices of cross-border encounter have transformed people for the better, building bridging social capital. One hundred and fifty years ago lively public spaces invited citizens to stretch away from their ordinary roles and personas, to loiter side by side with people from other walks of life, perhaps even make an evening together. One hundred years ago workers gathered regularly at public schools to debate and vote on issues of the day, from socialism to prohibition.

On the other hand, it has often been authoritatively asserted that elites know best, rational thinking leads to only one plausible answer, partisanship equals corruption, and in war time a nation must agree. These ideas have functioned as walls against disagreement—and still do so today. Indeed, the last of them went on to become a keystone of U.S. political culture with the onset of the Cold War, helping to shape a profound disagreement freeze. This in turn set the context for the rise of the administrative state, where bargaining became institutionalized as a substitute for political engagement about ideas. It was in this setting that America's two major political parties made a series of politically polarizing decisions—in the 1950s, 1960s, and 1970s—that so shape our world today. This is the subject of the next chapter.

# CHAPTER 3

# Argument after World War II

The false rhetoric of our current politics is based on a thoroughly misleading view of what actually happened during the 1960s.[1]

—E. J. Dionne, Jr.

By the time World War II was over, the United States had finally embraced managed capitalism. There were millions of small business, but most production was in the hands of large corporations. They raised money with the help of other large corporations, and all labored under the guidance of, and in concert with, the elaborate, enormous, fragmented government—the megastate. What came in the next several decades was a series of polarization-inducing moves of policy and campaign rhetoric, engineered by the two major political parties and their various coalition partners: federal government agencies, powerful interest groups, and state and local governments. This chapter offers four conclusions about these events. First, the polarization that emerged is rooted in major understanding gaps that developed during the period and which are sustained, first and foremost, by separation. America is segregated along multiple lines—race, political point of view, ideology, and economic class, for example—with little cross-border communication. Second, many different groups share responsibility for this sorry state, so there is not much point in assigning blame. Instead what is needed is more awareness of the degree of separation and its cost, so as to fuel a cycle of more cross-border compassion, more communication, and healthier forms of polarization. Third, the conventional narrative of the 1960s—as a time of excess followed by 1970s' backlash—mostly misses the mark. Fourth, pseudodisagreement and standoff, based on posing and/or conversation-stopping myths, are now the order of the day; public political talk tends to stroke identities and mobilize select constituencies while doing little to illuminate or guide the actual process of governing.

A caveat is in order. While this chapter emphasizes misunderstanding as a major problem of the current political scene, it by no means claims that polarization is *all* about misunderstanding. People disagree for many reasons, including truly divergent interests, different beliefs, and simply because they are competing for power. This is just as it should be. Unfortunately, the disagreements of the second half of the twentieth century also have deep roots in unnecessary disagreement failure.

## THE CONVENTIONAL NARRATIVE

During the Cold War the Democratic Party enjoyed year after year of majority status in the Senate and the House of Representatives. Kennedy's presidential victory in 1960 gave the Party even more control. What did it do with this power? In a way this is the wrong question, as the Party didn't "run" things so much as preside over the inner workings of the administrative state, in which power was shared among elites from both major political parties, politically organized representatives of the corporate sector, and, to a lesser extent, the leaders of big unions and political not-for-profits. To know, then, what government actually did during the time in question requires one to look at details: e.g., budget amounts, where the money went, and degrees of policy enforcement. What people often look at, however, when trying to assess what leaders are up to, are policy titles, prominent court cases, and the grand promises made in public. This sort of gaze is, in any case, the source of the commonly accepted story of the 1960s; this being that the government, led by the Democratic Party, veered too far to the left and thereby initiated a white, working-class backlash that eventually broke up the "New Deal coalition" of voters and brought the Republicans to power. This is what I call the conventional narrative.

The more liberal version of the conventional narrative holds that, while Johnson's Great Society accomplished a good deal for blacks and women, it did little for middle-class whites who were upset about high crime, high taxes, and a decline in family values. The more conservative version holds that the Democrats, entranced by the idea that a new era of economic abundance had dawned, actually did little of value for anybody besides themselves and their elite allies. Their policies, the story continues, went beyond the pursuit of equal opportunity to the quest for equal results and, to make matters worse, the liberals who were running the party, lacking in both personal morality and patriotism, initiated a decline of the nation's core values. The result, concludes the narrative, was a combination of welfare explosion, affirmative action, too many rights for the accused, excessively short prison sentences, gay rights advocacy, increased rates of divorce, legalized abortion, and high crime rates.

Both versions of the conventional narrative emphasize a public perception, especially on the part of the white middle class, that the Democratic Party and the federal government were playing favorites. Thus *Chain Reaction* (1992), by

Thomas Edsall with Mary Edsall, makes the claim that the Democratic Party became identified with women, minorities, and gays.[2] Likewise, E. J. Dionne, in *Why Americans Hate Politics* (1991) says, "It is a simple and undeniable truth of American politics that the Republicans gained a great deal both in the South and in white enclaves of Northern big cities because of the reaction of the Democratic Party's stand in favor of civil rights."[3] This reaction, says Dionne, gave support to the conservative narrative that liberals were arrogant and hypocritical elites, out of touch with ordinary people. "By the 1970s, liberalism" had "come to be seen as a set of exotic commitments felt strongly by the well-educated members of the upper middle class."[4] The "culture war" was on.

The history laid out in this chapter shows this narrative to be accurate when it comes to shifts in public perceptions and the ways they played out politically but fundamentally wrong about what happened. The policies and actions of the 1960s and 1970s U.S. government did not, when taken in sum, add up to a liberal revolution.

## A REINTERPRETATION OF PUBLIC OPINION

Before I turn to the direct evidence in support of this claim, I consider the conventional narrative itself. More specifically, I reconsider the public opinion data, with the help of Jennifer Hochschild's 1995 study of the idea of "the American Dream." She begins by breaking down the dream into four separate tenets: (1) citizens should have equal opportunity, (2) economic prosperity for all citizens and their families is possible under current conditions, (3) whether or not people achieve success in doing so is in their own control, and (4) such success is justified only if achieved in a virtuous way. When she turns to the data, Hochschild uncovers three important patterns. First, Americans overwhelmingly support the first and fourth tenet; they support, in other words, the normative vision of the dream. They see it as a moral vision. Second, when asked about themselves and their families, majorities in every group studied (black, white, Hispanic, rich, middle-class, poor, etc.) report optimism about the future; they "consider the American dream" to be "a description of their own lives." In fact, on this count blacks score noticeably higher than whites and have done so consistently at least since the 1940s. In 1990, 39 percent of blacks said it was "fairly likely" or "very likely" that they would someday be rich, compared to 25 percent of whites, and in 1986, 62 percent of blacks reported being optimistic about their children's future, compared to 50 percent of whites.[5]

Third, and conversely, Hochschild reports that Americans disagree with each other considerably when it comes to the realities faced by *other* people besides themselves. Thus, "over half of blacks but only a quarter to a third of whites think our nation is moving toward two separate but unequal societies."[6] Also, "[b]lacks are almost three times as likely as whites to agree that 'society gives some people a head start and holds others back.'"[7] Likewise, a 1991 Gallup poll reported that 60 percent of whites, but only 33 percent of blacks, believe that "compared with whites, blacks have equal or greater job opportunity."[8] And a 1995 *Washington*

*Post* survey found that "55 percent of whites (compared with 29 percent of blacks) mistakenly agreed that the 'average African American' is as well off or better off than 'the average white person' in their enjoyment of jobs and education."[9]

The last finding clearly confirms the perceptual side of the conventional narrative. It seems that many whites did, as Dionne says, feel personally beleaguered and perceive blacks to be rather well off. This is consistent with the notion that a "white backlash" led to the political ascendancy of the Republican Party. Notice, however, that Hochschild is careful to call such perception of black success "mistaken." Indeed it is; whether one looks at income levels, wealth levels, life expectancy, quality of health care, or unemployment rates, the average African-American is clearly worse off than the average white person and has been so throughout the time in question.[10]

The data also suggest that many of those who *do* notice that blacks are, on average, worse off than whites come to the conclusion that blacks are themselves at fault. On this subject Hochschild again uncovers a racial divide. According to a 1992 survey, 55 percent of whites, compared to 45 percent of blacks, agree with the claim that many of the problems blacks suffer under are "self-inflicted."[11] A 2003 Gallup poll found that 60 percent of whites do not think American society is "divided into haves and have-nots," 61 percent of blacks have the opposite view; 56 percent of whites think that money and wealth should be more evenly distributed, and a whopping 80 percent of blacks approve of the idea.[12] Similarly, a June 2007 Gallup poll found that only 30 percent of blacks are satisfied with the way blacks are treated, a mere 8 percent are "very satisfied," 67 percent are dissatisfied, and 38 percent are "very dissatisfied." On the other hand, no less than 75 percent of non-Hispanic whites think of "white-black relations as good."[13]

Hochschild usefully interprets the data as creating two "quandaries." For typical whites the quandary is that they're worried about their own future but strongly believe in the likelihood of a good future for others. They're apparently clinging to their faith in the American Dream despite their personal situation. The effort to deal with this possible contradiction leads some (anywhere from a tenth to a third) to believe "that compared with whites blacks have more opportunities, are less vulnerable to economic upheaval, receive better health care, are treated better in the courts and the media, and are more likely to obtain good jobs and be admitted to good colleges."[14]

Many blacks, says Hochschild, face a quandary of their own. They're pessimistic about the chances for blacks as a group but optimistic about their own prospects. On the one hand, they know that many blacks are now middle-class, some are upper-class, and old-style racism has been largely defeated. They also know, however, that the black working class is hurting. Seeking, like whites, to believe in the American Dream and to avoid racist conclusions about fellow blacks, some conclude that whites are to blame.

Hochschild sums up the situation this way: "Many middle-class African Americans see white placeholders denying them their earned and deserved success . . . [while] many whites see middle-class blacks making excessive demands and blaming their personal failures on a convenient but non-existent enemy."[15]

Put in the language of the American dream, "[w]hites believe it works for everyone; blacks believe it works only for those not of their own race."[16]

By my lights, this way of putting it frames the situation as one of disagreement failure. It also helps to make sense of a third quandary: how is it that the conventional narrative has so much staying power, given that (as I have suggested and show in the pages ahead) the U.S. government did not, all in all, do any favors for the poor and minorities during the 1960s and 1970s? One answer is the argument of this book as a whole, that people rarely share perspectives and experiences outside the circle of their immediate friends and relatives, much less across borders of race and class, so even simple misunderstandings can and do stubbornly persist. Another reason, more to the point here, is that the conventional narrative finds support in people's desire to believe in the American Dream, no matter the facts.

On the racial front this thinking takes the form of the assumption that separation and segregation are caused by "prejudice," rather than, say, economic structure or government programs aimed at management of the economy rather than race per se. A prejudice-only lens can't reveal the Jim Crow laws of the American South as a hierarchical economic system that exploited poor whites along with poor blacks while providing a living and a way of life to many; they appear instead to be purely the result of racism. The lens likewise can't reveal racial differentials in the rest of the nation as rooted in structural realities, like the closing of factories and working-class whites acting (at times viciously) to protect their property values amidst neighborhood decline; instead it points the finger at discrimination. What the prejudice-only lens *does* do is fit with the American Dream, or the dream that's been dreamed thus far. To dream anew requires cross-border, interracial dialogue—disagreement and all.

## THE RELATIVE INVISIBILITY OF STRUCTURE

While the persistence of an understanding gap between whites and blacks and appeal of the prejudice-only lens is partly the result of people's desire to believe in the American Dream, it is also a result of the fact that structural sources of individual failure and success are by definition hard to see. Consider the effects of location. If a person lives in one part of town rather than another they might thereby lack the connections needed to get a good job. They might also lack safe housing or a way to get to where the work is. Or consider the structure of the workplace: an unprejudiced employer might benefit financially by creating or catering to racial animosities among the employees, perhaps by means of giving black workers different jobs than white workers or hiring blacks in order to replace white workers who are on strike. Consider also that for generations many economically vulnerable working-class whites in the North, seeking to distance themselves from those below them in the economy and hang on to their faith in the American Dream, did so by looking at economic difference and seeing race instead, in effect allowing race to serve as a cipher for class status. Consider, finally, that slavery and Jim Crow were first and foremost labor systems, based on extracting profit, with prejudice present largely as a rationalizing corollary, an effect as much as a cause.

One of these structural forms of racial injustice deserves a bit of elaboration here because of the lessons it contains regarding encounter and dialogue. In the agricultural South of the first half of the twentieth century the divide-and-conquer labor system functioned by paying poverty wages to many whites while otherwise treating them much better than blacks. The latter were virtually en-slaved by company stores, usurious interest rates, worthless scrip, and complicit law enforcement, all of which put them in endless "debt" to their employers. Few know today that many whites both understood the nature of this labor system and opposed it. The United Mine Workers, for example, took a clearly antiracist line, with black and white workers standing shoulder to shoulder in the effort. The union suffered heavy repression at the hands of the organized planter class, who largely controlled local government, but nonetheless often rose from the ashes to reorganize and push back once again. How did this happen in the "racist" South? It happened because the owners needed to hire blacks in order to get enough workers and also because *all* of the mine work was dangerous. In other words, divide and conquer strategies to extract more profit were not usable; blacks and whites worked side by side in dangerous conditions, and thereby developed bonds of encounter and mutual activity.[17] Cross-border encounter worked some of its characteristic magic.

Structural realities are especially hard to see for those looking through a lens of individualism. In that case irrational prejudice is likely to jump to mind when one tries to imagine the sources of race problems. At this spot in the conventional train of logic there is a fork in the track. Some lean toward the idea that whites were, and still are, racist as a group. Why else would nonwhites still suffer dispro-portionately? Others consider racial prejudice to be largely a thing of the past, deducing from this that truly daunting racial barriers must also be a thing of the past and concluding that any remaining race-based disparities must be caused by nonsystemic factors, such as a lack of good education or personal effort, misguided government programs, and unique personal tragedies.

There is, in other words, little room for critique of the economy in the con-ventional narrative. Suffering at the hands of markets is seen, when noticed, as a "side effect" of prosperity, as a result of temporary "adjustments" and "dislocations" that will of course be remedied over time by new investments, provided of course that the affected individuals make an effort. These views find their most succinct expression in the work of conservatives. Shelby Steele, for example, argues that the Martin Luther King, Jr., phase of the Civil Rights Movement brought an end to systemic racism.[18] It's time, according to Steele (who is himself black, by the way), for blacks to give up the status of victim and acknowledge that they can and should succeed on their own merits. Too many African-Americans, he says, look to keep whites "on the hook" by wielding the accusation of racism, whether it's there or not. This can bring a seductive feeling of power, but it can never bring real power, success, or freedom. For sure it will bring paternalistic assistance and breed dependency.

Many commentators more liberal than Steele make similar assumptions about recent history. Consider, for example, an August 2007 *New York Times* op-ed piece by Joshua Green, a senior editor for *The Atlantic*. Writing in response to the August 2007 resignation of Karl Rove, the controversial Republican strategist, from his position as President George W. Bush's political advisor, Green described the conservatives of the 1980s as truly against big government, unlike those of Bush's generation: "In seeking to establish a lasting conservative majority, Mr. Rove violated one of the central tenets of modern conservative ideology: the idea that government cannot effectively refashion American society." Correspondingly, Green remembers old-time liberals as architects of excess, writing, "Like a 1960s liberal in love with the abstract merits of a guaranteed income, Mr. Rove misread the mood of the country and tried to do too much." Never mind that Nixon, a pragmatic Republican, was the only American president to propose a guaranteed income; Green remembers the 1960s as the age of failed social engineering and asks his readers to draw the appropriate lessons: "Of course, there is a bright side. If nothing else, Mr. Rove has strengthened the conservative critique of what happens when you try to engineer great societal changes through government policy. Perhaps conservatives can find some solace by telling themselves they were right all along."[19]

## TRUTH IN THE CONVENTIONAL NARRATIVE

The facts do not fit the assertions of Steele or Green. The *actual actions* of the U.S. government of the 1960s and 1970s did not work to help traditionally oppressed groups. Or, rather, some did, but some clearly did not. In fact some amounted to nothing less than as assault on racial equality. To help me situate and defend this claim, I need to first briefly recount what the government *did* do to help the downtrodden during the period in question.

The high-flying rhetoric of the "Great Society" was not all fluff and spin. There was plenty of spending and a good deal of new commitment to helping the poor and the disadvantaged. Landmark laws included the Civil Rights Acts of 1957, 1960, and 1964; the Voting Rights Act of 1965; and the Fair Housing Act of 1968. New agencies and bureaus included the Civil Rights Division of the Justice Department (1957), the Civil Rights Commission (1957), the Office of Civil Rights (1964), the Office of Economic Opportunity (1964), and the Equal Employment Opportunity Commission (1964). The scope of the federal government was significantly expanded by the creation of Medicare, Medicaid, Food Stamps, and expanded disability benefits (1965). The Peace Corps was created in 1961, and Head Start legislation was passed in 1965. Vista, the Job Corps, and the Community Action Program were created in 1964. In 1965 the Johnson administration created affirmative action with executive orders (11246 and 11375), which favored minority bids for federal construction dollars. Home-buying subsidies and tuition subsidies flowed to veterans of World War II, the Korean War, and the Vietnam War. And, finally, many a judge and justice struck down de jure forms of racial segregation, ordered school districts to integrate by busing, and granted new rights to welfare recipients and those accused of crime.

One reason for all the activity was the perception that there was lots of money available. Aggregate economic numbers, from 1945 to 1975, were better than they had been in any other 30-year period in the nation's history. Overall growth, job creation, productivity, and home ownership rates had reached new highs. The recessions of the time were shallower, fewer, and shorter. While there was more poverty than there is today, the poor were by most either unseen or thought of as a special population, unfit or uniquely disadvantaged. Hopes were high, in part because real wages for hourly workers went up during the period at the same time as the income distance between the top fifth and the bottom fifth went down—something that has not happened before or since. And the percentage of those owning their own homes rose significantly.[20] In short, the middle-class dream of America seemed to be coming true.

This prosperity was, moreover, partly the result of the new government programs. Social Security, Medicare, and Medicaid "virtually wiped out" poverty among the elderly.[21] Workers benefited from postwar government support for labor unions. Veterans and their families used subsidies to buy homes in the suburbs, and they spent union wages buying consumer goods. Life expectancy rose, and, since the battle against smallpox and polio was mostly complete, it seemed that the increases were at least in part the result of Medicare and Medicaid. Over 22 million preschool-aged children had participated in Head Start as of 2005.[22] On the racial front, old-style biological racism was largely defeated. Inferior race theorists became simply unwelcome on the mainstream political stage. Some segregated schools were integrated. Record numbers of blacks registered to vote and voted. And segregation in public transportation was conquered. In other words, the government appeared to be doing great things, and the economy was humming along as well. Problems of unmet needs and unfairness still existed, but the assumption was that they would soon be taken care of. Indeed, it was widely believed that the "end of ideology" was at hand, to be ushered in by the new era of endless economic surplus.

The conventional narrative is also on the mark in declaring the 1960s as a time of changing values and a questioning of authority. Certainly many evangelical and fundamentalist Christians, and many others, recoiled in shock when confronted with public experimentations with psychedelic drugs, declarations of free love as a philosophy of life, and public displays of nudity. The Vietnam War and the protests against it made this divide into a chasm, raising deep questions about what it means to be a patriotic citizen and throwing the entire revolution into relief, as if it were a yes or no question. In this context the Watergate scandal was also polarizing, leading some to a more radical, pessimistic liberalism and others toward anti-big government conservatism.

Even leaving aside the more flamboyant and obviously polarized aspects of the time—some of which were, after all, both overemphasized by the press and less radical than they seemed to be—there was real revolution. There were profound changes—or profound new questions asked—in the realms of music, art, gender, the meaning of work, and the relation of humans to the environment. True, these changes are still contested; there's still plenty of opposition or discomfort and uncertainty. And it's not easy to say where the changes will go from here or where they should go, particularly in the light of the commercial forces that they have unleashed and that have, arguably, co-opted or even corrupted "the 1960s" to a significant degree. Nonetheless, many aspects of the revolution are now fully established in American culture, even taken for granted.

It needs to be remembered, however, that the Great Society programming was actually rather moderate, even conservative. Many of the policies bore little resemblance to official titles and rhetoric. (One would think that conservatives attuned to the ills of big government would consider this possibility more often.) The War on Poverty's Community Action Program, for example, was traditional in its emphasis on training and inspiration rather than jobs, benefits, and neighborhood investment. It was rooted in what was then called "manpower theory," which considered unemployment to be the result of individual characteristics and which embodied a "fundamental optimism about the capacity of the private sector to absorb surplus labor."[23] The private sector, moreover, was brought into the programming in traditional, megastate fashion: government money was funneled to private interests and local politicians who were to "empower" the poor; money did not flow to the poor directly, and much of the spending never reached them. Finally, the Vietnam War was expensive and thus the antipoverty effort was seriously underfunded to begin with. For example, the entire annual budget of the Office of Economic Opportunity (OEO), which encompassed Vista, the Jobs Corps, the Community Action Program, and Head Start, was $1.7 billion, "in its best years."[24] By contrast, between 1960 and 1970 the government spent between $4 and $6 billion per year on the space program (i.e., on NASA),[25] and the total social security bill for the year of 1970 was $31.9 billion.[26]

Moreover, if by "welfare" one means cash assistance to the nondisabled and nonelderly poor, then welfare benefits (per family member and adjusted for inflation) went down steadily beginning in the early 1970s. The *total* spent on welfare did go up but not until the 1970s, when Nixon was in office, and this occurred not so much because liberals planned it or the state intentionally implemented it as because more of those who were eligible chose to apply, welfare rights lawyers and court decisions made it harder to throw people off lists arbitrarily, and more were eligible because of recession.

Similarly, the provisions of Medicare and Medicaid in no way match the rhetoric of "Great Society" or "War on Poverty." There is no denying that these programs are expensive and also that they count as major innovations in American policy history. On the other hand, most of the benefits flow to the elderly (some of them "poor" by virtue of living in a nursing home), a good deal of the funding is funneled through private providers who take their cut (a la the megastate), and the degree of care provided often leaves something to be desired.

Next, a glimpse at the antidiscrimination initiatives at the center of controversy reveals a mixed record. There was indeed a successful revolution against de jure forms of discrimination in transportation, accommodations, public facilities, and voting (albeit with some worrisome setbacks in recent years when it comes to voter registration), but much less was achieved in the areas of housing and employment. And most of the women and minorities who benefited from affirmative action were already in the middle class or were members of small constituencies targeted by courts as deserving of specific redress. In the words of historian Carter A. Wilson,

> Although these policies have eliminated the more direct and blatant forms of discrimination, they have had much less effect on institutional forms of discrimination. Racial discrimination in the housing market leaves blacks concentrated in the central cities, and discrimination in the labor market keeps black unemployment rates disproportionately higher than white rates, even among blacks and whites with the same levels of education.[27]

Consider, for example, the mid-1970s Congressional initiative to commit 10 percent of federal construction dollars to minority contractors. Whatever one thinks of this program on the merits, it's safe to say that a good portion of the money involved flowed to those who already had relatively well-paying jobs, and it is clear that the total amount involved was not enough to alter the construction industry taken as a whole.[28] The building trades remained a mostly male realm in which the high value placed on fraternity meant that, generally speaking, a person needed supporters already in the business in order to get hired as anything besides a low-wage, casual day laborer. Residential segregation and the lack of border-crossing interactions left many members of minority groups without these connections. Thus it was that, from the 1940s through the 1960s, "Detroit's black day laborers gathered at an informal outdoor labor market on the city's periphery, known to local whites as the 'slave market.'"[29] The men would bring their tools and hang out, hoping to be one of the few chosen that day by white contractors who came in their trucks looking for a few day laborers to be paid at less than union scale. The result was a system which not only failed to open the trades to blacks but also worked to actively undermine concurrent desegregation efforts, as the site of men milling about on the street was widely misunderstood, and disapproved of, by middle-class Detroiters, black and white, thereby driving an additional wedge between the already separate worlds of experience.

Another brand of affirmative action were court-ordered remedies for blatant, repeated acts of discrimination, as when a union or employer excluded blacks or women and then continued to do so surreptitiously, even after being ordered to change its ways. The resulting cases sometimes earned headlines that suggested a frontal attack on racism spearheaded by liberal judges, but in fact most of the rulings applied to one organization at a time and reached only a few people. Most blacks and women received nothing as a result, unless one counts the additional modicum of resentment faced by some from their fellow employees who wrongly suspected that they were "unqualified."

True, most affirmative action efforts fit into another category, that of "unmandated" workplace and university programs used for hiring staff and/or admitting students. Most of these policies have, however, been rather mild in their design. Some amounted to next to nothing, as in the placing of job ads in a few new places. The rare, more radical initiatives made use of quotas, but the norm has instead been the setting of goals. All in all, the results have been modest. The nation now enjoys a more representative ethnic and gender mix among both professionals and college students. Many women and minorities who qualified for middle-class and professional jobs reaped some benefit. But little changed for those in the nonprofessional, wage-earning strata or who occupy the bottom rungs of the nation's occupational hierarchy. Thomas J. Sugrue's analysis of Detroit again sums up national results:

> [I]n the private sector, companies and workers continued to resist affirmative action programs, and blacks have remained underrepresented in skilled and white collar work... By and large untouched by affirmative action programs have been the displaced working class and poor black Detroiters most in need of assistance.[30]

All in all, affirmative action programs were like the other War on Poverty programs: they suffered from accommodation to the logic of the megastate. Like defense contracting, government funded research and development, urban renewal, and highway spending, they existed in the gray area between the realms of the public and the private, partaking in both. Like agricultural policy and economic management, perceived problems were addressed by making adjustments in the allocative process of bargaining. Thus it is not surprising that most of those who actually benefited were already in the middle class and up. Nor is it surprising that a host of resentments and misconceptions were mobilized among those not included in those circles and that this in turn meant a hardening of opposed positions that amounts to disagreement failure.

Even this look at the successes of 1960s liberalism might make one wonder if Dionne goes too far when he says (in keeping with the conventional narrative) that Democrats and liberals "failed to understand that the burdens of achieving racial justice were being borne disproportionately by their traditional supporters among the less affluent whites."[31] This seems to say that racial justice was achieved. The fact that this is wrong becomes even more obvious when one turns to the attack on racial equality that took place at the same time.

## SAYING ONE THING AND DOING ANOTHER

The pillars of the "war on the poor" were urban renewal, the construction of the Interstate Highway System, government home loan policies, and the variety of tax breaks that subsidized corporate movement away from city centers. While the national public talk focused on generous liberal programming, development policies devastated hundreds of neighborhoods and impoverished thousands of people. I don't mean to say that the politicians of the day were lying (although there was some of that to go around, as always) so much as that different policies were being pursued by different parts and levels of government, with lots of wishful thinking in the mix, including excessive faith in simplistic theories of poverty and the trickle-down theories of economic growth.

First, consider urban renewal. Beginning around 1950, city after city adopted comprehensive proposals to "revitalize" their "blighted" central areas. Less euphemistic phrasing can be found in Mindy Thompson Fullilove's *Root Shock: How Tearing Up City Neighborhoods Hurts America, and What We Can Do about It* (2004). She reports that the program, "between 1949 and 1973, bulldozed 2,500 neighborhoods in 993 American cities. A million people were dispossessed."[32] In other words, the reality was that the residents of many a poor neighborhood were evicted, their apartments and homes were destroyed, and new housing—most of it private—was erected in its place. This was war on the poor.

One city's experience is carefully described by Sugrue in *The Origins of the Urban Crisis: Race and Inequality in Postwar Detroit*. "Four of the city's most important redevelopment projects—the Gratiot redevelopment site, the Brewster and Douglass public housing projects, and the Medical Center Area—were premised on the destruction of some of the most densely populated black neighborhoods in the city."[33] The Gratiot project was typical in that it was the result of a planning process that brought government and developers together, and the goal was to create private housing, "thus appealing to conservative real estate and business interests in the city."[34] Funds were made available when Congress passed the federal Housing Act of 1949, and the first residents were evicted in 1950.

Urban renewal worked synergistically with a contemporaneous boom in urban highway construction, accelerated by the passage of the Federal Aid Highway Act of 1956, which underwrote the construction of the Interstate Highway System. Over 40,000 miles of road were built by 2004. Most middle-class neighborhoods had enough political clout to avoid condemnation, bulldozing, and dissection, but poor neighborhoods typically did not. Thus it was that in Detroit, the "Oakland-Hastings (later Chrysler) Freeway blasted through the black Lower East Side, Paradise Valley, and the Hasting Street business district, wiping out many of the city's most prominent African American institutions, from jazz clubs to the Saint Antoine branch of the YMCA."[35] And in Newark, according to one community activist, the city's "Route 280 was done to stop the movement of African Americans north."[36]

The twin initiative of roads and renewal had everything to do with the nation's movement to more automobile transportation, suburban development, and urban sprawl. This process had benefits (and beneficiaries), but the net national loss included thousands of small businesses shut down, homes and apartments razed, and untold numbers of jobs lost. Plans were often announced years before crews arrived, rendering many a home and business worthless, just like that. Owners were unable to sell. People had nowhere to go. Vital inner-city neighborhoods were destroyed.

For many reasons, the costs of this transformation were paid disproportionately by blacks. For one, African-American poverty was more urban than white poverty and thus more visible to the nonpoor. Many middle-class residents—often white—associated blacks with poverty, didn't want to see the poor, and feared them. Highways were effective weapons to keep them at a distance, and this affected the highway planning process. Also fewer blacks were homeowners, and even those who were often did not live in buildings that could be picked up and relocated. And the new roads facilitated the movement of large companies, jobs included, out of the city centers, and many a black family could not get housing in the suburbs because of a series of exclusionary practices, motivated out of racism or just the racism-in-effect of concerns about property values.

What happened to the displaced? In Gratiot, where slums were "cleared" for development, about one-third of the dislocated families eventually found spots in inferior public housing. Most moved in with friends and family who lived in already overcrowded, overpriced, and/or dangerously unsafe apartments.[37] Many were both bewildered and angry.

> Harvey Royal, who lived along the route of the future Edsel Ford Freeway, wrote, "I think it would have been so much nicer to have built places for people to live in than a highway & just people in the street..." Maud W. Cain, a widow who lived in a one-room apartment behind a storefront on Hastings Street, expressed her desperation about finding an affordable apartment when she was relocated for highway construction. "I do not have money to rent a $75.00 house [with] no heat."[38]

The experiences of Royal and Cain were invisible to many, in part because of the mode of thinking that lies at the heart of mainstream economics and which infuses much discourse about development. This thinking looked at aggregate results as if they were *the* result. Thus Albert Cobo, an anti-integrationist Republican elected mayor of Detroit in 1950, was speaking for many on both sides of the aisle when he said, "Sure there have been some inconveniences in building our expressways and in our slum clearance program, but in the long run more people benefit. That's the price of progress."[39]

Whatever one thinks of the morality of adding up costs and benefits (as if all the people who paid the costs also reaped the benefits), there can be no gainsaying the fact that Cobo failed to acknowledge the real costs. What he called "inconvenience" was in fact devastation for Royal, for Cain, and for thousands of others. Part of the problem was an intense housing shortage. This was due in part to a wartime shortage of construction materials for new housing. In addition, Detroit was one of many cities that had to absorb thousands of new residents over the course of several decades—the population rose by 220,000 between 1940 and 1950 alone.[40] Aside from returning veterans, the newcomers came because of the tremendous demand for labor, which was created in turn by the end of the Depression, wartime spending on military supplies, postwar military procurement, cheap oil, the displacement of agricultural workers in the South, and the dominant position of the United States in the global economy.

Many of the newcomers were black, and many—especially those who came during and immediately after the war—got good jobs. Before that time blacks had often gone unhired in big industry or were used as strikebreakers, feeding the fires of racial animosity. But during the war the demand for workers was too great, and, moreover, the United Auto Workers and other industrial unions switched gears and began supporting civil rights and black inclusion in union locals. Many locals resisted this interracial approach to organizing, but arriving African Americans could nonetheless "expect to find jobs that had been closed to them in the South [albeit often the least desirable jobs, as janitors and in the paint booths], and wages that far surpassed those in the best paid southern industries."[41] Unfortunately, housing construction could not keep up with the rising population. The building trades were still reeling from the reduced demand of the Depression and had also been hit with wartime shortages in labor and materials. For a long time supply did not come close to demand, especially when it came to the needs of the working class; "builders preferred to construct homes for well-to-do buyers."[42] The situation for blacks was especially desperate, as most were intensely—sometimes brutally—excluded from homeownership and a move to the suburbs.

Sugrue tells this story in amazing detail, generous in many directions. Think of a home-owning black family being charged usurious interest under a nonequity accumulating "land contract" who then find themselves without enough money to properly maintain the property, and who eventually lose their home when late with a single payment, all because the Federal Housing Administration (FHA) and the Home Owners' Loan Corporation (HOLC) wouldn't give them the subsidies and guarantees needed to get a normal mortgage, in keeping with its policy of preserving "racially homogeneous" neighborhoods.[43] Think of a white low-wage family whose only investment is tied up in a modest house, whose only chance to move to the suburbs is to sell that house, and who sees a black family moving in next door as a dire threat to their equity and therefore their future. And think of the realtor threatened with the loss of their realtor's license if found in violation of the Detroit Real Estate Board's "Code of Ethics" if they sell a home to a black family in a white neighborhood.[44]

> Although Detroit had a stock of . . . homes that blue-collar workers could afford, blacks were systematically shut out of the private real estate market. White real estate brokers shunned black clients and encouraged restrictive covenants and other discriminatory practices that kept blacks out of most of the city's single-family houses. Bankers seldom lent to black home buyers, abetted by federal housing appraisal practices that ruled black neighborhoods to be dangerous risks . . . . The result was that blacks were trapped in the city's worst housing, in strictly segregated sections of the city.[45]

Under these conditions the city's offer to assist displaced residents find housing was downright insulting. There simply wasn't enough housing to go around. To quote one advocacy group of the day, "By not building a supply of low-rent homes on vacant land sites...the city is ignoring the plight of thousands of Detroit families living in sub-standard housing, doubled or tripled up with relatives, or otherwise in need of a decent place to live."[46]

In the meantime, a majority of working-class Americans were reaping the benefits of a host of government spending programs or otherwise sharing in the bounty of the booming economy. Consider the contradictions: Social Security payments had begun for many, but those who had been domestic servants or agricultural workers were not eligible. The Servicemen's Readjustment Act of 1944 (the GI Bill) was followed by the Veteran's Adjustment Act of 1952 and the Veterans' Readjustment Benefits Act of 1966, and these laws provided temporary readjustment funds, college tuition payments, and low-interest, zero-down payment home loans for thousands of veterans of World War II, the Korean War, and the Vietnam War. Many black servicemen were, however, unable to take advantage because of institutionalized opposition to "disturbing the character" of a neighborhood.

I do not draw attention to this pile of contrasts to shame whites or to deny agency to blacks. The world already features too much use of conversation-ending, antidisagreement strategies of simplification and identity-support. Instead my purpose is twofold. I seek first to better reveal the roots of today's polarization in the understanding gap that formed in the crucible of divergent postwar experiences and failures to communicate. Second, I aim to undermine the conventional narrative and thus point the way to more productive forms of communication. To this end, it is important to note that the policies just discussed did the bulk of their transformative work well before the black riots of the 1960s, well before the 1970s when the number of welfare recipients grew quickly, and well before the heyday of the black power movement and affirmative action. The conventional narrative is, however, not only well ensconced in the reference world of public symbols and discussion. It is also an appealing half-truth that seems to make sense of many powerful events. It will not be easily displaced by mere facts.

## SEPARATION AND THE UNDERSTANDING GAP

Consider again the situation in the Detroit of 1950. More than anyone else, blacks had few housing options. Landlords, many of them of the absentee variety, could therefore overcharge black tenants for dilapidated apartments. The few blacks who owned homes often could not get loans to repair them, producing more dilapidation. Overcrowded buildings produced lots of garbage, but the city trucks still came but once a week, and the result was smelly piles and rats in the streets. What were bankers, white city residents, and city officials likely to conclude, upon seeing the resulting blight? Structural forces are hard to see, but smelly garbage is hard to miss. What many did conclude was that "those" people don't take care of themselves." This attitude lent support to the discriminatory practices that had helped to create the problem in the first place. All in all, it was a vicious circle of misunderstanding.

On the other hand, for many African-American city dwellers the postwar experience was one of high-flying expectations followed by free fall and a loss of hope. It must have felt like a kind of total betrayal. After all, blacks were just as sold on the American Dream as were others: they could not easily see the barriers faced by many a white worker. Blacks had, moreover, been cast for generations (without their consent and in ways mostly beyond their control) as first and foremost "black," and therefore, when trying to grasp what was happening to them, what could they conclude but that "whites" were, as a group, responsible?

In other words, when Martin Luther King, Jr., shared his dream for equality, the Supreme Court announced that segregation by law was illegal, Johnson announced the War on Poverty, and the economy was humming with new jobs and thousands of new homeowners, Americans of all stripes had every reason to believe that access to prosperity was at hand. But after all was said and done—after urban renewal, affirmative action, busing, and the rest—many blacks came to sense that the system was rigged against them. In the meantime those who looked over their shoulder, from the prosperous suburbs back at "welfare recipients" still in the city, typically didn't know how much of their own prosperity was due to aid programs begun in the 1950s. Again, structural forces are hard to see. What members of the prosperous working class could see was that they had worked hard. Their success would, then, seem to them to be a result of their own efforts. And many also believed that an immense amount of government help was flowing, or would soon flow, to the poor and to blacks. To many, especially to those whites still in the ranks of the vulnerable or who were themselves among the newly impoverished, this did not seem right.

In a nutshell, some thought most whites were doing well financially, while blacks were kept out of the circle of success by racism, and others believed that blacks were the ones getting unfair advantages. Each of these visions contained inaccuracies and misunderstandings. Both dehumanized the Other and obscured common ground. Both led people to be less than receptive to dialogue with their opponents. There have been, and are, many rallies, protests, guilt-tripping racial sensitivity workshops, sermons, yelling sessions, and managed debates, but there has not been enough disagreement-friendly dialogue. No wonder, then, that the visions of half-truth and error persist as key elements in today's culture war.

It needs to be said that more generous ideas of self and other, of us and them, might well have triumphed over these excessively negative judgments for the simple reason that people are all human and are therefore prone—under the right conditions—to see through to the humanity of others. Unfortunately, the gulf was not just one of differing opinions, backgrounds, and stakes in the economy. It also stemmed from geographical separation and supported that separation. As Sugrue puts it, "Perceptions of racial difference were not . . . wholly, or even primarily, the consequences of popular culture. In the postwar city, blackness and whiteness assumed a spatial definition."[47]

As an example of misperceptions that persist, consider the issue of the remaining black-white gap in economic and educational achievement. To many of my students, it appears as mysterious, as explainable only by means either of racist conclusions about blacks or racist conclusions about whites. They don't want to come to such conclusions but have a hard time imagining any alternatives. So it is that they sometimes ask me, "How come blacks who migrated to cities didn't succeed as the earlier waves of newcomers had?" In the classroom I usually decline to answer directly, instead suggesting a comparison of what various authors have to say. But if pushed far enough, I say the following:

> First, don't romanticize: some immigrants went home, or suffered unduly, or died young of work-related disease and injury or starvation. Second, many blacks did "assimilate" in just the way meant. Taken as a group, blacks tried as hard as other groups, and millions did move from exploitation as agricultural workers into working-class and middle-class jobs in the industrial economy. Third, the barriers faced by blacks [outlined above] were more total than those faced by many others. Blacks looked to move en masse into the urban/suburban world at a different time in American political and economic history than did, say, Italians or Poles. And blacks also walked into a different identity script of fear and exclusion.
>
> Fourth, and perhaps most importantly, one doesn't get very far if by summing up the barriers faced by migrant blacks with the all-or-nothing word of "racism." More specifically, when thousands of American-born blacks left the dying economic system of indentured servant agriculture— the de facto slavery of Jim Crow—to enter the economy of modern wage labor, most came without tools, land ownership, entrée into unions, college degrees, or industrial skills and therefore had to join the fray at the bottom of the economic totem pole. Also, many arrived in the big city in the 1950s just when industrial jobs had begun to leave for the suburbs and the South.

It's hard to get this complex message across, for one because the notion of affirmative action is out there powerfully in people's mental landscape, and this notion implicitly contains the promise of opportunity; it says that the economy can provide for all, once those on the outside get "affirmed." If even liberals who have been the proponents of affirmative action believe this one can hardly blame the millions of Americans who suffer from anxiety about a needed promotion or about having enough income for wondering why other people need special help. Indeed, the structural situation—the shrinking middle class—encourages those who are anxious about money to suspect or believe that maybe someone else got the job that should have been theirs. Affirmative action pushes this resentment button.

## THE RACE CONNECTION

But, the discerning reader might ask, why have I been speaking so much about race? Americans disagree, after all, about many subjects, and most of them have no direct connection to race. Abortion, gay marriage, sex on television, terrorism, textbooks: the different opinions people hold on these subjects don't line up neatly with racial and ethnic background, nor is there any reason why they should.

The short answer to the question is that I don't have room to talk about everything. The longer answer is that the race story tells the bigger tale because race perceptions play a role in so much else American, including the formation of the liberal/conservative divide (the Edsalls are correct on that point). Many pro-life advocates, for example, who see choosing to have an abortion as selfish, also see welfare receipt, the gay lifestyle, having a child out of wedlock, and benefiting from affirmative action as selfish. And some of these issues concern, or seem to concern, race. The various issues come together as concern about the nation's putative turn away from virtue and towards hedonism, a decline that is connected in many minds to liberal policies on race and justice. Liberals have hurt America, the thinking goes, by being "soft." They are soft on foreign policy, soft on crime, and soft on personal responsibility. And this failing is crystallized in the positions liberals usually take on race.

It is also important to remember that race is something most Americans quickly notice, for understandable historical reasons. Shades of economic difference are often not as easy to see, and the culture includes a strong tradition in favor of not seeing them. The poor and the rich alike wear blue jeans, and the prevailing ethos declares someone "middle-class," no matter what her income and wealth, as long as she works for a living and believes in moving up. Because of these cultural realities many nonracial parameters of separation and segregation—income, age, religiosity, sexual identity, sexual style, and more—get perceived through the lens of race. For example, people, when looking at (thinking about, encountering, or talking about) people from different income groups, often quickly see "black," "Hispanic," "white," "native," and "Asian," instead of income per se. This process tends to hide class relationships. In a similar move, questions about economic development, government and business, and basic equity often disappear from view, only to reappear as issues of personal behavior such as commitment to marriage, commitment to hard work, personal behavior, and reliance on welfare. And these are issues that have already been connected, in many minds, to race.

Earlier we glimpsed the complexity of the race-class connection in concrete terms by considering the dynamics of residential segregation in Detroit, but 1950 was a long time ago. Consider, then, an event in Boca Raton, Florida, of 2003, when many residents turned out at a city council meeting to oppose Habitat for Humanity's attempt to build two affordable homes in the community.

> Unidentified Woman #1: "There is no need to put a home on that neighbor . . . on our neighborhood—excuse me—that would depreciate the neighborhood."
>
> Unidentified Woman #2: "I am totally against Habitat housing. I've put a lot of money into my home, and it's the last thing I need to lose my appreciation for Habitat Housing."
>
> Unidentified Woman #3: "A typical Habitat home would be a step back for my neighborhood."[48]

One homeowner, Patricia Mathis, spoke more diplomatically: "I don't know that anyone is against the Habitat philosophy, but the philosophy, what we understand it to be, is you go into neighborhoods where these homes would be fitting for those neighbors. That's not the situation here."[49] Would the building of the less expensive Habitat houses in fact lower local property values? Probably, but in all likelihood for no other reason than the fact that some people believed they would, and they acted accordingly, leading to increased attempts to sell and/or fewer attempts to buy. The quoted homeowners in Boca Raton might have responded quite differently had they been occasionally party to some serious conversation with people like their potential new neighbors. And in that case the new houses, if built, would have been less likely to negatively affect the investments of neighbors. As it was, Habitat for Humanity had to look elsewhere.

I interpret this event in basically nonracial terms as revealing feelings of distrust and concern for personal safety in the face of encounters with newcomers, as well as class-rooted ideas about who is "fit" to live where. True, such feelings and concerns play into, and help sustain, the nation's long-standing dynamic of racial separation, but the fact remains that race is just one of many lines of separation that breed misunderstanding and thus more separation. Conversely, it's also just one of the many cleavages that would become more productive and less demonizing, or perhaps fade away, if more people were to create practices of cross-border encounters that take place over time, include conversation, and allow for disagreement. What's needed on the race front is, in other words, nothing other than that which is needed on other fronts: cross-border public conversation rooted in the celebration of encounter.

## FEMINISM AND THE UNDERSTANDING GAP

While I make race a central example, American culture is also replete with misunderstanding when it comes to feminism. As with race, so with gender: people's thinking is often guided by a misleading narrative of excess and backlash. As with race, genuinely opposed views exist on the various issues at stake— issues like gender roles, abortion, sexual freedom, marriage, and daycare—but the current situation is also marked by the empty polarization of disagreement failure.

The women's movement of the late twentieth century stands as one of the most successful revolutions in human history. Its major goals—equal pay for equal work, access by women to public lives on par with men, control by each woman over when and if she has children, and the equality of women's and men's right to sexual pleasure—are now widely accepted in the United States as rightful, even if many are yet to be fully achieved in practice and despite the heated disagreement on the subject of abortion. Somehow, despite this success, the popularity of the movement took a nosedive in the mid-1970s. This was in part because it came to be seen as asking for more than equality, in part because it came to be seen as an elite cause, working on behalf of ambitious professional women, and in part because it came to be associated with radical change in general—something many Americans had developed anxiety about in the face of protest, the violent backlash against protest, economic depression, double-digit inflation, and an increase in public displays of sex, sexuality, and nudity.

E. J. Dionne tells this story succinctly and generously in his "Family Politics" chapter, making it clear that the backlash had little to do with feminism's actual position on issues and quite a bit to do with skillful opponents and bad luck. The movement came into its own just as the major recessions and double-digit inflation of the 1970s hit with a vengeance. For the first time in some thirty years, real average wages stopped rising and the numbers of well-paying working-class jobs began to dwindle.[50] Economic insecurity was nothing new, but it had been largely hidden from the majority by postwar optimism, by a focus on aggregate numbers in public discussions and professional economics, and by the positive experiences of many wageworkers. By 1975, on the other hand, the tables had turned, and many were newly anxious about the future. To some it seemed that the crash of the American Dream could only be the fault of all the recent changes they knew about, feminism being one of the most visible. What made matters worse was that many of the immediate benefits of the women's movement flowed to professional women and other college graduates. Many working-class women didn't have the chance to choose to work for cash; they had to do so, just as many doors to meaningful work were closing. So it was that, as Dionne puts it, "[c]onservatives successfully cast feminists as the defenders of the professionals and the scourge of 'ordinary women.'"[51]

On the other hand, assumptions and techniques within the feminist movement contributed to the ways it was perceived. First, one group of activists (following the lead of antiracism efforts) emphasized rights, e.g., the right to protection against rape, equal pay for equal work, discrimination-free hiring, and access to safe abortion. This is hardly surprising, both because rights thinking is American to the core and because it's not clear that persuasion would have gotten anywhere on its own. Unfortunately, rights are by definition all or nothing. To call something a "right" is to declare it beyond discussion and compromise, to announce that the claim being made trumps other sorts of claims—such as that something is merely "good" (e.g., the traditional family or mom and dad identities). Because of this, rights claims tend to close off discussion. And in the 1970s women's rights claims made those who might have been defensive anyway feel all the more confronted. It didn't help matters that part of the positive identity (such as it was) that had long been offered to women by the culture was that of a nurturer, meaning precisely someone who does not make claims for herself, so that she can give to others.

The other problem with the rights strategy was that it tends to lead to the courtroom, and courtrooms are not dialogue-friendly places. Instead they are adversarial on many levels. To start with, in court people do not represent themselves but bring claims to an advocate (a lawyer) whose job it is to speak on their behalf. It is manifestly not the lawyers' job to listen to the other side and consider its arguments. Instead their obligation is to serve predefined interests no matter what, within the limits of the law. Moreover, the very structure of a courtroom, with competing lawyers who make no compromise as each of them appeals to a third party (judge or jury), makes the claim that there is a single objective truth of the law as it applies to the case at hand. The implicit faith is that the process of confrontation, not dialogue, is best suited to bring that truth forward.

The other wing of the women's movement focused not on rights but on consciousness-raising. The goal was new gender roles and personal relationships. It was understood that people needed to give up deep-seated ideas of what it is to be a man and what it is to be a woman, of machismo as male and deference as female, of strength as force and women as beauty. These notions, along with others, had to go, and, it was felt, they would go if people only worked at it hard enough. This was an opportunity for dialogue if ever there was one. And, indeed, there *was* lots of it. Many people took time to work things through, to grapple with difficult questions. Many adjusted their views of others, made new friends, redefined their lives, conquered old gender stereotypes, and in general experienced themselves in new and better ways as a result.

Unfortunately, some of the consciousness raising was flawed in that it was assumed that there was a single, better, "higher" consciousness to be reached, and if anyone didn't find this truth at first, he or she should try harder. This top-down, "vanguard" idea of truth is inherently arrogant. It can be downright oppressive, as it was during the Cultural Revolution in Mao's China, or its imposition can be subtle, as when a pseudodiscussion invokes guilt or encourages confession without demanding it, as when men are assumed to have an inner patriarch to defeat and whites to have an inner racist to expunge. One thing is for sure: the idea that people need their consciousness "raised" is not truly welcoming to those who disagree. They are at least not welcome on equal terms but instead invited to a sort of "workshop." A workshop is not the same as a discussion among equals.

In feminism's defense, the above-named flaws were, and are, merely the flaws of America. Looked at that way, the problem with the movement in the 1970s was not that it was "too radical" but that it was not radical *enough*. Since that time, moreover, the women's movement has become exemplary when it comes to dialogue. How many groups of committed activists debate each other with the intensity and the openness to many points of view of contemporary feminism? I am hard pressed to think of any that come close. Feminists are self-critical and take a wide variety of positions: some defend pornography, others critique it; some defend women's traditional identities, others criticize them; some call for universal rights, others say the very idea is Eurocentric. Unfortunately, few outside of academic circles have access to these debates (with some theorists encouraging this by their use of difficult language), and in any case the walls of polarization that have been created by the repetitive deployment of the conventional narrative are by now higher than most people can climb—at least without a new disagreement movement.

## LOVE OF CENTER VERSUS THE VITAL EDGE

One obstacle to a disagreement movement worth its salt is the widely believed notion that "moderate" views are best, that a healthy politics requires the cultivation of a "vital center." Interestingly, when Arthur M. Schlesinger, Jr. used these words in 1948 he was calling for the *expansion* of the range of groups and ideas

that were recognized as legitimate. He intended, for example, to encourage conservatives to distinguish between the "noncommunist left" and the communist
left, and to accept the former in dialogue, even as they excluded the latter.[52] In
reality, however, the idea of the vital center has not been inclusive in its effects.
Even Schlesinger himself saw unity as essential, which indeed was one reason
why he endorsed the exclusion of "radicals" from the political process, and it is in
this spirit that his phrase is now often invoked. Dionne, for example, says that,
while the pro-New Deal consensus celebrated by Schlesinger might have been
"boring" it was also "practical," and Dionne ends his political history by calling
for a "revived sense of common citizenship" based on a "new political center."[53]
Americans need once again to be "practical" so as to "move . . . politics away
from the moralistic concerns of the upper middle class, whether 'Goldwaterite' or
'McGovernite.'" The public discourse needs to rekindle a "moral sense . . . lacking
in American public life today."[54] They need, according to Dionne, to come together around the truths that have become obvious, such as the notions that mom
and dad traditional families are best and that work should be rewarded.

Dionne does not always make himself clear, as when he simultaneously calls
for less "moralism" and for more "moral sense," and I don't agree with him when
it comes to which truths are "obvious," but I have no problem with his taking
a stance on where the country should go. What I do have a problem with is
the way he hallows the center. Even if certain views command a majority or in
some substantive sense lie "in between" other competing views which are more
"radical" in some positional sense, they might not be better views than those
positioned closer to the edge. Arguments should triumph on their merits, not
because of their position in the polls or their location on an imaginary line. In
practice, admiration of the middle as such accomplishes nothing except putting
a people at risk of failing to move valuable perspectives from the "edge" so as
to make them part of some "center" of the future. Friedrich Hayek, writing from
a conservative, pro-free market angle, understood this well: "the argument for
democracy presupposes that any minority opinion may become a majority one.
New views must appear somewhere before they can become majority views."[55]

What, however, of Dionne's claim that a nation needs a degree of unity in
order to enjoy a "common sense of citizenship?" Isn't this a reason to elevate the
middle? Don't the views that reside there stand the best chance, independent
of their other merits, of forming the basis for consensus? This argument does
not stand up to scrutiny for two basic reasons. First, sometimes radical views are
actually closer to other opposing radical views than they are to views that lie
logically between them, and this means that sticking to either the center or the
majority view may actually lead to less unity, not more. I, for example, favor total
public financing of campaigns over a system with no rules at all besides disclosure.
In fact I consider the latter idea to be all the way on the "other side" and a terrible
plan. But I have to admit that no rules at all would be a big improvement over
the current maze of regulations and public and private financing, which gives an
advantage to those who can afford to pay experts to find loopholes. If, perchance,
a substantial number of people came to agree with me (no need for us to be

the majority) and were mobilized on the issue perhaps the nation could bring extremes closer to the center by adopting one of the extremes.

Second, and more fundamentally, the expression of strong disagreements in the public sphere, including radically divergent views that leave little room for compromise, does not necessarily put people's sense of shared citizenship at risk. People can feel connected in other ways, and in fact often do. People can be connected by virtue of their joint participation in argument. Or the fact of living together within a nation—and paying taxes and obeying laws as a general rule while sometimes protesting them peacefully—can form the basis for a sense of community. In other words, it can be enough for a people to agree about some things, in order to disagree strongly about others. They might, at the end of the day, feel connected enough to know they are member of a collectivity they endorse. In fact one can imagine a scenario in which more engagement in disagreement is supported by the celebration of the "vital edge," making for widespread endorsement of the system and commitment to the community. This is, of course, nothing less than the argument of this book, that the nation—and the world—is now in exactly that position and that the effort to include extremes in public discussions will not only improve policy but will also provide a renewed sense of community and membership, as more people feel included in the process and as people learn to see their political opponents in a new, more generous light. The argument is that, in this day and age, the pursuit of moderation is both self-defeating and unnecessary.

One final word on this subject, for the moment: those inclined to favor the "reasonable middle" might respond by pointing to the conventional narrative as evidence that movement toward extremes did in fact undermine national community. The problem with that claim, however, is that, as has been shown, the conventional narrative is wrong in a crucial respect: extremism—of the left or of the right—never did find its way through the maze of the state into policy.

## CONCLUSION

The point of this chapter and the last has been to use broad brushstrokes to put a few clichés and debilitating falsehoods to rest, such as the idea that life used to be great before it went downhill and that Americans lack political interest and rational ability. U.S. history teaches that no clearly immoral, singular force, coming from outside of some true America, caused today's state of empty polarization. It teaches that the American people are no less moral than they used to be. And it teaches that they are not in the thrall of a "devaluing" perpetrated by amoral liberals or in a depraved condition thanks simply to offensive lies and immoral greed facilitated by conservatives. Instead changes in work life, where people live, forms of entertainment, the structure of capital markets, and strategies followed by the major political parties have combined with long-standing anti-disagreement principles in the culture to bring the nation to where it is today. These antidisagreement principles are that each individual has full control over their fate, elites know best, rational thinking leads to one right answer, true community requires unity and can be based on personal choice, and partisanship equals corruption. Standing against these principles, and able to provide hope if people pay attention, are many shining examples of Americans who understood, and stood up for, the idea that a true democracy requires disagreement-friendly beliefs and practices.

The direction the nation has traveled in recent decades—thanks to this mixed legacy—has been away from unscripted, risky, public conversation as a socially legitimate and regular part of people's lives, towards greater social and physical distance between the perspectives, neighborhoods, and classes. Carnival-like town squares and hotel lobbies, with people from many social ranks milling about together while on holiday; thousands gathered at a political speech and making it a festival; rowdy political conventions which really decided something; and barn-raisings where neighbors who maybe didn't like each other nonetheless completed a task together: these have been replaced by privatized leisure, the use of television to consume what other people do and say, the provision of needs through private buying, and political action as little more than voting and giving money. The current ways of completing political tasks are for the most part both nonconversational and inaccessible to view. One might go so far as to say that the nation lacks a true public realm and that the populace is therefore akin to a mere population—at any given time more or less exploited, better or worse managed, well or poorly entertained, and granted more or less by way of strictly individual freedoms—but not a truly free people.

CHAPTER 4

# United We Stand and Conspiracy Thinking

Conspiracy theories link structural and historical forces to subjective political action by elites who prefer to confer and operate out of the glare of transparent daylight, in the opaque twilight of deep politics.[1]

—Daniel Hellinger

The historical accounts of the last two chapters support the claim that the empty polarization now plaguing U.S. politics is to a considerable extent the result of misunderstandings, communication shortcoming, and separations. To put it another way, they support the claim that today's political differences are not expressions of unbridgeable philosophical and theological differences, that there is no "clash of civilizations" (to use Samuel P. Huntington's misguided phrase), and, therefore, that cross-border talking has the potential to transform many a situation for the better.[2]

True, most of the world's separations and misunderstandings constitute formidable obstacles to the very cross-border talking that might best address them. This is in part because misunderstandings are still understandings of a sort, functioning both to shore up identities and to make sense of events. Identity-connected notions, moreover, connect viscerally to place. Perception, geography, and appearance get linked in mutually sustaining ways. While geography can and does change and given identities can potentially be sustained by new ideas and less demonizing allegiances, it's also true that new, identity-challenging experiences and information about other people are sometimes extremely threatening. In part to ward off such challenges, people erect all sorts of obstacles to better disagreement. This chapter tackles two of them: conspiracy thinking and the philosophy of "United We Stand."

## UNITED WE STAND

One Monday morning, in the summer of 2007, I caught some radio news that included a statement made by President George W. Bush earlier that day: "Withdrawing troops permanently, based on politics, not on the advice of our military commanders, would be contrary to our national interest."[3] I have no reason to doubt that Bush was asserting what he believed to be true. I also suspect, without animus, that he was "doing" politics by dismissing an opposing view as "politics." What matters here, however, is that by doing so he invoked a commonplace assertion about partisanship and the national interest, the notion being that the former is best left to one side in the interest of the latter, especially when it comes to foreign policy. To do otherwise, the thinking goes, would be both weakness and error.

Thirty minutes later I again encountered this "United We Stand" idea, this time during *On Point*, a National Public Radio call-in show. The guest, Republican presidential candidate Mike Huckabee, was contrasting terrorists with the United States by saying that whereas "we" believe the Soviet Union fell because of an arms build-up that it "couldn't keep up with," "they" believe that the Soviets lost "the will to fight" because of the persistence of the insurgent opposition in Afghanistan.[4] Huckabee went on to say that Al Qaeda now plans "to wear us down" in similar fashion. His conclusion was that any declaration of intent to withdraw from Iraq would be a disaster because it would undermine the necessary U.S. display of will and unity.

I leave aside the question of why the Soviet Union fell (I am not in Huckabee's "we" on that one) in order to consider the validity of United We Stand. In invoking this idea Bush and Huckabee join a long line of American political leaders, from both sides of the political aisle. From John Addams to Lyndon Johnson, they all insist a people must stand together as one nation when it faces the rest of the world; that's where the value of disagreement reaches its limit, especially during a war effort. When considering this hallowed idea, two lines of thought present themselves. First, one can ask about plausibility, given the rules of logic and the realities of human psychology. The other tack is to ask what history has to say. Starting with plausibility, a problem appears right away: It seems that United We Stand cannot be *generally* true or *generally* false. Instead its validity must depend on the situation. It must depend, for example, on the worldview and motivation of "the enemy." Would a given suicide bomber be deterred by the unity of the opposition? Maybe, but the opposite might be the case. Indeed, when it comes to contemporary nonstate terrorism, the opposite seems likely. There is, after all, every reason to believe that such terrorism proceeds (as does much warfare violence) by virtue of heavy doses of demonization and abstraction. Those to be killed are scripted as unredeemable, as having stepped across a line into a nonhuman zone of pure evil. Or their reality as separate individuals is abstracted away until it disappears from view; they become merely "the enemy,"[5] as when the people working inside the World Trade Center on September 11, 2001 were seen by their attackers as mere representatives of "America," the latter being understood as a total enemy, out to destroy Islam and install Godlessness throughout the world. Would terrorist planners with such a view be deterred by the perception that this enemy was steadfastly unified against them? It seems likelier that they would be newly motivated.

To turn it around, one can also ask if terrorism would be aided by a show of disunity among the ranks of their perceived enemy. Maybe, but again the opposite could also be the case. Quite a few Muslims who are not terrorists feel that their way of life and their religion are under attack by Western, secularist policies.[6] This moves some to sympathize with Al Qaeda and to see it as an army fighting on their behalf. What if said sympathizers learned that thousands of U.S. citizens were arguing about the validity of their government's policies on terrorism, the Middle East, the location of military bases, and global development? Wouldn't this undermine the process of abstraction intrinsic to terrorism? Wouldn't this weaken the rationale offered by Al Qaeda for its actions, thereby also weakening the support networks it relies on? Even if one only answers "maybe" that's enough to support the conclusion that disunity could conceivably function at times as a source of military strength rather than weakness.

Huckabee himself offered support for the latter view when he said in the same interview that terrorists who attack in the name of Islam seek nothing less than "theological war," that their "purpose of life is to establish a religious kingdom on Earth," and that to get there they aim to kill all those who cannot live within and endorse that world. This worldview, Huckabee added, stands in contrast to America's approach to Islam: "we" are "perfectly willing to let them live where they live."

The last remark raises several questions. Who is "we" exactly, and don't some of "them" live "here"? Don't some tolerant folks live "there"? And how many Americans are as tolerant as Huckabee declares? Have U.S. national policies in fact suggested a live and let live approach? Is that how Muslims around the world understand the U.S. decision to invade Iraq? But the issue on the table is unity, so the question I address here is, if terrorists think as Huckabee says they do and if they are honored to die in pursuit of their goals, why would a display of unity and willpower do anything to stop them?

## THE NEED FOR DISSENT

Another issue to consider is cost: even in those cases when unity would have a valuable deterrent effect, it might be a bad idea for other reasons, for example, by leading to the adoption of poorly conceived, perhaps even ultimately disastrous policies. In fact this is likely, as Cass R. Sunstein makes clear in his recent book *Why Societies Need Dissent*.[7] Individuals, it turns out, have deeply conformist tendencies. They want to please those around them and be liked by those whom they admire. Also, their very perceptions of reality often fall into line with what they imagine to be in the minds of others around them. Because of this people are, under certain conditions, remarkably prone to misunderstanding and error, regardless of how smart or well-educated they are. With groups the problem is even worse. On the other hand, the voice of even a single alternative voice can break the spell, leading to error correction and better decisions. Thus it is that societies need dissent.

In making his case, Sunstein serves up a host of useful concepts. A "social cascade," for example, is a chain reaction that starts with the actions of just a few people. "Others then follow them, thinking that these initial movers are probably right or wanting to gain social approval."[8] If this second round of doers is observed in turn, followed in turn, and so on, it can create a wave of activity or opinion that reaches far and wide. Social cascades have led to nationwide shopping sprees, new fashion crazes, and the rise of urban legends about Halloween candy. They have helped to bring new and better laws to many a state on a pressing subject but also resulted in brutal, irrational acts of prejudice and discrimination. In any case the dynamic at work is conformist and the aggregate result considerably— sometimes entirely—accidental. Most importantly here, cascades can deprive society of useful information that many possess but keep to themselves.

To see how this is so imagine a CIA intelligence specialist who has reason to doubt the conclusion of a colleague about weapons of mass destruction in Iraq. He respects his colleague, or he depends on her for promotion; also his doubts are not conclusive, and the colleague's interpretation is plausible. In this situation he might not air his concerns. When the right moment arrives to do so, he might find his tongue doesn't quite get there. Now imagine a third colleague who observes the consensus of the first two. Thinking that each of the others has made an independent decision about the threat, he becomes convinced, and so on. In the end a decision might be made that, if only the people in the room had shared what they knew or believed, would not have been made.

Many of Sunstein's examples concern health care, a realm of activity where even the experts can never know enough about all the possible approaches, modalities, and research and where many judgment calls have to be made—like whether to proceed with surgery, what medicine is likely to be safe or effective, how much lifestyle and the food industry is involved, etc. There are many values to balance—such as the patient's quality of life, likely length of her life, risk of malpractice litigation, time needed for other patients, and what insurance will pay. In this situation it makes sense for physicians to rely to some degree on the opinions and the decisions of other physicians and even nonphysicians. On the other hand, if many of those others are likewise relying on others, the result could be a cascade of bad medicine, the blind leading the blind: "Some medical practices, such as tonsillectomy, appear to have been adopted without a great deal of scientific support, and extreme differences in tonsillectomy frequencies (and other procedures) provide good evidence that cascades are at work."[9]

Sunstein makes a distinction between cascades based on uncertainty of information and those based on the power of reputation, but, as the above examples indicate, the two forces are often combined. In the political sphere these group dynamics contribute to a phenomenon called "ideological amplification." This is when deliberation about a topic among a group of mostly like-minded people causes views to shift, not toward the median point among the perspectives represented but towards greater ideological severity; the "deliberating group ends up taking a *more extreme position* italics in original than its median member took before deliberation began."[10] Consider, for example, a simulation study described by Sunstein. Some 3,000 subjects were first polled to determine where the opinions of each fell on the subject of the proper severity of punishment for those convicted of crimes. They were then divided into "juries" of six, each of which was instructed to deliberate until it reached a unanimous verdict about punishment in a hypothetical case. The effect, says Sunstein, "was to create both a *severity shift* for jurors inclined toward high punishment and a *leniency shift* for jurors inclined toward low punishment [italics in original]."[11] In other words, the group process amplified the original majority point of view.

Conversely, the same conformist dynamic often causes "ideological dampening." This is when people in minority positions within a group moderate their positions in the direction of those around them. For example, when a conservative Republican judge joins a judicial panel with two Democratic judges, the decisions of the Republican often move in the ideological direction of the others. And a single Democratic judge on a panel with two Republicans is similarly likely to move toward her colleagues. Such behavior is not irrational. It can save time and energy to follow the clues of others, and in politics, as in medicine, individuals often lack the information needed to make a confident decision independently. "If we aren't sure what to do, we might well adopt an easily applied rule of thumb: follow the crowd."[12]

One of Sunstein's claims is that ideological amplification leads different groups further and further apart, ultimately contributing to political polarization. In fact he goes so far as to claim that humans are subject to a "law of group polarization,"[13] and, following from that, he suggests that it's wise to be wary of "too much" public deliberation. This news, if true, is disturbing, for one because it seems to undermine Sunstein's own call for dissent, seeing as it can be read as a warning against listening to people's political opinions in the setting of a group. Isn't speaking and being heard in such a context the very essence of dissent or at least an aspect of its life support system? Are people supposed to dissent but not deliberate?

One way to reconcile this apparent contradiction is to conclude that Sunstein is an advocate of a romanticized, individualist version of dissent, of freedom for lone individuals who speak against groups from the outside. Perhaps what Sunstein wants is protection for whistleblowers and witnesses; perhaps he wants people to value intellectuals who write books criticizing the system. That's all well and good, but if he also wants a culture of dissent even within organizations, as he says he does, then it seems as if his argument is somewhat defeated by the very law he discovers. And, absent the experience of hearing different opinions within their groups and discovering them useful, how many people will support the lone critic anyway?

Fortunately, there is no law of group polarization. What Sunstein has discovered is instead a *tendency* in a *particular society* at a *particular time in its history*, not a law. Moreover, the particular society at issue, the United States, just happens to be marked by a great degree of separation and segregation of age, class, perspective, race, and more, as well as by rather high degrees of distrust across group lines. And, most importantly, the tendency actually observed is a movement toward polarization after deliberation *among the like-minded*. Sunstein puts it this way: "like-minded people, after discussions with their peers, tend to end up thinking a more extreme version of what they thought before they started to talk."[14]

The news brought by Sunstein, then, is good. There is nothing *inherently* polarizing about deliberation. The presence of even a single, strong dissenting voice in a group faced with a decision can change members' perceptions and decisions entirely, usually for the better. Organizations that manage to cultivate a culture of dissent are far more likely to avoid blunders. On the other hand, the news is also that societies need more than dissent, as the latter is often understood as the voicing of a singular opinion; instead they also need disagreement, meaning engagement and argument in cross-border conversations.

To get back to the question of leaving politics at the water's edge, when it comes to basic plausibility, United We Stand does not fare well. Even to wisely decide if, in a given situation, there is a need for unity requires disunity at some level; it requires spirited conversation, with dissenting voices raised. True, in theory such dissent could take place only amongst high-placed decision makers who are sworn to secrecy. But how likely is it that in practice there will be enough dissent in such settings, given the law (tendency) of ideological amplification among the like-minded? It is not likely, and—I might add—it becomes even less so if in addition the decision makers believe in United We Stand.

## UNITY, THE MEDIA, AND THE VIETNAM WAR

This brings us to the second approach: how has United We Stand fared in history? A problem here is that the failures and successes of national policies always have multiple causes, so one can never say for sure if it was disunity that led to failure or unity that led to success. Indeed, it is often not easy to agree even about how unified any nation is or was at a given time. On the other hand, people do make claims about what particular events have to say, and it makes sense to ask how strong these arguments are.

For example, did the American mass media lose the Vietnam War by spreading doubt and pessimism about the odds of U.S. success? Many answer yes or did so in the 1970s and 1980s, when that idea helped to cement United We Stand as a staple assumption of American politics, thereby also shaping today's understanding of what it means to be "liberal" and "conservative." The controversy over the media role has centered on coverage of the Tet Offensive of 1968, when the U.S. enemy—the National Front for the Liberation of South Vietnam, also known as the Viet Minh—launched a major attack on the Saigon government and U.S. forces. Tet was a military failure: the attacking army suffered heavy losses; there was no general uprising against the Saigon government, and in the end the Viet Minh controlled little new ground. On the other hand, the event was the beginning of the end for the United States, as it contradicted claims that the conflict would soon be over and thus brought the public into the circle of doubt about the viability of the war effort that was already well formed among the U.S. war planners.

Peter Braestrup was one of many who complained that the media helped to lose the war for the United States at this crucial juncture by being overly "adversarial" and "pessimistic" in their reporting. Robert Elegant was another, arguing that "[f]or the first time in history, the outcome of a war was determined not in the battlefield, but on the printed page, and above all, on the television screen."[15] This view was first disseminated by conservative organizations such as Freedom House and Accuracy in Media, but it quickly became accepted in the mainstream, often in a more moderate version, as when, for example, John Corry "defended" the press by calling it "unmindful" rather than "unpatriotic."[16] Critics of the media were especially upset about the leak to the press—and subsequent reporting—of a high-level debate that took place within the Johnson administration after the offensive had been mostly turned back and General Westmoreland responded by asking the president for 206,003 more troops. Some of the architects of U.S. policy thought such an increase would send the wrong signal, telling the world that the United States had just lost ground when it had not, and others said that the higher troop numbers would only be matched by the enemy. When this debate became public it was, said the critics, harder for Johnson to present a front of optimism and unity.

The message that the press lost the war found a ready audience for many reasons. Some Americans simply wanted to find a way to support the troops. Also, every war brings the concept of duty to the fore, and some take this as injunction to endorse whatever the nation's leaders have to say. By this thinking, the press failed in its duty. Then there were those who simply did not like losing. Finally, one way to grasp the meaning of war—and reduce it to more manageable proportions, morally speaking—is to take the game/contest analogy too far, as if there are clear "sides" to every conflict, and the point is simply to "win"—rather than, say, to pursue the objectives that led to the war, or were used to justify it in the first place. Thus winning for some becomes an end in itself; each death in its name intensifies the desire that the nation continue the fight and increases the force of the imperative of rooting for one's team. Therefore the American media should have cheered for American victory.

Such is the psychology of warfare, but did the press in fact help lose the war for the United States? One way to consider this question is to look at *Manufacturing Consent*, the leftist classic by Edward S. Herman and Noam Chomsky.[17] Why, one might ask, look there? Wouldn't a "moderate," and thus more "neutral," source be better? This is one of the antidisagreement fallacies I hope to put to rest with this book. The fact is that "bias," if it means a strong point of view, often leads to better information, and a careful reading of Herman and Chomsky reveals lots of just that. They apply a "propaganda model" to the question at hand. This model predicts slavish support by the mainstream media (the broadcast television networks and public television) for elite points of view, and it likewise predicts the quashing of reporters' perspectives—whether liberal or conservative—whenever they appear to the ownership to threaten advertising revenue or put them at risk of a "flak" attack. "Flak" is the theorists' name for accusations of bias and/or lack of patriotism coming from those in a position to be heard—from well-organized and well-funded corporate interests in particular—and which is therefore likely to undermine media credibility and ultimately reduce their audience share.

What Herman and Chomsky find using their model is that, first, the main-stream media were, if anything, more patriotic than neutral, in that they never gave voice to the truly harsh critics who called the war an "invasion" of South Vietnam by the United States, who denounced U.S. policy as "imperialist," who expressed doubt about the idea that Vietnamese communism was an extension of Soviet communism, or who said that the conflict among the Vietnamese was actually a nationwide struggle between nationalists and ex-colonial collaborators rather than between "North Vietnam" and "South Vietnam." Instead the U.S. press, "with rare exceptions . . . gave an account of the war as perceived by the U.S. military on the ground or as offered in press briefings" and also said that "Washington's version prevailed until elite divisions within the United States expanded the range of tactical debate."[18]

Herman and Chomsky also conclude that by the time the media contributed to the appearance of the war going badly for the United States, it had been in fact going badly for some time. This is not to say that the United States was "losing" in a conventional sense—as it indeed never did lose in that sense—but rather that the U.S. armed forces were not winning and that the Saigon government was losing what little public support it had among the Vietnamese. It was, in other words, clear that there was no end in sight for the United States except to withdraw, that the only way to keep Vietnam from unifying under the leadership of those who ruled in Hanoi was to maintain large numbers of U.S. troops, sustain ongoing casualties, continue destroying Vietnam's villages and plant life, and continue killing large numbers of North and South Vietnamese.

By the way, the left-wing critique of the media offered by Herman and Chomsky is not the opposite of the oft-heard right-wing argument that the U.S. mass media are overwhelmingly liberal. Different people look for different things and use different definitions. Therefore they notice different aspects. (See the next chapter for more on this subject.) A newspaper that gives more coverage to right-to-choose arguments than right-to-life arguments about abortion might also report on business only by noting how well the markets are doing, never once giving mention of the left-wing critique of the business world in general and rarely covering mildly pro-labor perspectives. To a socialist the newspaper is conservative, and to a social conservative the newspaper is liberal. Each is right about something, and, since few on each side of the issue talk much to those on the other side, their respective perceptions tend to stick. I have more to say about this in the next chapter, which addresses the role of the mass media in today's disagreement failure.

If one suspects that Herman and Chomsky cooked the books or failed to see evidence they didn't want to see, one might want to read their chapters side by side with, say, Peter Braestrup's Freedom House-sponsored study of Tet media coverage, *Big Story*.[19] Alternatively, one might turn to the work of more politically moderate historians, survey findings about support for the war, comments made by U.S. military leaders of the day and since, and the recently released transcripts of White House remarks made by President Johnson and others.[20] They mostly back up what Herman and Chomsky have to say. Many point out, for example, that even before Tet the word was out that Vietnam was a "quagmire." The 1967 polls, while reporting majority support for continuing the effort, revealed that a plurality already viewed the war as a "mistake." And Daniel Hallin, in a 2003 Chapel Hill presentation about war and the media, echoed Herman and Chomsky when he said that "the media were more followers than leaders in the changed of opinion and policy on the Vietnam War."[21] Hallin goes on the say that "the coverage of the Vietnam War was actually highly supportive of the war in the early years" (before Tet), that the television coverage was "highly sanitized," with "little blood and gore," and that "television is generally wary about anything that will be politically controversial."[22] Importantly, he adds that media coverage became more pessimistic only *after* troop morale had already declined and thus could not have been a cause of that decline. This media turn was, he argues, caused by their tendency to focus on the troops, to tell sympathetic (and politically safe) stories about them as individuals. Thus, when most troops were enthusiastic about the mission the press seemed optimistic, and when troops began sharing doubts the press coverage sent a more pessimistic message.

Then there are the words of Lyndon Johnson, spoken to Senate Majority Leader Mike Mansfield in 1964: "I'm doing my best to hold this thing in balance just as long as I can. I can't run out. I'm not going to run in. I can't just sit there and let them be murdered. So I've got to put enough there to hold them and protect them [the Saigon government]."[23] This suggests that the war was not going well four years before Tet. Thus it is that foreign policy analyst Leslie Gelb, by no stretch of the imagination a leftist of any kind, remarked in 1972 that "[n]either the Americans nor the Vietnamese communists had good odds for a traditional military victory in Vietnam" and that "stalemate was the most likely outcome."[24]

Another reason to be suspicious of the "media lost the war" thesis is that foreign policy experts and military planners find the idea attractive for reasons that have nothing to do with its truth or falsity and thus have seen reason to propagate it. Their concern is the specter of a loss of faith, on the part of the general public, in the wisdom, benevolence, ability, and power of the U.S. government as an international actor. Absent such convictions, it is thought, public opposition will unduly interfere with the foreign policy establishment in the future when it tries to lead the nation into necessary military action. Henry Kissinger famously called such public skepticism the "Vietnam Syndrome," and the term has stuck, as if being skeptical about what leaders say about matters of war and peace is foolish, an attack of irrationality, a kind of posttraumatic stress disorder.[25] In the context of the Iraq War, the idea has resurfaced from the mouths of many a liberal and conservative, as when, for example, ABC's White House correspondent Terry Moran, in 2005, spoke to Hugh Hewitt on the latter's radio show:

There is, Hugh, I agree with you, a deep anti-military bias in the media. One that begins from the premise that the military must be lying, and that

American projection of power around the world must be wrong. I think that that is a hangover from Vietnam, and I think it's very dangerous. That's different from the media doing its job of challenging the exercise of power without fear or favor.[26]

It is worth pausing to think about the assumptions embedded in the notion of the Vietnam Syndrome. First, it is taken for granted that there is a clear "national interest" at any given time, a notion which in turn assumes that individual and group interests do not diverge on foreign policy questions—that all of the people (multinationals, wageworkers, importers, exporters, child raisers, defense workers, soldiers, homemakers, etc.) are one in relation to those outside the nation's borders. It assumes that the line between foreign and domestic policy is a relatively clear one. It assumes that experts know what the national interest is and will endorse it. And it assumes that those experts will be in charge and should therefore have the "room to move" to make and implement policy as they see fit. What these assumptions add up to is that democracy is constraining and unnecessary in the area of foreign policy.

The idea that nations cannot afford democracy on foreign policy is especially scary now that all nations live in the zone of credible terrorist threat and presumably will for the foreseeable future. Also, many traditionally "domestic issues" (domestic wiretapping, educational curriculum, interrogation policies, and more) can plausibly be said to connect to the "war on terror" in one way or another. Together these ideas suggest that democracy is simply outdated. There seems, using the logic of Vietnam-Syndrome thinking, nowhere to draw the line in defense of democracy as a first value.

## UNITED WE FALL AND NGO DINH DIEM

Fortunately, the story of the Vietnam War lends support to democracy as a first value rather than to United We Stand. Disagreement, it turns out, is not at all the same as hesitation or appeasement. Instead it's a way to make good decisions likelier, especially in the typical real-world situation where the national interest is debatable and where experts can be, and often are, wrong. The U.S. war planners of the Vietnam period were, as it turns out, wrong about a good deal, and they lacked a healthy process of disagreement, so their mistakes did not get checked or corrected. They did not adequately understand guerilla war, for example. They did not know (or did not want to know) that the "North Vietnamese" enemy was inspired by anticolonialist nationalism as much or more than by communism. They did not understand Vietnamese communism, imagining it as rooted in Russian and/or Chinese influence when it was very much Vietnamese. And they apparently brought to the conflict a stubborn gut belief that the United States could never lose any war if it did not lose its will to win, thereby ignoring other analyses of the odds for success.

One particular episode is telling: Stephen Kinzer, in his book *Overthrow*, tells the story of the 1963 decision by the Kennedy administration to covertly organize a coup to overthrow the regime of Ngo Dinh Diem in South Vietnam. In 1954 Secretary of State John Foster Dulles had sent Diem, an anticommunist Vietnamese Catholic living in Belgium, to Saigon so he could be installed by the United States as the prime minister of "South Vietnam."[27] This was part of the Eisenhower administration's effort to prevent elections from taking place, since it was not ready to accept the almost certain result of the election of Ho Chi Minh, a Vietnamese nationalist who, while a fan of Thomas Jefferson, was also a declared communist. By 1963, however, some U.S. leaders had come to see the repressive Diem as a liability rather than as an ally and thought he had to go. Others, including President Kennedy, Robert McNamara, and Robert Kennedy, thought that the coup was a terrible idea, but they authorized it nonetheless, and they deeply regretted it after Diem was dead and the situation in South Vietnam turned for the worse for the United States. How did this happen?

It happened because a few people (Assistant Secretary of State Roger Hilsman, Undersecretary of State Averill Harriman, and acting Head of the State Department George Ball) who wanted the coup to happen knew enough to get the ball rolling at a time when three of Diem's supporters (Secretary of State Dean Rusk, Secretary of Defense Robert McNamara, and President Kennedy) were not in Washington. It happened because Ball let the president think that Rusk had agreed to the coup plan, when he had not yet done so. But, in the final analysis, it happened because a meeting of the inner circle, held on October 29, 1963, ended inconclusively, and the coup supporters took that as a green light. "A broad array of top officials voiced doubts about the coup, including JFK himself, without any actual effect on the course of events."[28] Many in the room thought the coup a bad idea, but there was no vote. No one said to put the question off until a decision was more firmly reached. Kennedy did not ask for a clear yes or no from anyone. In the words of historian John Prados, "President Kennedy does not announce a clear decision, but the group proceeds as if the United States does support the coup."

All in all, the event provides, as Kinzer says, "a textbook example of how not to shape policy."[29] The group did not have a culture of spirited disagreement. No one wanted to second guess others with a firm no or demand that people support their stance more convincingly. They were all, it appears, somehow operating under the cloud of United We Stand, and as a result they took action without really meaning to, and many of them regretted it ever after.

## ONE MORE EXAMPLE

In 1948 a U.S. government administrator named Luther Gulick published a small book called *Administrative Reflections from World War II*. During the war Gulick served in multiple capacities (on the National Resources Planning Board, in the Departments of Treasury, Commerce, and War, on the War Production Board, at the United Nations, in the Bureau of the Budget, and on the White House staff), and after the war he studied U.S. government reports about war planning in Germany and Japan. From all this he drew fifteen lessons and, in summing them up, praised the American war planning process system precisely on the grounds that it allowed debate, relative to the nation's dictatorial wartime opponents. First the German and Japanese governments suffered from delay, divisiveness, excess secrecy, and bad decision making. "The action of the totalitarian leaders was irresponsible and disastrous in the nth degree [italics in original]." Failures were "hidden and denied behind a wall of censorship and discipline." The U.S. government, on the other hand, benefitted from the fact that "[b]road plans are more valid when they have been subject to the kind of review and criticism which democracy alone affords."[30]

If United We Stand has so few facts behind it, why is it so popular? Three words come to my mind: emotion, nationalism, and gender. It can feel good to see oneself as part of a unified whole. This is all the more the case in wartime, when in all likelihood the very existence of the whole is declared to be at risk and when fellow group members are putting their lives on the line, and some of them are killing and being killed. Soldiers need to believe in the cause if at all possible. Even if a given soldier's performance is not at all compromised by dissent within the ranks or by his own doubts, it may nonetheless make them heartsick, doubling their grief for fallen comrades and adding bitterness and anger. Those not in the battle will want and need to offer emotional support to their friends, family members, countrymen, and countrywomen who are. And finally, there is an old tradition that says that a good man is a warrior, and a good woman is someone who supports the warrior-citizens. These are identities: they can provide meaning; they can provide psychological and sociological glue that people live by; they can see a person through a time of stress. They thus have staying power independent of facts, logical justifications, and accurate estimates of costs and benefits.

To all of this I offer this entire book in support of the proposition that there are other ways of belonging and believing more consistent with spirited disagreement and thus with good policy making. One does not have to be warrior or a cheerleader to be a good citizen or to be a good man or woman. It will not, however, be easy to move towards these ways. United We Stand is just one of the obstacles. Conspiracy thinking, because of its erroneous conceptualization of power, is another.

## CONSPIRACY THINKING, COMMAND CENTER POWER, AND CAPILLARY POWER

The phrase "conspiracy theory" is most often used to refer to what might better be called "grand conspiracy theory," meaning any claim that a small group secretly wields tremendous power over a wide range of disparate events and territories, perhaps over the whole world, and uses this power to carry out a malevolent plan of further domination and total exploitation. Appearances, by this way of thinking, are never what they seem: apparently disconnected events are connected; the signs of the work of the single source of evil are everywhere, even though they are not easily understood. Millions of people are fooled, some unwittingly acting in support of the cabal, while others knowingly commit crimes of the highest order, in order to advance the conspiratorial cause.

Each grand conspiracy theory is actually several, as the assumption of successful secrecy allows theorizing to spin into endless variation. One believer's list of conspirators includes the "talking heads" in the mass media, "International Bankers, Secular Humanists, 'Progressive' Educators, New Age Gurus, The United Nations, American Politicians, Secret Societies, Fabian Socialists, Darwinists, [and] Marxists," all of whom are said to be "working in concert to construct the New Age World Order."[31] Others consider the World Bank, IMF, NATO, and European Union to be the key players. Some point the finger at certain families: the Rothschilds, the Du Ponts, the Rockefellers, and the Morgans. Then there are conspiracy theorists who include the Europeans kings and queens in the picture. And at least a few people believe that "the Illuminati" are busy setting up internment camps around the United States, so as to imprison dissidents once their worldwide coup is underway. Again, no one can say for sure who's in the conspiracy, as by definition they act in secret. But, as Robert Alan Goldberg points out, there is a pattern:

> The script has become familiar: Individuals and groups, acting in secret, move and shape recent American history. Driven by a lust for power and wealth, they practice deceit, subterfuge, and even assassination, sometimes brazenly executed. Nothing is random or the matter of coincidence. Institutional process, miscalculation, and chance bend to the conspirator's single-minded will.[32]

Such scripts provide endless opportunities for believers to "read the signs" and also to enjoy being among the few who are in the know. In the language of one astute theorist of the subject, grand conspiracy theory mobilizes an "endless desire for a totalizing method of mapping and understanding an order where power seems always elsewhere;" its discourse produces "an incessant chain of interpretation" for those who are on the trail.[33]

Grand conspiracy theory should not, however, be confused with the idea that a relatively small number of well-situated elites are planning, or have at times planned and executed, covert actions, in order to get, maintain, or increase their power over someone, with regard to something. Sometimes such claims are made without the assertion of any unity of evil. Sometimes there is, likewise, no assumption that an absolutely innocent populace would live in a power-free world of automatic consensus and virtue, if only the bad guys were defeated by the light of truth. Some theories of concentrated power are, in other words, neither kooky nor about the pleasures of theorizing and secrecy; they are specific claims, grounded in observation, to the effect that some people have power over others by means of their deliberate planning and action.

There are, for example, analysts who argue that policy making in capitalist societies is dominated (not completely "controlled") by a relatively cohesive group of politically active corporate elites and members of their rich family allies,

   If power is not located in some secret bunker or penthouse, where is it, and what is it? First a technical definition, derived from the work of a host of theorists, including Steven Lukes, Michel Foucault, Wendy Brown, and Eric A. Schutz: dominative power is present when some people substantially benefit compared to others, with regard to the quality of their lives, and do so by virtue of the way their respective options are defined and limited, unless those ways of defining and limiting (1) are natural and inescapable or (2) are freely chosen by all concerned as a result of their participation in a fully informed, democratic, deliberative process.[42] Another way of saying this is that dominative power exists when a social and cultural edifice (including ideas, specific forms of authority, economic opportunities, education, unhealthy environments, etc.) does harm to some people and when less harmful options either exist or would exist if people were to inclusively share ideas and concerns and act on the conclusions they came to as a result of those conversations.

   This definition raises many thorny questions, including whether anyone can ever be said to have interests they're not aware of, such that it's possible to say they are being "harmed" by a system even if they don't know it—that they "would" have chosen otherwise if they were more aware of various options. Fortunately I don't need to address that issue here. Even if one cannot convincingly make the claim that "true" interests exist or no one can ever know for sure just what is in fact in someone's true interest at a given time, one can still define power as including the shaping of the way people see their interests and options. And to do so is to allow for consideration and acknowledgment of the cultural and structural forces that put some groups on top relative to others, that leave the lives of so many nasty and short, and that often stand in the way of more democracy and justice.

   I have just spoken of what power "is," but what forms of it, so defined, operate in the contemporary world? Michel Foucault provides helpful language: power today is capillary, multiple, structural, discursive, and subject forming.[43] Put another way, societies now depend on the relatively smooth functioning of enormous organizations, intense levels of complex coordination, the consumption of staggering amounts of human and natural energy, and globally extended forms of organized violence. For this reason and others, power is rarely (and never routinely) a matter of pure force and total control; instead it's an artifact of the positions people occupy in organizations, the identities they form in their different cultural and organizational locations, and the ideas that circulate to offer justifications for those organizations and attach authority to those positions. The use of violence and the threat of its use are part of the equation, but so is the generation of beliefs, especially about what's legitimate and what's not. Everyone is ruled by "discourse" to one degree or another; everyone is influenced by ways of talking, depicting, and imagining themselves and the world.

   Power is, in sum, something like what Antonio Gramsci called "hegemony." It depends on legitimation; it's organizational and situational, and it almost always comes with built-in limits. This means that those who benefit most from its structures are in their grip just as much—or more—than those who benefit minimally or not at all. The powerful are, in other words, socially shaped like everyone else. They have to dance to one tune or another in order to stay in their positions of influence, and there is no center from which a small group could ever knowingly run the show in grand fashion, themselves free of the control they wreak upon others. Instead power, circulating through an uncountable number of channels (capillaries), reaches every person, never in exactly the same way. Finally, and perhaps hardest to accept for Americans, the sort of freedom possible in the real world is (by this view), itself a creature of power. It's created and limited by prevailing arrangements and discourses: never total, and never entirely abolished.

## THE POPULARITY OF COMMAND CENTER/CONSPIRACY THINKING

While the capillary, discursive notion of real-world power has rather convincingly defeated the command center idea in theory books on the subject, it has not triumphed elsewhere, in part because the latter notion has appeal that goes way beyond its truth value. When connected to conspiratorial ideas, it can bring the dense complexity of power down to manageable size, thereby helping people make sense of that which befalls them. It can be satisfying or reassuring to think that pure good is realizable and to locate oneself on that side of the moral equation, to see the good as requiring no-trade-offs, as a condition in which each person is entirely free and also at one with the community. It has the appeal of conspiracy theory described by Goldberg, giving "hope, unity, and purpose in a world that often seems beyond the reach of the powerless. It factors into the deep discontent men and women feel about their leaders and the direction they have set for the Republic."[44] Command center conspiracy thinking (CCCT) can, finally, be fun; it can provide people with endless opportunities to look for, and perhaps uncover, layers of secrecy and intrigue. "Conspiracy theory clearly wants something: it is a never-ending practice that combs the past and the present for evidence of some transcendent, all-explanatory thing."[45]

From the point of view of CCCT, what would government, politics, and community action look like, if all the negative forms of power were somehow defeated? Just as Karl Marx had nothing at all to say about how communism will work in practice, believing that its nature will be apparent when it gets here and that freedom and community will flower automatically once capitalism becomes worldwide and then collapses of its own contradictions, so also CCCT is not helpful when it comes to what good forms of collective action look like, if and when any evil command centers have been taken out. The few images of postconspiracy government it does generate are more mythical than practical, bearing resemblance to Rousseau's imaginary legitimate "social contract," on the one hand, and to the frontier communities of Western movies, on the other. The "town" is small, the citizens are virtuous, and the legislature gathers but occasionally, perhaps when it's time to make basic laws, feel some togetherness, dole out legal justice, or send men off to heroic war.[46] Virtue, it's presumed, will flower, and virtue is enough to run the show. The management of the money supply, who gets the government contracts and zoning variances, how collective actions will be financed, how disagreement among the virtuous will be managed: such details are unimportant.

Were George W. Bush, Dick Cheney, and Donald Rumsfeld in the thrall of command center simplicities when they failed to adequately plan for a post-Hussein Iraq? Maybe. Is Charles Murray, a libertarian who wants to abolish almost all of government, in the thrall of CCCT when he says that we the people should just "do things ourselves"? Did command center thinking keep him from saying a word about how this might work in practice, about how a people could act together without somehow utilizing the threat of coercion implicit in government, which he is dead set against?[47] Perhaps. What is more certain is that CCCT is prevalent.

Consider the following statements, for example. The first three are from the 2004 Democratic Party platform, and the next four are from the 2004 Republican platform:

[W]e need to create a "New Total Force," a military prepared to defeat any enemy, at any time, in any place.

In the Bush administration, energy independence doesn't get a thought. Their energy policy is simple: government by big oil, of big oil, and for big oil.

We face a global terrorist movement of many groups, funded from different sources with separate agendas, but all committed to assaulting the United States and free and open societies around the globe.

The taxation system should not be used to redistribute wealth or fund ever-increasing entitlements and social programs.... Many Democrats, however, believe the government has a right to claim the money earned by working Americans.

We...welcome declarations from responsible leaders of both parties that our nation will persevere in our mission there [Iraq], not cut and run.... We condemn inconsistent, ambiguous, and politically expedient statements on that point.

Today, because America has acted, and because America has led, the forces of terror and tyranny have suffered defeat after defeat, and America and the world are safer.

Every nation must make a choice to support terror or to support America and our coalition to defeat terror.... There is no negotiation with terrorists.[48]

Several elements of the command center idea appear in these words. "Safety" is about leadership; it's about being on the right side (the "responsible" side) and then acting with dispatch and resolve. On the other side is "the enemy": terrorists, Republicans who "don't give a thought" to energy independence, or Democrats who want to "cut and run." In any case the "global terrorist movement" is seen as united against the forces of the "free and open societies."

True, one cannot say, based on these quotations alone, that power is for certain assumed to be a thing purely possessed, rather than something that lives off shared ideas and arrangements, costly even to the power holders. On the other hand, the hints are there. For example, in the real world there really is no such thing as "total force," but the idea plays a big role in the platforms: such force, they assert, must be wielded by "responsible" leaders who have the character to "act" and "lead," who steer clear of the "ambiguous," who have made the "choice" to win, and who won't "cut and run," among other things. It's as if the issue faced by the world is who will, in the end, purely possess power: those bent on evil, pursuing pure self-interest and otherwise devoid of character, or the good guys who believe in freedom and possess virtue. In this battle each person and nation is "either with us or against us" (another political declaration of recent years). In this vision, force and the threat of force—rather than listening, learning, and doing one's best based on difficult choices and less than total certainty—are seen as holding moral order together.

Conspiracy thinking also creeps into antiracism discourse, even that which is otherwise very nuanced about power and generous in its ethics. For example, in May of 1998, while President Clinton's "dialogue on race" initiative was underway, National Public Radio aired an episode of *Making Contact* called "The Color of Racism." Host Phillip Babich joined Travis Lee to interview Mikal Muharrar, Sharon Martinez, Keri Anderson, Amy Little, Hiley Grossbecky, and Monica Castellon about race in America. The arguments made are worth looking at in some detail:

> Muharrar: You have a booming prison industry in this country that is quite sinister, because you literally have a policy, where on the one hand economically deprived communities have people in it—a rising number of those people are women, who are being funneled into the prison system, and other economically deprived communities who are largely white have prisons built in their communities and these prisons then become the foundation stone for economic development.
>
> Babich: Do you believe then there's more than just, I guess, a bias at work? That there is some conscious direction behind people in poor communities, blacks, African-Americans, Latinos going to prisons.
>
> Muharrar: Absolutely, and it's clearly public policy, and it's clearly often labor policy . . . . [H]ow are we going to control, you know, groups who are being marginalized? And it's clearly related to national politics, because you have a situation where, as I said before, whole communities are benefiting. Whole white communities, rural communities are benefiting. You have a situation where Wall Street now, the privatization that's occurring in terms of the prisons, I mean, it's like prisons are a boom industry. People are being told to invest in prisons. So, yes it is in fact public policy. Yes it is, in fact, conscious decisions, and it's conscious decisions that are not new. It just continues a historical practice. You know, if you look at the patterns,

for instance, of overrepresentation of minorities, you know, in prison, in among the poor, you know, among those who are—who have been receiving welfare. These are clear historical outcomes. It cannot be denied that they are historical outcomes. But America is very mythic. America is a very mythic place. The idea of America is very mythic. So America is kind of like living in the eternal present. An idea of a history that you have to really confront and address is like cut off all together [sic]. You can never confront the real reasons, because to confront the real reasons means you have to really confront what the United States of America really is about and what its contradictions really are. And they're not willing to do that.

Babich: The term white supremacy you use—maybe you can elaborate a little bit more. I think that most people think of white supremacy as groups like the Aryan Nations, or white supremacist ideology promoted by Hitler. Is that what you're talking about?

Muharrar: [T]he reason I use the term white supremacy is, because the term racism is too nebulous, you know, there's black racism, there's reverse racism, there's white racism. You know, it doesn't identify who is the leading group, you know, that is benefiting the most from the present structure. White supremacy is a term that deals with the history. It deals with the fact that it's a structure where white people—people who historically has been designated to be white, you know . . . benefit.

Babich: I'd like to get your opinion of President Clinton's handling of racism in America today, and also your thoughts on what needs to be done so people can address racism at large and also their own personal racism.

Muharrar: It's very good to have these diverse voices, but I don't think that the President's initiative is one that will bring us into any better social policy, public policy—especially since he's been leading a number of efforts that have harmed the very communities that he is now claiming to champion. He's very—in many ways it's a very cynical manipulation and it's insulting the notion of racism that is being projected to the American people. One that doesn't get to the structural disadvantaging of various communities, but one that reduces the whole race dynamic to one of conversation.

After these remarks the program provided some description of a thirteen-week course called "Challenging White Supremacy: A Workshop for Organizers" said to be "geared toward primarily white activists and organizers who want to be more conscious of their own subtle forms of white supremacy; and more importantly who want to eliminate institutionalized racism." Anderson's comments are as follows:

One of the things, um, I think that I take into my daily life from this workshop is the concept of . . . challenging other white people. And really . . . bringing it home to white folks that white supremacy is not about skinheads and clan members . . . . White supremacy is absolutely about the very invisible systems that continue to privilege me and privilege you, whether we like it or not, whether we know it or not, as we breathe and sleep every single day. And that very same system continues to oppress, and unprivilege [*sic*], and murder and imprison people of color.

Anderson and Muharrar are often on the mark, presenting power as structural, discursive, capillary, and subject-forming. Thus Anderson speaks of "invisible systems" that privilege some at the expense of others rather than of, say, white people choosing to privilege themselves, and Muharrar takes note of the mythical, history-blind quality of American culture as a force that renders racism invisible and calls white supremacy a "structure" from which white people benefit, thereby avoiding attributing total control to willful white dominators. Unfortunately, the command center vision clearly wins out in the end: The racist effects of the prison/criminal justice system are said to be the result of "conscious decisions," as if some rich whites sat down and designed the edifice in an effort to maintain racial and racist wage and opportunity differentials and as if those who invest in prisons do so as part of a scheme to keep blacks in a subservient position in the United States. And Clinton's race initiative is spoken of as a form of "cynical manipulation." Given this thinking, it is not surprising that the workshop on white supremacy is designed to correct the consciousness of white organizers. Granted, they are not taken to be true power wielders located at the center, but they are nonetheless understood to harbor racist attitudes; they have a chance of being on the right side if they own up, if they truly "want to eliminate institutionalized racism."

A similar pattern can be gleaned from a 2001 presentation made by Beverly Daniel Tatum, the author of *Why Are All the Black Kids Sitting Together in the Cafeteria?*

Now this is a gathering in which I know the focus is people of color and sometimes, speaking as a person of color myself, sometimes when we think about this misinformation, we think about the misinformation that has been targeted toward us. So for example speaking as an African American woman, I can say, I can think of many ways in which African American women have been stereotyped in the media to the extent that we've been omitted from the curriculum. I can think of lots of ways I have been left out or misrepresented. And that, those messages, those inaccurate messages get reinforced by social institutions . . . . And so, when I talk about racism as a system of advantage, we can see clearly that some people are systematically advantaged, others are systematically disadvantaged, but within that system, within that cycle, we all have individual choices to make, and to that extent, we all have some power. So I would challenge you all to think about what is your own sphere of influence in the course of your daily lives, who do you influence.[49]

Tatum is insightful in her grasp of racism as a discursive and structural "system of advantage" that benefits some compared to others, but her wisdom on this score is undermined by her use of the words "targeted" and "misinformation." To "target" a group is to consciously pick them out, in this case as victims of power and exploitation. To engage in a campaign of "misinformation" is to consciously lie in order to achieve a particular result. This is command center thinking. Does Tatum mean it? Did she intend to assert that stereotypes in the media are deliberately planted to maintain white advantage? Maybe, but I doubt it. More likely, command center thinking just slipped into place, as it so often does.

## CONSPIRACY THINKING AS AN OBSTACLE TO DELIBERATIVE DEMOCRACY

Conspiracy and command center thinking constitute major obstacles to disagreement success. The twin notions tend to reduce the idea of useful political action to either keeping or changing the guard. From the point of view of command center thinking conversation with the opposition is pointless. And if one adds to the mix the conspiracy idea that good outcomes emerge more or less automatically, as the spontaneous product of the people once the power centers have been found and disabled, there is that much less reason to deliberate, even with those on one's own side. Lost from view is the crucial fact that the maintenance of good society requires ongoing collective work, that getting things done (even among the "good guys") requires the regular butting of heads in public conversations of various kinds.

There is a kind of talk that remains important from the command center point of view. If the wrong people are in power somewhere, then those who believe their lies and half-truths, while not themselves at the center, need to be reeducated. The resulting conversations will, unfortunately, tend to take the form of the aforementioned "Workshop for Organizers," rather than dialogue. They will tend towards "training sessions" and "consciousness raisings," complete with elements of indoctrination and guilt tripping. Regularly held sessions of public disagreement, on the other hand, could serve to undermine the us–them simplicities of command center thinking, reveal more complex aspects of power, and support the spread of generous, compassionate notions about people, what is right and wrong with the world, and what needs to be done. Participants in such sessions might learn, for example, that most actual power is connected to positioning within an organization, and that such power over others typically comes with its own forms of subjection. This learning might, in turn, support disagreement practice.

Perhaps one reason for the rarity of such disagreement is people's suspicion of those who are politically active, especially those who are organized and perceived by others to be politically successful to some degree. They're often denounced as "special interests," where this term means a group that possesses power out of proportion to its size and pursues selfish goals, as if its members were deserving of "special" (better) treatment than others. Why such denunciation? The United

States is, after all, a society that celebrates itself as a democracy and routinely issues appeals for increased political participation. The answer may seem obvious: American "democracy" is, in fact, marked by low levels of popular political participation, and it's also true that small, well-financed groups have undue influence, whether by virtue of their social and economic position, their campaign contributions, or their ability to influence public opinion. But the questions still stand: Why blame anyone for pursuing their interests as they see them, or for pursuing other political goals? Why is it their fault if they succeed? Why are their motives questioned? Is it wrong to have interests? It's not clear why this should be so.

My view is that conspiracy thinking has a hand here. It offers a fantasy version of good government as a politics-free condition, and it generates images of power-hungry scheming by malefactors. Therefore it lends support to the idea that politics is an inherently suspicious activity, a nasty business of favor trading and ambition. Those who are organized and active are, then, easily smeared with the special interest label.

Many of the defenders of interest group activity take a "pluralist" stance. Political science textbooks which specialize in American government are still dominated by pluralism, a defense of the country as democratic that arose in the 1920s and hit the heights of its popularity in the 1950s. Pluralism reiterates, while also shifting, arguments made by James Madison and other framers of the constitution. It argues that the American political system utilizes and constrains selfish activity by means of the checking and balancing of one group by another in a conflictual bargaining process. Whereas Madison worried about the dangers presented by "factions" and hoped that the system would render them and the federal government weak, pluralists speak in more neutral terms, arguing that organized "selfish" groups provide needed information to legislators and that special interest activity, when added up, represents the American people rather effectively. To pluralists, interest group ferment is a crucial supplement to the electoral side of politics, in which the public-at-large acts from a more general, rather than a "special," standpoint, serving there as judge and jury, making final adjudications.[50]

The pluralists are right to say that the pursuit of self-interest in politics has a useful role to play. Deal making is not inherently bad and generally speaking (perhaps always) each person's conception of their self-interest has something to offer; each side has its truth. The pluralists are wrong, however, to assume that self-interest plays an entirely useful role as long as it is checked by bargaining on one hand and elections on the other. In fact, the facts of human nature suggest something else, that another check is needed, this being active disagreement.

It is, then, essential to avoid two pitfalls: conspiracy thinking on one side and the reduction of politics to bargaining on the other. The latter may be supportive of business-as-usual in the megastate, but it's hardly the politics of a free people. Freedom requires disagreements that challenge received notions of interest, sometimes reaffirming and sharpening them, and sometimes transforming them in new directions.

## ORWELL ALMOST RIGHT

Unfortunately, the world is in some respects moving in another direction, one that, in my darker moments, I call "Orwell Almost Right." OAR is a "discursive object," meaning a multisided cultural/social formation or, better yet, a dangerous confluence of developments. Its faces include (1) command center thinking; (2) the partial takeover of public space in electoral democracies by dialogue-narrowing discourses and money-narrowed election campaigns; (3) a dearth of physical spaces where different sorts of people can meet and mingle as members of the general public; (4) a shortage of social capital, thanks to past failures to engage citizens and issues across borders of difference and disagreement; (5) the dominance of state-centric foreign policy theories that close off discussion of what counts as the "national interest" and when such interests should take priority; (6) an eclipse of the rule of law both in theory and practice, marked by the increased use of collective punishment by state actors (including the United States) and the use of torture and surveillance as modes of "security"; (7) the rise of absolutisms of all stripes, from the religiously inspired terrorism of Al Qaeda to the U.S.-declared "war on terror"; and (8) the institutionalization and taking for granted of the goals of efficiency, economic expansion, and state expansion (the goals of the megastate, discussed in Chapter 2).

The word "almost" in OAR does not, by the way, mean that humans have yet to go all the way down the road to 1984. It means George Orwell was not right about everything. His novels suggest that the dangerous political power towards which the world moves is command center power. In the imagined world of 1984 there lurks the possibility of an ultrasecret group of controllers who are not themselves bound by the newspeak and doublethink that circumscribe the minds of others. This does not accurately describe today's withering of public space and absence of needed disagreement. In fact, no one controls it all; no one is free—though some are freer than others. Various forms of doublethink prevail—inaccurate dehumanization, half-truths about freedom, exaggerated views of the power of the media, a lack of faith on the part of many when it comes to their own ability to tell good argument from bad, and more—but these are spread in part by intention and in part by momentum. They are imposed, but they are also self-imposed. They are instantiated in the shared symbolic world of culture, and they are not adequately checked by educative forms of disagreement. There is no group free from their spell.

I don't go into detail here about all the aspects of OAR. Some get more treatment in Chapter 6. One that is worth mentioning at this juncture is the lack of adequate public space, where this refers to locations legally open to all, reasonably accessible, and encouraging of—or at least allowing for—unplanned and unscripted interactions between people. So defined, what the United States has is more like ersatz public space:

> The tendency toward excluding real social antagonisms and debate from the public sphere, and the logic of control that has come to permeate the

decaying institutions, structures, and spaces that compose what remains of civil society, leave little opportunity for "the citizen" to effectively, or affectively, engage with the state. Such engagement is displaced to the private realm of consumption, which has emerged as the model for political, social, and cultural activity.[51]

Real public space provides people with information about what it is like to be in other people's social and class locations, thereby supporting the formation of social capital and serving to counter command center and conspiracy thinking. As things stand now, CCCT is instead encouraged, consumed in lieu of better forms of citizenship.

Another aspect of OAR relevant here is the rise in the use of collective punishment as a policy tool. In true newspeak fashion, leaders justify such actions by invoking the sanctity of the rule of law. Missiles are aimed at the family dwellings of suspected suicide bombers who have not been found guilty or even formally charged by means of any judicially accountable, standardized legal procedure; bullets are shot into houses because insurgents might be inside; international sanctions are deployed when it is known they will cause the deaths of thousands of children; individuals are captured and detained for years, sometime without the release of their names simply because they might be in possession of desired information or because they were found in the wrong place. Such actions have contributed to a resurgence of revenge both as a feeling and as an ideal, as seen in the surfeit of pro-vengeance movie, television, and book plots in popular culture. This revenge ethic in turn tends to reinforce (and in the first place flows from) the all or nothing, us and them categories of command center thinking.

The eclipse of the rule of law is likewise linked to command center thinking. They especially connect with each other through the medium of foreign policy establishment-style abstractions that turn individuals into representatives of groups or nations, mere objects of security policy and/or revenge. Such abstraction is linked to conspiratorial ideas of power because the latter is itself a form of rendering flesh and blood into abstraction, as well as abstraction into flesh and blood. A person becomes a "terrorist plotter" or "a soldier in the army of atheist infidels." A movement becomes "Osama bin Laden" or "Saddam Hussein."

## CONCLUSION

Fortunately, OAR has plenty of opponents, from a variety of political camps. Some far-right conservatives are staunch defenders of the rule of law. Many far-left liberals are ready and willing to listen thoughtfully to the opposition. I have met many deeply religious individuals who call themselves fundamentalists and are very friendly to healthy disagreement. But such commitments and attitudes are by no means reliable vaccines against command center thinking. Indeed the latter often undermines the former. What is needed, then, is persistent talk about power that is both wise and accessible to nontheorists, talk that spreads the word that power is both necessary and dangerous, that it rules all to one degree or another, and that in today's world it often appears as the opposite of itself, as the humdrum pursuit of the goals of the megastate, goals that leave no room for politics. What is needed also is the promotion of the power of the people where this notion is understood, not as the opposite of the power of an elite conspiracy but as hard work done by disparate and differing individuals who act together to make things new, by means of unpredictable acting and forbearing, based on real and inclusive give and take and recurrent disagreement.

There are theorists who consider the just-described vision of participatory, pro-disagreement society to be both unachievable and dangerous, who believe humans are inherently prone to adopting a simplified view of power and placing their hopes and dreams in the hands of elites whom they consider of good character. According to these thinkers, the last thing anyone should do is encourage more disagreement and engagement.[52] I take on this argument in Chapter 6. In the meantime, there is the mass media to consider.

CHAPTER 5

# The Strange Case of the Mass Media

Generally speaking, . . . what appears in the media is most importantly shaped by forces outside of them.[1]

—G. William Domhoff

Many people believe both that the mass media have an essential role to play in support of democratic politics and that they fall short of the mark, thanks to political bias, a fixation with scandal, and an excessive focus on the bottom line. The critics of the media include many on the inside, as evidenced by reporter roundtables focusing on the failures of the press and retired journalists speaking out in despair about their former profession. Given the years of negative talk, why is it that the media don't launch in new directions in an effort to improve? One reason is that the media sometimes merely pretend to be self-critical; sometimes the teeth gnashing is just another show. Another contributing factor is the staying power of market forces; scandal will, for example, have an edge as long as it brings an audience and sells advertising. Another reason for the persistence of media failings is that the critics disagree about what changes are needed: some consider the media too liberal; others see them as too conservative. Different people, in other words, want to "fix" the media in different directions.

These explanations, even when taken together, are not enough. Yet another reason the media continually disappoint is the wider society's bias against bias, something dutifully mirrored and amplified by the press. The mass media are, in fact, not so much right or left as they are cowardly. They lean toward politically safe topics, heavily managed or downright staged debates, and the construction and presentation of arguments with the goal of entertainment foremost in mind. The U.S. mass media are, in sum, biased against disagreement.

Comprehensive documentation of this bias and its many exceptions is beyond the reach of this chapter, in part because "the media" include so much. Television situation comedy sends different messages to viewers than do late-night talk shows, and both genres tend to be more pro-disagreement than sports coverage. Rather than try to cover it all, I offer a pro-disagreement take on overall media performance and provide some representative examples. The situation is gloomy. Very little attention is paid by the mass media to the world of ideas, much less to truly competing ideas or the historical context needed to understand them. Radical ideas of any kind are particularly lost. Generally speaking, members of the public are better off looking elsewhere if they want to understand, learn, and make informed judgments about the issues of the day. And, what's worse, they often don't want to look elsewhere (at least not for the reasons listed), in part because the visions of satisfying human activity that fill media programs do little to communicate the idea that disagreement is a worthwhile aspect of life.

There is also good news. Pro-disagreement programs do find their way onto the screen and the radio. Also, movement in a more pro-disagreement direction is a reasonable goal, not an unreachable utopia. All other things being equal, it's hard to imagine liberals stepping up to give conservatives more airtime or conservatives pushing to hear more from liberals, leftists, feminists, or anarchists. On the other hand, a move towards more time for *all* concerned, in the name of disagreement, could be politically appealing to a variety of otherwise opposed groups.

Such a move would, however, require the creation of a more pro-disagreement society *outside* the zone of media production. It would require a more informed, engaged, and disagreeable public that demands and expects different things from the worlds of news and entertainment. This means that, in certain respects, the public would need to expect less from the media. Even in a world with zero bias (if such a thing were possible), it would make no sense to rely on journalists, who answer to deadlines on several issue areas at once and are by definition jacks of all trades, to adequately inform the rest of us. To be informed at a democratic level people need exposure to the views of politically passionate specialists on many sides. What's needed to improve the media is, then, nothing less than a more pro-disagreement society.

## MEDIA IN THE GRIP OF OUTSIDE FORCES

Committed conservatives are convinced that the media has a liberal bias, and liberals are just as frustrated with what they perceive to be a pro-conservative slant. Many feminists are critical of media depictions of women, while others ("masculinists"?) think the media is unfair to men. How is it that different people see such different things? Careful consideration of this question reveals the slippery nature of bias itself. It's not clear, for example, how bias can be defined—much less deployed in any investigation of the media—in a way not itself shaped by bias. Also, does "biased" mean having a political perspective, being closed to evidence one doesn't like, being wrong, being passionate, or some combination of all four? And doesn't everyone have a bias of *some* kind? If so, then maybe the media *should* be biased—but just in the "right" direction. And if that's the case then who gets to say which direction is right? Maybe, on the other hand, objectivity is the opposite of bias rather than one more bias, and humans can, therefore, strive for objectivity. But what, then, is objectivity? Is it the opposite of having a political position, or is it a kind of openness to new information and ideas? Is it the same as being right? The words bias and objectivity seem to invoke each other but in more than one way, so what's their relationship? Efforts to answer this question are complicated by the fact that the use of each term is frequently self-interested, deployed to praise friends or smear opponents.

A few distinctions can help make sense of this morass. First, the personal political views of reporters, editors, anchorpersons, entertainment writers, and network owners are one thing and media content is another. There is some evidence that, with regard to the former, media personnel are more liberal, on average, than the general public on some issues. On the other hand, one cannot thereby conclude that media *output* has a liberal slant. Many factors enter into what goes on the air or in print besides the personal views of the journalists involved. To know about media output, one needs to look at media output.

Another distinction of import is that between the coverage of different sorts of political issues. G. William Domhoff argues, for example, that mass media news reporting is somewhat liberal on social issues but conservative on bread-and-butter economic issues.[2] And why not? One need not endorse Domhoff's leftist politics to agree that questions about school prayer, gay marriage, multilingual education, and abortion are largely distinct from those concerning the minimum wage rate, regulations costly to business, tax rates, trade policy, and the like. True, conservatives on the first set of issues are to some extent allied with those in the second camp. But this alliance is not one of equal partners, says Domhoff. Economic conservatives enjoy the support of (and often come from the ranks of) the politically organized representatives of large corporations. As such, they have more political clout than social conservatives, and that clout is also less tied to public opinion. This is in part because their structural position gives them access to the policy-making process; government elites even go so far as to anticipate their desires without being asked—as in "Let's not upset the business climate." It's also because the corporate elite have substantial resources at their disposal they can use to try to penetrate the media and shape public opinion. Unfortunately for the social conservatives, the corporate community has no position, as a group, on social issues. This or that CEO might be pro-life, but most could just as easily be pro-choice without it constituting a violation of the tacit understanding of their job. On the other hand, the job description for many a CEO includes working politically on behalf of the economic interests of the corporation (which for some means being pro-consumption, perhaps even pro-pornography, and these are hardly social conservative positions).

Add to this power situation the fact that a significant portion of the general public is liberal on social questions, and the bias picture starts to clear up.[3] The mass media are relatively free to reflect the socially liberal outlook of many of their workers, i.e., they have no reason to shy away from covering such points of view. On the other hand, these same media companies largely defer to (and are schooled in) the perspective of experts supplied by the economically based, often-united "power elite." Thus the media are, as Domhoff argues, often liberal on social issues but tend to be quite conservative in reflecting a pro-market perspective.

For example, the last forty years have been witness to a gradual rise in the number of black, brown, Asian, and female faces appearing authoritatively on television screens, whether on *The Cosby Show*, in advertising, or as anchorpersons, but in the same time period there has been little (some would say nil) mainstream coverage of truly left-wing (rather than merely liberal) positions on economic issues. Even those who watch the news, and read headline newspaper stories carefully, might nonetheless be unaware—for example—of debates about whether the public should have a say in investment decisions; about the validity of the neoliberal trade philosophy enforced by the IMF, the World Bank, and the World Trade Organization; about what should count as national progress (GNP, GDP, or something else); and about the motives and interests that lie behind U.S. foreign policy.

Why is the distinction between social issues and market issues so often ignored in talk of media leanings? One reason is selective viewing: people are quick to notice media bias when it cuts away from their own point of view but tend to miss it when they agree with it. Liberal ideas generally appear to liberals as factual or as the truth, and the same goes for conservatives. Thus it's not surprising that a 2007 telephone survey found that 49 percent of self-identified liberals believe the major television networks "have a conservative bias," but 62 percent of self-identified conservatives see things the other way around.[4]

One set of influential authors who ignored the two distinctions noted above are S. Robert Lichter, Stanley Rothman, and Linda S. Lichter. They conducted a series of public opinion investigations in the 1980s that compared journalists to businessmen and the general public. One of those studies led Rothman and S. Robert Lichter to conclude that journalists are on average more atheistic, educated, narcissistic, and ideologically liberal than most people and more likely to think that adultery is not immoral, that income redistribution is necessary, and that the legal system favors the wealthy. These characteristics, the authors also conclude, affect "the manner in which they [journalists] perceive and report 'reality' to other elites and the general population."[5] But on what is this crucial finding based? It's not clear. It was not based on content analysis. No news broadcasts were analyzed. No newspaper articles were parsed. Instead journalists were asked to read imaginary news stories, written by the researchers, and respond by summarizing them briefly. The summaries, when coded for ideological slant, were rated as more liberal than those of the businessmen in the sample. Journalists were also shown pictures and asked to write brief stories about them, and the results were likewise deemed to be more liberal, e.g., more often portraying minorities or low-status figures as victims of oppression or being negative about society and opportunity. Rothman and Lichter then deem these findings to have "implications for the manner in which they [journalists] report the news to general public."[6] In other words, Rothman and Lichter ignore the distinction between media content and the personal views of journalists.

True, a failure to demonstrate liberal content bias doesn't prove none is present. On the other hand, claims of bias shouldn't be made lightly, given that they sometimes contribute to their own falsity by acting as a form of pressure that pushes media away from story lines and investigations that might generate complaints. Such a dynamic is easy to imagine: American reporters, owners, and editors work, after all, in a society in which many people define "objectivity" as the opposite of lending support to any viewpoint, even if such support is purely factual. They also face pressure to guard their industry position, to keep or increase audience share and advertising revenue.[7] And most of them care deeply, as individuals, about their professional reputation. They are, then, intensely concerned to maintain a reputation of objectivity, and because of this accusations of bias, especially those promulgated by people in a position to be heard, are a serious threat. In other words, media decision makers are vulnerable to "flak," to use Ed Herman and Noam Chomsky's term. And in order to minimize damage, they adjust their activities; the fear of flak influences program content.[8]

According to Domhoff, Herman and Chomsky, and others, this is exactly what happened in the last four decades.[9] The mass media were accused of being liberal, and partly as a result, they became more conservative. Or rather, as pointed out above, they did so in certain issue areas, those of concern to the politically organized corporate community. The latter group became newly mobilized during the mid-1970s, in response to falling profit rates, increased competition, and anxiety about inflation. They united in a political campaign to weaken unions, increase their greater access to foreign markets, reduce the government's regulation of financial transactions, and reduce government aid for the low-paid and the unemployed. And, says Domhoff, the corporate community got much of what it wanted, in part because the mass media dutifully reported their concerns as if they were the very definition of the "problems" of the day.

One need not agree with Domhoff's claim that the United States is dominated by a "power elite" to side with his claim that the media are largely beholden to outside forces. They are beholden and as a result mostly fail to provide the diverse information and ideas needed to support feisty, informed public debate. Instead they pass on, and amplify, the perspectives of elite "flakkers," advertisers, and consumers.[10] The first two groups set broad limits on what counts as acceptable content, and consumers enjoy a modicum of buyer power within that zone.

The notion of media that are pushed around fits with the pattern of Vietnam War coverage described in the last chapter. News programming began to include bad war news only after U.S. elites became divided about the viability of the U.S. effort. More evidence came to light in a study of newspaper coverage of politics conducted in the mid-1990s.[11] Matthew Gentzkow and Jess M. Shapiro compiled a list of political position-linked phrases used by liberal and conservative Congresspersons respectively (e.g., "death tax" vs. "estate tax" and "undocumented aliens" vs. "illegal aliens"). They then measured the rate of appearance of the phrases in 417 newspapers (in news stories, not editorials), the political leanings of the buyers of each newspaper, and the political leanings of the newspaper owners. They found no significant relationships between a newspaper's slant and the political party to whom the owners gave money. They found no significant relationship between a newspaper's slant and that of other newspapers owned by the same company. What they did find was a relationship between the phrases used and the views of the readership; newspapers, they concluded, "are targeting their slant to their customers' demand."

One limitation of the study is the way it circumscribes "slant" within the bounds set by those who make it into the halls of Congress. In other words, Gentzkow and Shapiro didn't look for the views, angles, or phrases routinely used by pacifists, anti-free trade types, Earth First members, feminists, social union organizers, anarchists, nudity clubs, or anyone else too on the edge to get representation in Washington. These phrases would presumably be red flags for high-powered flakkers and high-spending advertisers. Maybe they didn't appear in the news stories at all. The work of Gentzkow and Shapiro does not, therefore, amount to a challenge to that of Domhoff or Herman and Chomsky but instead fits nicely alongside. Taken together their theories suggest that consumer preferences have a real but limited influence on media content.

But even if consumers are a force to be reckoned with from the point of view of editors, media buyers are not independent players who simply "get what they want." Consumer "preferences" are heavily shaped by whatever options are currently on display in the market and by each consumer's own unthinking adjustment to the fact that buying is basically a one-at-a-time type of action. What one "wants" is, in other words, in part a product of an estimate of what the realistic choices are, and this estimate is in turn shaped by what's on the "shelf" and what other people are buying. And that "structure of consumption" is partly the result of the decisions made by similarly situated (also adjusting to the outside) buyers, not to mention choices that were made years before by buyers, governments, and industries. If a transportation system is built around cars, for example, it makes sense for consumers to think about what kind of car they want, not what kind of train they want.

Correspondingly, individual buyers of the news live in an antidisagreement culture, without much exposure to radically differing, in-depth analyses on pressing subjects. These consumers influence what editors put in their newspapers but presumably become liberal or conservative newspaper buyers in the first place in part because of how newspapers and other sources have presented the world to them. And the journalists and media owners who present this world are themselves constrained by flak and, like their consumers, lacking in exposure to a broad world of ideas. It's a circle. As with opinion polls, it's more or less the blind leading the blind. And together they revolve around the version of the political "center" that has been created (for the most part) by flak and advertiser caution.

Flak could conceivably come from many directions, but conservative flakkers—some corporate, some Christian right, some neoconservative, and some otherwise in "the movement"—did enjoy certain advantages in the late twentieth century. They could, and did, cite the work of Rothman and the Lichters, over and over.

They had millions of foundation and think tank dollars to work with. And they had a ready audience, as many citizens were simmering with resentments and/or anxiety or otherwise looking for answers, in the wake of the brutal recession and inflation of the early 1970s and the travail of the Vietnam War and Watergate. Conservative flakkers wisely framed their media-attacking messages in terms of values, and liberals were somewhat hamstrung in this regard, thanks in part to their (part fictional and part real) association with the corporate-dominated, Democratic Party–controlled administrative state, a state that was unable, as such, to address issues in terms of values. It functioned as a system of interest group bargaining among moneyed elites and found itself mute when it came to public concern about religion, crime, and personal behavior.

Finally, and most importantly here, those who declared the media liberal benefitted from the pro-authority cowardice of the media themselves. For example, when the postwar U.S. government seemed to be doing great things for minorities and the poor but was actually doing otherwise, the media failed to respond. They dutifully repeated official promises, focused on ground-breaking Supreme Court decisions, covered riots, and took note of enormous protests, but they did little to explain the full parameters of urban renewal, the selective devastation wrought by Interstate Highway construction, or the antiunion policies that were gaining power in the worlds of business and law and inside the U.S. Department of Labor. In this context, when conservatives declared the media to be but one part of a nihilist liberal juggernaut that was at the root of the nation's decline, journalists were put on the defensive. They didn't want to seem "anti-American," and their instinct to bend with the wind, combined with their location in a largely antidisagreement culture, led them to embrace, and then repeat, the attack upon themselves. They sold programming by asking themselves "hard questions" about their own flaws. They moved into the "Shock Radio" business. The culture war had begun.

## BIAS AGAINST BIAS

Public conviction that the mass media are liberal may have weakened in recent years, thanks to the rise of more overt forms of conservative programming (Fox television, Shock Radio, and the like), Republican control of the White House and (for a time) of Congress (making it harder to seem a victim of bias), the disaster in Iraq, and the liberal counterattack led by political comedy (e.g., The Daily Show, Michael Moore, Al Franken, Stephen Colbert, and the like). On the other hand, the notion of the liberal media is still strong. A 2007 poll found that "[b]y a 39% to 20% margin" (leaving many in the "other" categories), "American adults believe that the three major broadcast [television] networks deliver news with a bias in favor of liberals."[12] And in 2003 a book claiming liberal bias climbed onto the bestseller list.[13]

Some readers might be tempted to attribute these beliefs to the machinations of a conservative media that, in a perverse and subtle fashion, perpetuate the myth that they themselves are liberal. This gets at an important point. A 1999 study found that the number of people who see the media as liberal was both large during the 1990s and grew during that time. It also found that this increase was mostly caused by the "increasing news self-coverage that focuses on the general topic of bias in news content."[14] In other words, media highlighted the issue of media bias, giving it valence for their audience. The authors of the study—Marke D. Watts, David Domke, Dhavan V. Shah, and David P. Pan—do not, however, see in this behavior any machinations of conspiracy. Instead they suggest a media dancing in defense of their credibility, making displays of concern about their many flaws, and adjusting content in response to outside pressures. The important question, in other words, is not which side the media are on but what it is that pressures them and in which directions.

When it comes to news reporting, the media's concern with outside power leads them toward a set of (mostly unwritten) rules: Avoid crossing those who have the power to impugn your credibility. Stick to the script. Add a twist that brings more audience share. Perform one's role as expected; be that anchorperson, journalist, weatherperson or sports analyst. Stick to the facts all have access to— even if they're not the most important. Get to those facts first. When possible, rely on official sources. Entertain; provide a human side to every story.[15] Look for personal scandal, tragedy, and heroism. Above all, maintain appearances. These rules are typically taken for granted as part of what it means to do the job, to be professional. They reside in the prevailing conceptualization of news. And their power is bolstered by cost considerations. Investigative journalism is expensive, as is the provision of time to reporters so they can study alternative viewpoints on a subject or so they can explain an issue at length rather than in a sound bite.

As a result, news programming prioritizes the immediate, unexpected, scandalous, and tragic, at the expense of the detailed, historical, and conceptually challenging. At the heart of the problem is what might be called a bias against bias. What I mean is that news decision makers worry about appearing to support or oppose political positions. Their behavior is significantly governed by the notion that supporting an argument is the same thing as bias, as if it were unfair or prejudiced to provide facts that might help a person decide what they should be for and against. The practical effect of this antidisagreement idea is to lead journalists, editors, and media managers to support prevailing prejudices, especially elite prejudices. The news media dance, in other words, to the tune of the most effective flakkers and at the expense of the detailed, historical, and conceptually challenging.

What, then, is bias, properly understood? It's the triumph of ego, self-interest, or preconception over sound methods and fair interpretations. It's what happens when someone's mind gets clouded in a way that distorts results. Clearly, journalists should avoid bias of this sort, but how can they do so while also avoiding bias in the other sense, as the lending of support to an argument? It often can't be done; thorough and unprejudiced thinking on a given subject frequently ends up supporting some positions and refuting others. I say, when there's a conflict, the first duty of journalists is to the truth, not to the appearance of neutrality. Likewise, the consumers of the news have a duty to demand—or at least not to impugn out of hand – news stories that challenge dominant views. Unfortunately, the bias against bias is deeply entrenched. Ours is an antidisagreement society.

## PRO-BIAS SENSIBILITY

To adequately support democracy, the media need consumers who possess three attributes. First, they need to understand the future as necessarily open-ended, as less than fully predictable. Such an attitude to truth—which might be called a common sense epistemology—is needed to counter the tendency to look at journalists as modern astrologers, as reader of tea leaves who tell others where to place their bets. Divination is not per se a bad thing and in any case is here to stay in one form or another, but a pro-disagreement society requires divination to be (implicitly) understood both as an inherently contestable enterprise and as most properly a product of dialogue. Members of the media audience would, in such a world, look for competing readings to emerge in heated conversations, and they would place their bets both on the ones that seem most convincing as well as on the process itself. They would, then, see themselves not only as the audience but also as the producers, and they would expect the search for truth to continue indefinitely.

Second (and along the same lines), the media need audience members who, generally speaking, believe that uncertain truth is still truth of a kind, that there are better and worse arguments on any given subject, and that they can tell the difference if they work at it. Such viewers and listeners would take it for granted that social understanding is neither the product of neutral experts who tell others "the facts" nor the possession of a mere pile of different, biased opinions.

Third, and most importantly, the media need a sizable number of consumers who come to the table bearing a pro-disagreement *sensibility*. This refers to a disposition, something that goes beyond that which is grasped intellectually to include an ability to maintain a degree of physical calm even amidst heated discussion. It's a way of being in the world where thought and feeling are linked in a pro-disagreement direction. It's a comfort zone and an expectation, a combination of confidence and humility.

This can be put it terms of faith. A pro-disagreement sensibility means combining faith with openness to alternative faiths, where "faith" means not religion necessarily but what William E. Connolly calls "existential faith," i.e., some sort of "elemental sense of the ultimate character of being."[16] Everyone has faith of this kind. In one way or another, everyone believes in something, be it in a law-governed universe, the reality of reality, the truth of feeling, or the redemptive power of God. "To be human is to be inhabited by existential faith."[17] To combine faith with openness is to have a pro-disagreement bent or what Connolly calls a "bicameral orientation" to life, an acceptance of "deep pluralism," which he describes as an "engrained sense that you should exercise presumptive receptivity toward others when drawing [your] . . . faith, creed, or philosophy into the public realm."[18] This means giving up on the false dream of a faith-free, neutral public space and instead aiming for a faith-friendly but agonistic public space. It means a public where people act together despite deep differences, thanks to their "toler-ance of ambiguity in politics," their "presumptive generosity," and their "courage to bear the agony of diversity."[19]

People do not come to have this sort of sensibility by magic or by accident, nor is its appearance per se a matter of intelligence, high education level, or personality. It is, rather, a fundamental possibility for all humans. It can and does grow under a thousand different stones, but to thrive it requires favorable cultural and institutional conditions. It grew in Boston as a result of the sustained conversation between three pro-life and three pro-choice advocates—described in Chapter 1. And it can grow elsewhere under the tutelage of such cross-border encounter. People can and do develop the sense that Reverend Anne Fowler developed, one of "hopefulness that people can tackle a very difficult, divisive, painful issue and be civilized and even friendly in the discussions."[20] Widespread, regular experience with cross-border encounter could, then, serve to build a world of pro-disagreement media consumers.

As things stand, cross-border disagreement experience is rare. And, not coin-cidentally, many people take truth for granted or look to find it once and for all, with no questions left to ask. Some find truth in a single, authoritative source such as a sacred text. Some find it in a born-again experience. Some scan the horizon (e.g., in newspapers and on television) looking for accounts that provide defini-tive, unquestionable facts that answer the pressing questions. Some then become cynical, even despair, as it appears to them that perspective is everywhere, that there are no bias-free facts to be found. And some then deal with this problem turning to relativism, by deciding that "it's all a matter of opinion, so my opinion is as good as yours."

All of these modes of finding truth contribute to, and embody, antidisagree-ment sensibility. Together they make for a world of consumers who tend to find the truths they're already looking for; who find a way, no matter what, to confirm what they already believe. This poses a problem for the media in general and for news broadcasting in particular.

## THE NEWS

The news—if this word means the review and analysis of the latest events by multitasking journalists—can never serve successfully as the primary way people become politically informed. Democracy instead requires a bazaar, a host of diver-gent, disagreement-based, bias-laced sources of ideas and information available to, and frequented by, the general public. In such a world "the news" will still be needed to provide background facts, history, and perspectives. Now, on the other hand, the news labors to maintain its credibility in a mostly antidisagreement society.

One scholar who understands the political news is Thomas E. Patterson. He points out that, on the one hand, "news" has long been defined as that which is "found in particular events rather than the underlying forces in society that create them." On the other hand, an "older, descriptive model of reporting" has, he says, recently given way to a more "interpretive" style. Whereas in the old days, journalists "sought to tell the reader or listener what had happened; the larger meaning was left to the audience to determine," the newer style is "a version of truth-telling," requiring "the journalist to see things that cannot be seen and to understand things that are not easily grasped."[21]

Two of the shortcomings with media truth telling noted by Patterson are that it often concerns the trivial, and the predictions it generates are frequently just plain wrong, even when being right is not that difficult. "If reporters had flipped coins, their attempts to predict the outcome of the 1976 Republican presidential race [the Republican primary contest] would have been just as accurate."[22] A third problem is that journalistic soothsaying is almost always *thin*, even when it's accurate and nontrivial. Patterson, citing Walter Lippman, uses the word "flimsy."

Patterson is not, however, simply blaming the media, pointing out, for example, that journalists are "ill-equipped" to do better. In part this is because they "labor at a hectic job, looking at the world in all its bewildering complexity through the narrow lens of events, leaders, and fast-breaking developments."[23] Another problem is that they labor within the bounds of a "commitment to impartiality" that defines facts as separate from values, and that's therefore leery of any reporting that might lead one position to look right and another wrong.[24] How, under these circumstances, can journalists possibly provide in-depth reporting about candidate proposals or party platforms? They can't, and they don't. Instead they provide clichés that are both "fleeting and inexact."[25] And they look for lies, hunt for hypocrisy, and ponder "integrity." It's not a pretty picture.

A fourth problem with media truth telling is that damage is often done even in those rare moments when a journalist speaks of something important, makes accurate predictions, and provides some in-depth understanding. Damage is done when newsmakers, ironically by doing well, reinforce the popular idea that unbiased, objective truth is out there somewhere, ready to be grasped by the very best soothsayers, found on some mysterious Mount Olympus of total objectivity. In other words, journalists who beat the odds and do well may thereby reinforce the audience's objectivist, passive, and disagreement-unfriendly tendencies when it comes to the news. This can only play into existing circles of disagreement failure. All look over their shoulder for clues; the clues of the powerful speak more powerfully, and the world of available facts and ideas remains narrow and thin.

The thin and narrow can be seen even in those news programs that are more in-depth and more pro-disagreement. Consider, for example, the November 2, 2007 episode of *On Point*, a National Public Radio talk show. Each Friday the first hour features journalists commenting on the events of the week, and that day's group consisted of William McKenzie (an editorial page columnist for *The Dallas Morning News*), Eleanor Clift (a contributing editor at *Newsweek* Magazine), and Jack Beatty (an *On Point* news analyst and a senior editor at *The Atlantic Monthly*). Program host Anthony Brooks introduced the first subject, the contest for the Democratic presidential nomination, by asking Eleanor Clift a question: "The Democrats debated on Wednesday; Hilary took a bit of a beating . . . . How did you score it?" Clift couldn't have been surprised by this classic "horse race" query, and she answered in kind:

> Democrats raised all the issues that the Republicans will raise if Hillary Clinton is the nominee . . . [I]ssues that Democrats talk about and worry about [are]: the fact that she sometimes seems too calculating, [and] whether she is electable; so I'm of two minds as to whether this a good fight for Hillary Clinton, getting her into fighting form for the general election, or whether this could seriously hurt her going as she goes forward if she becomes the nominee.

This is called "horse race" talk because the focus is on the front-runner and because it concerns who's ahead, who's behind, and the various candidates' chances as they go forward. The talk is not, in other words, about the intrinsic competence of the candidates or the validity of their respective issue positions. Clift speaks not of whether Clinton *is* too calculating but of whether she *seems* to be so. The focus is on how Clinton's actions and apparent attributes will "play" with the voters and, above all, on what happens next. Clift dutifully tries to read the tea leaves, though to her credit she reports that their meaning is, in the case at hand, unclear.

Clift is again queried after Brooks plays a clip from the debate during which candidate John Edwards criticizes Senator Clinton on the subject of Iraq.

> Brooks: [I]s that the kind of decisiveness that will cut into Hillary Clinton's lead?
>
> Clift: I don't think that's the sound bite where John Edwards really got at Hillary Clinton. . . . I think his more zinging attack has to do with her and her reliance on supposed special interests . . . He clearly needs to do something to sharpen his rhetoric to get back into the game. . . . He's now opened up this whole sort of character attack on Hillary Clinton . . . I suspect that he is going to be accused of being somewhat opportunistic.

The focus is again on strategy, appearance, and potential outcomes. Clift does, however, hint at substantive issues of candidate quality; e.g., who's beholden to special interests and who's opportunistic. What she doesn't do is provide any facts from outside the universe of "the race" that might help voters to answer those questions. She doesn't provide the background and history that might help someone decide if Clinton is "beholden" or if Edwards is decisive.

Substantive questions are not, however, treated as unimportant, as if winning were all that mattered. Instead their importance is implicitly recognized in a peculiar way, as if the quality of candidates were revealed through divination and deference to voters. It's as if the proper way for a journalist to help voters make good judgments is to (1) pick concerns supposedly on the minds of voters, (2) offer guesses about the judgments that the voters will make later on about the candidates in relation to those concerns, (3) likewise guess about how current events are likely to shape voter judgments, and (4) offer all this to the voters, whose votes will then reveal the substance, meaning the true quality of the candidates. Voters, in other words, can make good judgments by looking at each other's judgments.

In the case of Edwards, the logic could proceed this way: (1) because voters seem concerned with opportunism, (2) because polls show Edwards to be behind in the race, and (3) because Edwards' latest statement could be perceived as opportunistic and thus as possibly negatively affecting his future standing in the polls; voters can find out if Edwards *is* opportunistic by seeing if he "sharpens his rhetoric" in the future and by looking at how others react to him in the future. Reality is, by this logic, more or less collapsed into appearance; being ahead in a race is thought to reveal a candidate's quality, and appearing to be of good quality helps put a candidate ahead. The journalists' role is to occupy a spot on this circle of appearance/reality in a way that defers to voters or, to say it more exactly, in a way that defers to an imaginary world of voters as signaled by who's a front-runner and by opinion polls.

This is not an easy idiom to escape. Another *On Point* guest, William McKenzie, did get part of the way out when his turn came to comment on the "attack on Hillary":

> McKenzie: I think it is better to get this out of the way for her now. It's better to get her sea legs . . . The thing she needs to worry about, though, is this hangover from her husband's presidency, that they're just so calculating, and they're waiting to see which way the wind blows before they take a position. And I watched this debate and . . . I was astounded with how many times she dodged . . . for example this question about illegal immigrants and whether they should get driver's licenses . . . . I mean, just say something.

These remarks depart from the horse race idiom in several ways: McKenzie declares that Clinton actually *did* dodge, rather than merely *appearing* to do so; he shared his *personal* perception that Clinton seemed calculating; and he overtly criticized Clinton for failing to "just say something." McKenzie can, then, be accused of bias.

But this is unfair, for two reasons. First, the horse race genre is not as neutral as it seems. Instead it's biased toward appearance as an essential indicator of underlying substance, toward front-runners as most worthy of coverage, and toward whatever issues and perspectives are already being taken seriously in the narrowed public world called "the mood of the electorate." This phrase (which, by the way, appears on the radio show as a topic unto itself) is, while neither meaningless nor simply a lie, to some degree a phantasm shaped by flak, campaign contributions, survey question writing and analysis, lobbyists, economic elites working on government advisory panels, advertiser concerns about media content, etc. In an antidisagreement society that relies on a somewhat cowardly mass media to inform the people, "public opinion" has a manufactured aspect. Like the news itself, it's thin and narrow.

Another reason that it's unfair to accuse McKenzie of bias is that his remarks don't, in fact, fully exit the circular realm of appearance and divination. For one thing, his reading of Clinton as a dodger is a comment on her debate performance, not on her track record as a politician. The claim is that she dodged *questions*, not that she has stood for nothing, as a person or politician, during the course of her life. Also, McKenzie's feeling that Clinton is calculating follows Clift in reporting a perception. McKenzie simply uses his own observation in the way some other journalists use poll results. Most of his words remain inside the circle.

The circular horse race format is by no means all bad. It gives journalists a role to live up to, thereby supporting the cause (or at least the ideal) of journalistic independence. The format also implicitly shows respect for voters by, in effect, performing the idea that voters can both wisely indicate concerns and read appearances effectively (with the help of the news analysis). But the latter positive is also a negative. Because America is performed as already-a-democracy and because voter preference is elevated to the status of both sovereign and independent variable, several important paths of journalistic investigation are made unlikely. The performance of democracy is not consistent, for example, with question-raising about the validity of the political system in general (e.g., what did *not* get talked about at the debate, who was not present, why two parties dominate, etc.). And the elevation of apparent voter preference is not compatible with taking a serious look at issues that are not of concern to voters—but which might be (i.e., with a look at what each of the "losers" has to say). Finally, the emphasis on appearance leans journalists away from attention to things not connected to what voters already know about: e.g., the details of candidate track records or historical facts that may have a bearing on the validity of candidate proposals.

Within the limits posed by the situation, Clift and McKenzie do rather well. They manage to obliquely bring up legitimate questions about the quality of the candidates: Is Edwards opportunistic? Is he decisive? Is Clinton both calculating and a dodger, not truly for or against anything, just checking the wind? Neither journalist directly addresses these questions, but, one might ask, how could they?

## PRETENDING TO CONVERSE

Early in 2004 the U.S. economy was officially in recovery, but the job situation was dismal. President Bush, perhaps in an effort to convince voters he cared about the unemployed and otherwise had a sound economic policy, put together a series of "conversations on the economy." Thus on February 26, at ISCO Industries in Louisville, Kentucky, he had a "talk" with the owners and employees of several local family-owned companies, along with other local workers and at least one not-for-profit volunteer. The audience heard about the humble beginnings of a local pipe factory, the important needs being met by a compressed air and pump company, and the fact that a woman has no problem owning and operating a construction and excavation firm. Bush heaped praise on an anti-domestic violence advocate, as well as a collections specialist and an accountant. After president's speech each of these real Americans got a minute to say something about themselves, and Bush responded with warm jokes and supportive statements.[26]

I wouldn't pick the word "conversation" to describe what happened that day. The *Watertown Daily Times*—a newspaper published in a fairly Republican corner of northern New York, not too far from where I live—was closer to the mark in referring to one of the Bush gatherings as a "talk-show-type event staged by the White House."[27] Another apt analogy might be a game show: the grand prize for five was a moment of fame, plus contact with the president, and the runner-up award was the opportunity for millions of viewers to imagine the feeling of being suddenly thrust into such a setting.

I don't mean to single out Bush for criticism. I could just as easily have mentioned the "Americans" introduced by President Clinton during each of his State of the Union Addresses. The problem with such displays is that they are put forward as if they're in some way representative of a larger, imaginary encounter, as if they amount to a conversation with the entire nation. The suggestion is that the president has made contact with "America"; his finger is on the pulse; he empathizes; he knows what he's doing. That such talk-show-type events work as well as they do, politically speaking, reveal how much needs to be done to make feisty dialogue a regularized aspect of politics.

What about public opinion polls? Are they a form of political participation? Yes and no. Polls provide information citizens can use to help them think about issues, options, and candidates, etc. On the other hand, "America," like any other collectivity, is not a mere aggregate collection of separate individuals so much as a thing that gets formed in the imagination, an entity that exists if and when many people see it as more than an aggregate. This requires a degree of performance; America gets "performed" into being, made reality by people believing in it and acting those beliefs out somehow (even by protesting). There is, correspondingly, no such thing as "American" public opinion until enough Americans make a decision about what America believes. And the gathering up and collating of individual responses to various questions is by no means the most democratic way by which to form the national "we."

From the point of view of democracy, the primary problem with polls is that they do not represent the results of conversation. As Craig Calhoun puts it, "Public opinion research is more akin to the simultaneously developed field of group psychology than to democratic practice; it is an auxiliary science to public administration rather than a basis or substitute for true public discourse."[28] Questions are formulated by experts or by interested parties, perhaps to match other questions that were asked last year or to further various political and/or research goals. Answers are then given one at a time, by people with a variety of concerns in mind and with different degrees of commitment to, and investment in, those answers. And interpretations must be made and packaged, whether by pundits, pollsters, social scientists, or journalists. The result is a (somewhat vicious) circle in which the individuals being queried are in part reacting to what others seem to believe, those reactions are entering back into the production of those appearances of belief, people react to that in turn, and so on. In other words, public opinion, like every nation, can only come to be by means of performance. "Opinion polls in this sense are a performative genre. They do not measure something that already exists as public opinion, but when they are reported as such, they *are* public opinion [emphasis in original]."[29]

Fortunately, it's safe to say that few people consider opinion polls or televised meetings between presidents and common folk to be actual conversations. The same cannot be said, however, for the proliferating genre of ersatz political dialogue. I refer to events that are probably intended as—and certainly perform themselves as—actual debates held among equally situated participants on pressing issues but which are nonetheless too highly managed to truly count as such. Typically, the subject matter is defined so that any actual clash between truly different views is unlikely. Sadly, this can easily happen even when people bring good intentions to the effort, if and when their ideas about what counts as a problem take over.

Consider two examples: The "Great Discussion Program," sponsored by the Foreign Policy Association (FPA) and begun in 1954, is "designed to stimulate thinking and discussion in classrooms and communities across the country." Each year brings a new edition of *Great Decisions*, a book said to provide "balanced articles on eight crucial foreign policy issues."[30] Lesson plans are provided for teachers. Videos featuring "internationally recognized experts" on foreign policy are available. Question and answer interview transcripts with said experts are available at the click of a mouse. Teachers and community members are encouraged to form discussion groups. The FPA offers to provide such groups with publicity, a program handbook, tips for organizers and discussion leaders, a modest grant to support the expenses, and access to an opinion balloting process.

For whatever reason (no need to dwell on intentions or funding sources here), the "balanced articles" are, like the list of experts provided, much less than balanced. For example, when, in October of 2003, I clicked on "Iraq Watch, In Focus,"[31] I found links to the ideas of a current ambassador, a member of the Iraqi opposition to Saddam Hussein, and an ex-CIA agent, as well as to documents of the Senate Foreign Relations Committee. Of all the sources listed, only the remarks of Robert Baer, the ex-CIA agent, were even modestly critical of U.S. policy, and upon inspection they turned out to raise questions about the quality of intelligence—an important subject for sure but hardly a tool to help people to critically consider the foundational assumptions of their nation's foreign policy. Taken as a whole, the views presented by FPA instead merely reproduced the range of debate active within governmental circles of the time; they asked, for example, just how isolationist Americans can afford to be in this age, and just how multilateral or unilateral the nation ought to be while assuming that *of course* it should try to remove Saddam Hussein from power and *of course* it has a right to do so.

The problem is always with the "of course." What about the claim that the U.S. approach to Iraq was nothing other than an arrogant exercise of imperial power, justified by bogus claims about weapons of mass destruction, and bound to backfire by creating more anti-American extremism? Such views were widespread in some circles *well before* the U.S. attack on Iraq, and they provided a foundation for (and came from) the rise of thousands of activist groups in small towns and big cities around the nation. They were not, however, to be found in the FPA materials, perhaps because they were also not noticed (or in any case were not covered) by mainstream media outlets, who almost never ask protestors about what they believe and who rarely provide any time to foreign policy perspectives that are not voiced at high-profile government or think tank-sponsored press conferences.

Compared to what actual protestors had to say, the "opposition" point of view offered by the FPA was downright milquetoasty. Consider, for example, the words of Dr. Gary Milhollin, a nuclear weapons expert and director of the Wisconsin Project on Nuclear Arms Control, whose "criticism" is nothing but a request for more evidence: "I think there is a need for further evidence that the Iraqis are actively trying to conceal what they have . . . I think that will go a long way towards convincing people that Saddam has no intention of disarming."[32] Likewise, Charles Kupchan, a professor of international relations at Georgetown University, senior fellow at the Council on Foreign Relations, and member of the National Security Council during the Clinton administration, questions none of the Bush administration's basic goals or intentions, asking only that the nation proceed "with utmost care" and avoid being "blustery" lest others "lock arms against us."[33]

A similar pattern can be seen in an initiative called "The People Speak" (TPS). Sponsored in 2003 by the United Nations Foundation, the Rockefeller Brothers Fund, and thirteen other organizations, the program sought to foster "an ongoing discussion about the future of American foreign policy."[34] I went to Schenectady Community College to take part in one of the resulting dialogues, an event organized and hosted by Professor David J. Hennessy, an engaging and thoughtful political scientist who chairs the school's business and law program. Things got going slowly, as most of the audience straggled in a bit late, looking like students showing up at their professors' behest, and the presentations made were a bit hard to follow in places, perhaps because (as I found out afterwards) each of the two speakers was detouring away from their actual positions, in order to do their best to present "two sides." The talk did get lively, however, and many perspectives got aired, thanks largely to the ideas, and the chutzpah, of a few members of the audience who managed, in the few minutes at their disposal, to take the issues beyond the questions posed.

The chutzpah and sincere effort was necessary because the TPS debate resolutions were almost as narrow in conception as those provided by the FPA. Debate organizers were, for example, asked to debate one of the following propositions:

- RESOLVED, that the United States should use military force preemptively to meet the threats posed by hostile nations and groups seeking to acquire nuclear, biological, or chemical weapons.
- RESOLVED, that the United States should participate in military operations overseas only where vital American interests are at stake, not for democracy promotion or primarily humanitarian causes.[35]

Once again certain issues were not put on the table. With regard to the first resolution, how could any pro and con discussion of the claim manage to include the idea that the government might be wrong about which nations and groups actually pose a threat or that the government may have lied to the public about the subject? The language of the resolution rules these topics out by reducing the question to one of timing, to *when* the nation should turn to force, preemptively or later. Turning to the second resolution, how, in any argument about its merits, could one put forward a declaration asserting that democracy promotion is itself a "vital interest," rather than an alternative to the nation's vital interests? How, for that matter, could one ask if the current administration has any idea what is in the nation's "vital interests?" Once again, the questions being asked by the more critical commentators were ruled out by the language used. They were not noticed as worthy of debate, presumably because they were not then being debated within current leadership circles. They think that "of course" leaders know what the nation's vital interests are; and they were busy at the time debating isolationism versus activism and whether to act now or to wait a little longer. The FPA offering both reflected and reinforced that perspective, despite its appearance as real debate.

"Great Decisions" and "The People Speak" might be well-intentioned initiatives. And even if their sponsors, or some of them, are involved in a conscious effort to shape public opinion, I imagine that they believe in the messages they're trying to spread. This thought does not, however, reassure me. In fact it scares me, as it's hard to imagine a more effective way to discredit ideas than by *unthinkingly* leaving them out of an *otherwise* multisided and genuine discussion. That which is excluded ends up appearing unreasonable or otherwise beyond the pale of that worth consideration.

This is often the fate of pacifism, nonviolence, and anti-imperialism. These philosophies have a long and storied history. They are very much alive today. And proponents from each point of view had something to say, late in 2002, in firm opposition to the U.S. government's increasingly obvious plan to launch a military attack on the government of Iraq. Yet all three were left out of almost every prewar U.S. media discussion about the wisdom of launching the war. When they did receive media attention it was usually in ways that ignored and/or discredited the ideas at issue. The media did, for example, take note of some of the many political protests—where pacifists and anti-imperialists often carried the biggest banners—but framed them, in the usual ways, as locales where society's need to keep order has to be balanced against individual rights and as places where interesting but quaint or less-than-creditable characters appear (people who are "out there," "from the sixties," or "dangerous and irresponsible"). The ideas at stake were, in effect, discredited by exclusion.

All the organizers of the two above-mentioned dialogue initiatives had to do, in order to include a wider range of views, was to click on one of hundreds of anti-imperialist or pacifist-inspired Web sites, for example, that of the American Friends Service Committee (the national Quaker organization).[36] Instead they apparently either reflexively wrote off such groups, or they didn't know such groups existed.

I don't mean to go down the conspiracy road. I am not accusing the FPA or TPS of somehow trying to triumph politically by suppressing points of view that are at odds with their agenda. In a way it would be nice if the world worked that way: there would be bad guys to oppose, and the good guys would have a simple mandate to oust them from their privileged positions, thereby letting objective truth and goodness shine through. But a coup d'état is not the answer. Instead what's needed is difficult conversation. The people behind the FPA and TPS need it, and anyone who sees them as mere propagandists also needs it. But such conversation is lacking, so "experts" are often clueless, blind to issues or arguments of major importance. Moving in like-minded circles, caught up in self-sealing group cultures, they perpetuate narrow frameworks about "both sides."

Are dialogue initiatives like those of the FPA and TPS at least better than nothing? It's hard to say. Yes, because the public is thereby invited into otherwise expert conversations. And the public can surprise. At Schenectady Community College, for example, the participants managed, despite the restraints, to carry the discussion to unscripted places. We found a way to talk about the topics the TPA had failed to include: the morality of war on Iraq, the questions of who is truly a threat, the meaning of "the national interest," and so on. On the other hand, maybe the programs are not better than nothing, because so often what carries the day in the end is the way the issues are framed. Yes, alternative comments were made in Schenectady, but the discussion leaders kept to the road that the TPA had laid out for them.

Be wary, then, of what goes by the name of "debate." Sometimes similarly trained experts argue but only about the best method for reaching a goal they share. Sometimes election-year pundits have it out but only about the strategic merits of the various statements and actions of the front-runners. Even if important facts are thereby made available, the positions taken may nonetheless mirror those currently being taken among the already powerful, among people who by and large agree when it comes to essentials. And in that case any journalist covering the events will, in all likelihood, simply report what was said, thus reinforcing those elite positions.

## TALK RADIO AND SHOCK TELEVISION—BETTER THAN THE 6 O'CLOCK NEWS

In this context of media disagreement failure, angry, overtly one-sided "shock" radio is in many ways a welcome development. Here I have a bit of personal experience. Early in 2003 I got a call from WYBG, which broadcasts from Massena, New York, near where I live and work. The station, which regularly features *The Rush Limbaugh Show*, invited me to speak about Alternatives to War, a group of people opposed to the looming U.S. attack on Iraq and to which I belonged at the time. I agreed, expecting to get a few minutes to explain what the group was all about and perhaps a chance to announce our next event. But when I got on the air I instead found myself immediately under attack. I was interrupted in the middle of virtually every sentence. I had to struggle to get a word in edgewise. The host claimed, among other things, that the reason the Bush administration had been given no evidence of weapons of mass destruction was that the information was top secret. Then I was told that *Readers' Digest* had in fact published the proof that the weapons did exist. Before I could fully grasp what had just been said, much less point out that it might be self-contradictory, I was steered away from the subject of Iraq entirely by the host's sudden declaration that "everything" was the fault of the Arabs, who were said to have "stolen the Middle East" because they "want to drive the Jews into the ocean." Then the interview was over. The whole thing took less than five minutes.

Once I caught my breath I was surprised to find myself energized, even exhilarated. True, I was frustrated, but I had held my own under fire. I was often interrupted, but I had returned the favor to a degree, and I never got angry. I was not successfully baited. I never turned away from my nature. And it seemed to me (though I admit ego could be interfering with my judgment here) that I might have succeeded in getting at least ideas I believe in out to people who don't already agree with me. My guess, in any case, was that a lot more people paid attention to what I had to say than would have if I had simply been permitted to add to the "community calendar" with an announcement.

What about Rush Limbaugh's style of acerbic radio diatribe? In November 2003 Limbaugh returned to the airwaves to host his radio call-in show, having been on leave while undergoing treatment for an addiction to painkillers. Right away his angry political sarcasm, his all-problems-are-caused-by-the-amoral-liberal-elite-who-have-stolen-the-country thinking, was in full swing. Should he get points for promoting disagreement? Absolutely. True, demonization is the name of his game and listening to alternatives is not. But by creating a genuinely partisan space, Limbaugh helps to license impromptu speaking out, thereby highlighting the need for the expression of "crazy" opinion. On his show extreme views get airtime, even if they are almost all his, and there's nothing like an extreme view to stimulate real thinking, to make people want to respond, whether positively or negatively.

One way some have responded is with liberal political comedy. And at times this up-and-coming genre does a good job supporting disagreement. So it was on October 8, 2007, when talk show host, author, and political pundit Chris Matthews appeared as a guest on *The Daily Show*, a political comedy program hosted by Jon Stewart. The subject of discussion was Matthews' new book, *Life's a Campaign*, which purports to offer lessons for getting ahead in life based on the techniques used by successful politicians. On Stewart's show Matthews pointed out, by way of example, that Bill Clinton is "a good listener," half-jokingly adding that this is perhaps how Clinton got "so many women to sleep with him." Soon after this remark the conversation became less genial. Consider the following excerpt:

Stewart: I thought that it [Matthew's book] was a recipe for sadness, only because, and I say this to you honestly, as I read it, I thought, this strikes me as artifice. If you live this book, your life will be strategy, and if your life is strategy you'll be unhappy.

Matthews: People, to get ahead on life, are good listeners; they're optimistic people; they're very good at asking for help because they don't try to do it alone; and every time they ask for help, they get more people to invest in them.

Stewart: But that's not a campaign; that's common sense: listening to people, caring about people. There's stuff in here about "Attack somebody when no else is going to attack them."

Matthews: I never said that; I never said that.

Stewart: [after some back and forth about a book detail that was a bit hard to follow] It seems like what you're saying is doing what you think will win, not do what you think is right.

Matthews: Well, it's both.

Stewart: This seems to emphasize the former.

Matthews: It does; it's about . . . Will you come on *Hardball* [Matthew's show]?

Stewart: I don't troll.

Matthews: [raising his voice but smiling] You are unbelievable. You know this is a book interview from hell; this is the worst interview I ever had in my life . . . . You are the worst . . . You're afraid of this book.

In response to this last remark, Stewart laughed, maybe a bit sheepishly but also in mock denial. He then ended the interview with an offering: "I love what you do . . ." True, he was clearly half-joking, looking for laughs, but it was also clear that he wanted to say something nice, after the hard words that had been exchanged. "I really appreciate your trying . . . I'll come on your show . . . You can yell at me, 'Friends?'" The two men shook hands.

Stewart was, to be sure, catering to his audience, and Matthews was certainly looking for publicity. And it's also true that in effect the two men implicitly worked together toward these goals. But it would be a mistake to overlook the pro-democracy aspect of their conversation (or, for that matter, to be disdainful of entertainment as such). Matthews and Stewart jostled with each about difficult subjects on which they were at odds: morality, the proper priorities in life, and what truly counts as success. It was intense, but they shook hands afterwards. *The Daily Show* provides regular displays of such disagreement, of argument conducted in a confrontational, but civil and respectful, manner.

On the other hand, today's talk radio and talk television also have flaws when it comes to encounter. Stewart and Matthews compressed their subject matter into a five-minute exchange. To survive on WYBG I had to speak aggressively in a similarly fast-paced situation. Not everyone can do that, and maybe I didn't do as well as I thought. In general radio and television arguments are short, experts or hosts direct and dominate the discussion, and the differing ideas fly past one another. This is in part a technical issue; even the best such exchanges cannot fully substitute for face-to-face meetings when it comes to providing for the time-consuming process of finding common ground or achieving a deeper understanding of the issues at stake and of one's opponents. But the biggest problem with the ways political argument usually happens in the media is cultural, not technical. What passes for encounter is often just encounter for the sake of it, as Deborah Tannen, author of *The Argument Culture*, learned from her several television appearances: "I encountered producers who insisted on setting up a television show as a fight (either between the host and me or another guest and me)."[37]

Will humor and entertainment value be lost if the media move towards depictions of the exchange of ideas? Yes, but some will be gained as well. As today's comedy shows make clear, real disagreement need not be politically correct and boring. If Al Franken were to cohost *Saturday Night Live* with Rush Limbaugh sparks would probably fly. Even now, Michael Moore provides elucidative, pro-disagreement entertainment in some of his films. Moore is at his best when he engages, rather than simply pokes fun at, his political opponents. In those moments he leaves questions unanswered; he leaves his audience to ponder many sides of an issue. I'm thinking especially of his encounter with Charlton Heston in *Bowling for Columbine*. True, Moore goes after Heston for his anti-gun control stance, but he also announces in the film that he is himself a member of the NRA. And *Bowling for Columbine* similarly refuses to offer a definitive answer to its central question, "Why is the United States such a violent place." The film, in other words, is confrontational, provocative, and by no means neutral, but it's also welcoming of counterargument.

## IMAGES OF HAPPINESS AND SUCCESS

What counts as a good time? What methods work best to solve problems? What achievements or experiences make for the best life? Every day each American is bombarded with hints, assumptions, and possible answers to these questions, mostly in the form of images or narratives, much of it found in mass media productions designed primarily to entertain or sell products. Much could be, and has been, said about the cultural and political import of these productions, but here I offer only one idea: the media sends few messages that include disagreement as part of the success/happiness picture. More specifically, conversations that include disagreement are rarely depicted as worthwhile or satisfying. Also, on most of the occasions when such conversations *are* depicted as worthwhile, the subjects discussed are narrow, and the participants are not talking about ideas, much less radically differing ideas.

These observations are, I admit, not based on a systematic or comprehensive count of how often this and that depiction appears. In my defense, such a project is fraught with difficulty. For one thing, the number of discrete media depictions is enormous, ever-shifting, and ever-expanding. Also the relevant images appear in many genres, from commercials to news broadcasts to YouTube movies. Then there's the challenge of saying clearly where one depiction begins and another ends. And, finally, there's no way to specify what a given depiction "means" using strictly factual (nonquestionable, unambiguous, and entirely nonarbitrary) terms. Meaning doesn't work that way. Because of these problems and because of time and resource constraints, I have chosen to offer a brief image sketch based on my personal observation of media presentations, in many genres, conducted over the course of many years. And I invite my readers to try looking at the media themselves using this image sketch or to otherwise look at them from a pro-disagreement perspective and see if that angle makes good sense of it all.

I begin with a list of typical ways happy or fulfilled people appear in the media:

- Dancing, often in a sexually charged atmosphere or situation;
- Laughing and making small talk: e.g., summer campers, students on the way to class, and the like;
- Being in an audience and being entertained or deeply moved;
- Eating with family or friends;
- Experiencing the thrills of white water rafting or bungee jumping;
- Sharing and expressing romantic love;
- Winning, especially in sports, making the team win;
- Experiencing other forms of personal achievement, e.g., high school and college graduations;
- Happily playing at a casino or winning the lottery;
- Enjoying silence in the face of a beautiful, awesome natural scene.

I consider this list reasonably comprehensive, and nowhere in it do I see argument, disagreement, or the expression of ideas. It's not that this trio is missing entirely from the media. It's that they tend to appear in solo speeches and testimony, usually without any hint of personal fulfillment. The people depicted are often as follows:

- Angry or sad, telling reporters about violence that has just befallen them or their family;
- Delivering an angry, heated message to a large (maybe screaming, poster-bearing) crowd;
- Making a serious, official speech from behind a podium or on a legislative floor;
- Describing someone else's ideas very briefly while providing "the news."

Thus far I have not listed any depictions of actual disagreement encounter, where conflicting views clash. It does appear in the media, but where I mostly find it is as follows:

- Analysts arguing about sports: e.g., teams, players, rules, steroids, will, and character;

- Journalists arguing about politics, using a horse race idiom, and interrupting each other a lot;
- Political candidates who exchange views but do not ask each other any questions (as it's against the debate rules), and they rarely appear to enjoy themselves.

My claim is that Americans rarely see disagreement and political expression depicted in ways that suggest any link between such activity and either happiness or fulfillment. Those who want to find satisfaction in arguing should, based on the mass media, become sports commentators.

An important exception to the general trend are the many depictions of transformational, agonistic events in narrative drama—e.g., novels, plays, movies, and television series. On the other hand, the characters involved often are family members, friends, or lovers. Perhaps they are somehow reconciling after, or because of, a difficult round of sharing. Or the arguers could be members of a small team of closely bound coworkers, who function much like a family. What's still missing are positive images of an exchange of differing ideas between people who otherwise don't know each other or only know each other as neighbors or people who also live in the community. In sum, then, the images of success and happiness that appear in the mass media do little to support public cross-border disagreement.

## ON THE WEB

My friend Don emailed me not too long ago with a request. He was deep into a series of political arguments on the Net, and wanted some help in crafting a response. A flaming liberal, Don regularly logs onto conservative chat rooms to have it out. Sometimes he even changes his mind about something. Thus it is that, in the words of Al Gore, the "Internet is perhaps the greatest source of hope for reestablishing an open communications environment in which the conversation of democracy can flourish."[38] But Gore also rightly points out there's no guarantee that the Internet will, in fact, live up to its promise. Not everyone is as inclined as Don to seek out opposing ideas. Web sites specialize, making it easy for people to "talk" only among the like-minded. Also the word "browser" is misleading: it's easier to browse a newspaper than the Web, if "to browse" means to look around and thus hazard running into the unexpected, perhaps hearing a point of view you did not seek out.

The Internet, moreover, can never fully substitute for face-to-face meetings. Many of my students have taken part in online "class discussions," and they tell me that virtual conversation, even when done in full video, is not the same as being in a room together. It's not nearly as conducive to what Daniel Yankelovich calls the "magic of dialogue."[39] The magic Yankelovich refers to is what happens when people connect across a border thanks to the creation of empathy and an experience of each other's humanity. As Seyla Benhabib puts it, "Understanding the other is not just a cognitive act; it is also a moral and political deed." It's physically seeing and feeling the basic similarity, as well as the raw individuality, of another person. It's a "magic" moment that involves a paradoxical realization:

that person is unique, just like me. Such connecting usually requires not only an exchange of words but also gestures of openness, eye contact, and the like. And, while facial expressions can appear on a screen, in that location they don't necessarily seem to belong to real individuals; again as my students say, seeing the other becomes too much like "watching a movie." This means that, while the Internet is a valuable tool it needs, like the media in general, a pro-disagreement world around it and in it, if it is to fulfill its promise.

Here's a list of some good aspects of the Internet, from a pro-disagreement point of view:

- It offers the opportunity for bottom-up content uncontrolled by elite agenda setters;
- It lowers the cost of creating a communications network; members of the middle class and even the struggling working class can form a political network, if they can find the time;
- Labels can be more easily defied (thanks to anonymity), and coalitions can be more easily redefined and restructured;
- It makes it easier to converse with those who are not nearby (and might be across the globe); and
- It can make speaking up and being honest easier for some people (thanks again to anonymity).

On the other hand:

- It encourages enclaves and talking to the like-minded, which as we have seen (see Chapter 4) can lead to ideological amplification and to less correction of factual errors;
- It's not conducive to the development of shared identification and mutual commitment across borders; the encounters are electronic and thus more likely to be thin or instrumental;
- There is a higher degree of self-selection;
- There's no way to attend an online meeting without speaking and still get counted as present in the way one might in a face-to-face gathering; and
- It's not public in the specific sense that there is no open audience, there is thus less accountability, and this means there's not enough pressure on each individual to consider their contributions seriously, in the light of the goals of the event.

The moral of the story is that there's no way for technology to make the world more pro-disagreement. People have to do it.

## CONCLUSION

What the media needs, and what democracy needs, is a pro-disagreement sensibility in the populace, and this needs to be supported by a robust practice of cross-border public encounter. The media would, in such a world, be pressured, and also be allowed, to change for the better. Conservatives, liberals, and a host of radicals would get more opportunity to speak in their own voices than they do now. Every "side" on a given issue would be more pressed to speak well and to listen to its opponents. The media would serve up the disagreement food required by the public sphere. And the public would in turn feed the media with issues and perspectives. Is all this likely? Maybe. Is it possible? Absolutely.

CHAPTER 6

# Democracy as Conversation

The trouble . . . is that we have taken democracy for granted; we have thought and acted as if our forefathers had founded it once and for all. We have forgotten that it has to be enacted anew in every generation, in every year and day, in the living relations of person to person in all social forms and institutions.[1]

—John Dewey

The dialogue is the conversational and communicative fore that allows a person to achieve liberation from conventional, preconceived, and forever petrified descriptions, and to recognize and realize one's equality and freedom together with others, particularly through freedom in and of speech.[2]

—Dmitri Nikulin

This chapter situates this book relative to the thriving body of scholarly work that's come be known as deliberative democracy. The best versions of this theory recognize the imperative role of disagreement in citizen deliberation, and I go so far as to argue that disagreement needs to be put first as a value, that as a goal it's both more central and more practical than deliberation. With that in mind I consider objections to moving society in the direction of more disagreement. My conclusion is that the project is both possible and likely to be beneficial. The various objections point to real risks, but the greater threat, by far, is posed by *not* trying, by continuing to steer clear of "extremes," and continuing to leave political arguments to others.

## DELIBERATIVE DEMOCRACY

Sometime in the year 2003 my frustration with the state of the world began to crystallize around the idea of an underappreciation of disagreement. Just as I began to delve into the idea, Bruce Ackerman and James S. Fishkin published *Deliberation Day*. In that book they propose a two-day holiday from paid work during which citizens would do citizenship work. Specifically, they would gather in groups two weeks prior to each national election, "deliberate on the choices facing the nation" under the guidance of trained facilitators, and receive a modest stipend for their efforts.[3] They would thereby learn from each other, refine their views, and possibly influence the future policies of their nation.

This idea struck me in two ways. I thought it was worth looking into, something that might work. I also thought the very act of proposing a Deliberation Day valuable as a way to draw attention to underappreciated possibilities: that opinion based on deliberation might be different than predeliberative opinion; that "ordinary" people might be capable of remarkable, positive things if given the right opportunities; and that there must be productive, nonpolarizing ways for people to agree and disagree about politics that have yet to be fully considered.

I was also heartened to learn about Ackerman and Fishkin's "deliberative polling" work. The first step in a deliberative poll is to survey the opinions of a random sample of citizens. The chosen group is then invited, "at the expense of the project, to engage in a weekend of small group discussions and larger plenary sessions in which it is given extensive opportunities to get good information, exchange competing points of view and come to a considered judgment." After that the group is polled once again. Deliberative polls have at this point been conducted on many occasions—and on many topics. "The resulting changes of opinion," says Fishkin, are often dramatic."[4] To the point here, while participants sometimes change their positions on this or that policy, thanks to their deliberations, the most consistently observed change has been in their evaluation of those on the "other side." They often come to see their opponents in a more generous light; they are often struck by the plausibility or reasonableness of arguments they previously understood little or looked down upon in one way or another.[5]

My encounter with the work of Ackerman and Fishkin spurred me in several ways. First, I became more decisive in my commitment to "disagreement," as opposed to "deliberation," as the best way to conceptualize (and sell) needed change. As I try to make clear throughout this book, one of the most challenging tasks of our time is to bring a wider range of perspectives into the public realm while also bringing people there both to hear them and give them voice. The concept of "deliberation" is thus too limiting: it carries an implicit injunction to be "reasonable;" it suggests "thoughtful" contributions to a collective train of thought; it implies people making sure to say things that are "productive" and "relevant." I'm all for thoughtfulness and relevance, but in practice these concepts will often feed dynamics of exclusion; people will frequently seem "out of order" just because they have something to say that's hard for others to hear.

Ackerman and Fishkin also turned my thinking toward what might be required to bring the creation of a disagreement/deliberation holiday within the realm of the possible. On this subject, I didn't have to start from scratch. I knew about the classic theorists of "participatory democracy," from Jean-Jacques Rousseau to John Stuart Mill. I knew of Carole Pateman's foundational 1970s work in that area. I knew about John Rawls A *Theory of Justice*, in which he purports to derive principles of justice from an imaginary conversation of sorts.[6] And I knew about Pateman's and Rawls' contemporary, Jürgen Habermas, who argues that the way to temper the instrumental rationality of social systems (which can only treat humans as so much material to be managed) is to tap the more emancipatory rationality found in the sphere of noncoerced, fully inclusive human conversation. All acts of communication, says Habermas, however imperfect, imply allegiance to an ideal of emancipated, egalitarian communication; they imply a dynamic of persuasion without manipulation, an "ideal speech situation." This notion, he goes on to say, while never fully realized in practice, provides both a goal toward which humans should move and a legitimating principle of collective decision making.[7]

What I didn't know was that a host of political theorists had already responded to these developments by reviving and transforming participatory theory into "deliberative democracy." The basic premise of this body of theory is that deliberative, public conversation is the first principle of legitimate decision making; it generally improves the quality of decisions made; and it cultivates and honors the fundamental values of reciprocity and mutual respect.[8] "The people," the various theories also claim, only fully exist *as such* if and when they participate in a deliberative public realm. Without that empowering, opinion-strengthening element the best the people can be is a mere "electorate," and correspondingly, all they can hope for from politics is mere "aggregative" democracy.

The last term refers to the adding up of individual "preferences"—however thick, thin, manipulated, thought-out, farsighted, or shortsighted—through some sort of voting (e.g., for representatives or referenda), and treating those votes as authoritative. In practice this means a system dominated by big money and public relations campaigns that sells candidates by targeting select voters and then tapping their various emotional buttons.[9] Don't misunderstand: people's preferences deserve respect; indeed such respect is one of the principles of deliberative democracy. On the other hand, thinly held preferences can be shortsighted and easily manipulated, and the public policy generated by tapping into such preferences through elections, in the context of a mass media consumer society, are potentially disastrous: unjust wars, failures to plan and act for the long term, the pork barrel accumulation of policies that add up to deficits and a lack of revenue to address new and pressing problems, and more.

Fareed Zakaria's *The Future of Freedom* follows in the footsteps of James Madison, Friedrich Hayek, and Samuel P. Huntington in labeling social and policy ills like those listed above as the result of "too much" democracy.[10] But what is democracy? Zakaria uses the word in two ways, with considerable waffling back and forth. He uses it very narrowly to refer to any practice of using competitive elections to fill political offices, and he also uses it more broadly to refer to all forms of pandering to, and expressions of, preference. He uses the latter idea to speak of the new degree of attention paid by professionals (such as lawyers) to consumer demand, the growth of money market fund opportunities for the middle class, the proliferation of opinion polls, and the increased number of lobbyists

living inside the beltway as if they were all examples of the rampant spread of the
rule of the people.[11] In so doing, he equates the ownership of a tiny fraction of
shares in a retirement fund mutual account with the possession of real power over
the future direction of society. And by means of such logic he manages to declare
human history is in "the democratic age." He's able to assert that democracy is
"out of control,"[12] that the nation has "too much of a good thing," thereby threatening liberty, prosperity, stability, and security.[13] Never mind the undemocratic
role of money in elections, the fact that the most influential lobbyists represent
rich corporate leaders and owners, and the structural power held by big business
due to their investment clout. Never mind all the reasons that Zakaria himself
calls many apparent democracies a sham. Never mind, in other words, all the
reasons that a host of theorists now argue that the United States is not very
democratic.[14] There's still "too much" of it, and the proper answers, according
to Zakaria, are to cleave to constitutional limits on popular power, create more
government agencies run by "independent" experts, renew respect for authority
and even aristocracy, and inject more free market discipline into government
policy.

Zakaria's book offers trenchant insight into many contemporary problems. He
knows a good deal about the specific situations of dozens of countries around the
world, and he's also a good writer, so his book is educative and reads convincingly. But his overarching framework is a problem. For one thing, it's not clear
how all his "solutions" could possibly fit together; it's not clear how free market
policies can do anything but increase the "democracy of consumerism," meaning
pandering to whatever sells. More to the point here, Zakaria confuses aggregative
pseudodemocracy with the real thing. John S. Dryzek, a deliberative democrat,
sums up the movement of theory away from aggregative thinking this way: "The
essence of democracy itself is now widely taken to be deliberation, as opposed
to voting, constitutional rights, or even self-government," where "deliberation"
means communication that induces "reflection upon preferences in non-coercive
fashion."[15] Amy Gutmann and Dennis Thompson likewise speak for deliberative
theory in arguing that such reflection is valuable because it encourages people "to
take a broader perspective on questions of common interest" while also promoting
"mutually respectful processes of decision making" and helping to correct policy
mistakes.[16]

So it is that, while Zakaria sees a world falling apart under the strain of
untrammeled preference, deliberative democrats see a lack of settings where
people might solidify and/or change their preferences, where they might make
those preferences both more truly their own and more likely to add up with other
preferences in coherent, thoughtful ways. This does not mean that deliberative
democrats want everything to be up for discussion. They recognize that not all
decisions can be subjected to a public exchange of reasons for and against. Also,
while they believe that deliberation should be *encouraged* in many arenas of life, it
should not, say Gutmann and Thompson, be *required* "beyond what is necessary
for citizens to live freely while also respecting the basic liberties and opportunities
of their fellow citizens."[17]

The theorists of deliberative democracy have many practitioner allies. The National Coalition on Dialogue and Disagreement, for example, hosts a biannual meeting of dialogue specialists, people who spend their working time helping to resolve disputes, working with community activists to create "Issues Forums" where citizens gather to talk about opposing arguments on pressing local questions or convening "World Café" discussions, where people sit in small groups around tables to talk about an issue and then rotate to other tables, where they do it again. Dialogue activists also help many corporations to move in a cooperative, dialogic direction, create dialogue spaces on the Internet, and bring "stakeholders" together to help communities make difficult decisions. They hawk "open space technology, a simple set of techniques enabling conference participants to organize their own panels on the spot, in accordance with their various concerns. And dialogue practitioners help organize "citizen juries," also known as "citizen congresses" or "consensus conferences," whereby a cross section of citizens, often randomly selected, gather together in order to consider an issue or proposal. The jurors listen to expert testimony, read background materials and position papers, spend days deliberating under the guidance of facilitators, and then issue a policy recommendation or issue statement. In Denmark, among other places, this process plays a role in governmental policy making.

The many theorists and practitioners of dialogue and deliberation don't agree with each other about everything, nor should they. One of the issues in play is whether deliberative democracy is most fundamentally a form of government rather than a practice of discussion and argument. Gutmann and Thompson see it as "a form of government in which free and equal citizens (and their representatives) justify their decisions in a process in which they give one another reasons that are mutually acceptable and generally accessible, with the aim of reaching conclusions that are binding in the present on all citizens but open to challenge in the future."[18] Ethan J. Leib likewise calls for the creation of a "fourth branch" of government in which randomly selected citizens deliberate in "civic juries" convened regularly to consider specific issues and make law.[19] Citizens thereby engage in "actual institutionalized decision-making about *policies*, not *politics* [italics in original]," leading to the formation of what he calls "will" rather than "opinion." The latter—the formation of mere opinion—is the likely result when people exchange views as if a decision was in the offing when it's not. As Leib puts it, "non-fictive will-formation should be central."[20]

I don't fully agree. While it's true that a government cannot be considered fully democratic unless authoritative public deliberation plays a role in its operations, there are other benefits that come from public discussions where no decision hangs in the balance, and these discussions are more foundational. In the words of John S. Dryzek, "[a] vital public sphere is essential . . . because a flourishing civil society provides both a resource for future democratization of the state and a check against reversal of the state's democratic commitments."[21] To say it another way, I can't imagine people starting where Leib asks them to start, politically speaking. I can't picture today's busy, often stressed out, often consumption-oriented citizenry supporting a constitutional amendment to create a new branch of government.

What I can imagine is people going in the direction he wants them to go if they start by creating a pro-disagreement movement of culture and practice.

Another area of theoretical disagreement is disagreement itself. As Gutmann and Thompson put it, there are consensual theories and there are pluralist theories.[22] The proper goal of deliberation, according to the consensual theories, is comprehensive agreement about what counts as the common good. Even if such agreement must remain elusive in reality, as some concede, anything less is thin by comparison. Agreement should be the goal and communities ought to come as close to it as they can.[23] Pluralists like Gutmann and Thompson, on the other hand, embrace disagreement as both inevitable and valuable; they rightly see no inherent contradiction between community and the presence of significant moral differences. And they see a degree of danger in any effort to put an end to such differences. As they put it, a "democracy can govern effectively and prosper morally if its citizens seek to clarify and narrow their deliberative disagreements without giving up their core moral commitments."[24]

## THE MISSING PUBLIC

If a "vital public sphere" is essential, what more exactly do these words mean? Nancy Fraser, in an essay called "Rethinking the Public Sphere," usefully argues that any democracy worthy of the name requires multiple "publics" that come to be in multiple public spaces. By a public space she means (citing Habermas' foundational work in this area) "a theater in modern societies in which political participation is enacted through the medium of talk."[25] Put more fully, Fraser understands a public space as any site where individuals come together to engage in discourse about matters they consider to be of common interest, where violence is off-limits, where no topic is ruled out in advance, where disagreement is both expected and accepted, and which is open to the general public (or at least open to a wide range of people, with some degree of unpredictability with regard to who shows up and with no undue costs for attendance). Such spaces can conceivably (and in a democracy should) reside within the government (as in a legislative hearing), but the "public realm" they constitute is logically distinct both from the government and the market sector of buying and selling. By gathering and exchanging ideas, feelings, reasons, and the like in this realm, individuals make more real their existence as distinct individuals while also existing with others as a single entity, as a group (a public) that can act in concert in the political realm and can (if need be) be meaningfully "represented" by someone else.

One reason that multiple spaces are needed is to provide room for many sorts of people to defend their interests and also get heard doing so. They can serve, in other words, as voting booths of a sort, in this case shaping public opinion instead of directly determining election outcomes. But they are also needed to take citizens beyond the aggregation of preexisting preferences by providing space for them to show something of who they are to others, to enact themselves, and thus to exist in ways they otherwise would not. They are needed, then, to support the reflexive, libratory process whereby people rethink who they "are" and thus think anew about what's truly in their interest and the interest of others.[26] This process can make for the formation of a single people that consists of many peoples, a public formed from many overlapping publics, each itself formed relative to particular issues and identities. As Nicholas Garnham puts it, "a single autonomous public sphere is not sufficient."[27]

Fraser contrasts her way of looking at the ideal public sphere with the liberal-individualist view and civic-republican views. The former reduces the public sphere to a bargaining session, as if every person already knew what she truly wanted and needed ahead of time, prior to political discussions. The civic-republican view, on the other hand, sees the public realm as a place where citizens learn "civic virtue," meaning that they come to care about and identify with the whole and therefore put aside their particular interests to pursue the common good. Both of these views are antidisagreement in important ways. The liberal-individualist view gives people a vision of themselves as consumers, as unphilosophical preference-maximizing machines, pointing them away from serious conversation about, say, the nature of the good life. The civic-republican view assumes that at any given time there is a single, clear, common good, that there are no genuine conflicts of interest or incommensurate but legitimate philosophies at work in the society. Fraser's view is more agonistic: a people can constitute a public even as they disagree about—and argue about—what counts as the common good. Those who bring up unpopular notions and ideas in public are not thereby "divisive" or "selfish." Instead they're being citizens.

Part of what makes a public space public is that the participation is noncoerced and there is some degree of accountability. By the latter I mean that the participants are somehow available to answer for their words and (relevant) actions. This can mean that those who are present end the discussion by making a decision that binds the larger community—by making law; but it can also mean only that they are asked (or could be asked) to defend what they say. In either case the public is not the same as the private. There's overlap, the private can become public at times, and what happens "in private" can be brought up in public as an issue. But, as Harry C. Boyte points out, "[p]ublic life is a realm of difference, public work, accountability, respect and recognition, negotiation and bargaining; private life is an arena of intimacy, spontaneity, similarity, and loyalty."[28]

Based on these definitions, the contemporary United States—like many a nation-state—has a public deficit. It lacks the spaces and practices needed for its populace to constitute itself as a public, as opposed to a mere electorate. It remains stuck in what Lizabeth Cohen calls *A Consumers' Republic*, a state in which at best each individual merely gets to choose—but never to make.[29] The role of citizens is little more than that of a consumer who chooses among options that are themselves chosen by others and which include only those things which are capable of being chosen by one individual at a time (unlike, say, clean air). Citizens as consumers are vulnerable to manipulative marketing techniques, as they have little recourse but to make choices based on popularity, emotional appeals, and indirect evidence such as the apparent trustworthiness of leaders. American citizen/consumers have little to zero chance of reaching beyond their immediate circle of friends, family, and coworkers to shape the way others perceive them or to figure out—in person—how they ought to perceive others; thus they often play no meaningful role in shaping what "America" is thought to be and, following this, in shaping what "America" is.[30] In the words of Matthew A. Crenson and Benjamin Ginsburg, "America is becoming a nation of emphatically private citizens—customers and clients who find it difficult to express coherent, common interests through collective political action."[31]

The traditional American response to perceived lacks of democracy has been to try to make the political process more representative in one way or another. Thus many now call for term limits, new campaign spending limits, same-day registration, and the like. As desirable as some of these measures are, they can't conjure up a general public. No matter how free and fair the press is, no matter how good the voting system is, and no matter what people's legal rights are or how well they are protected, the citizen's role will remain limited to that of audience member and judge and politics will remain akin to commercial advertising. Without cross-border, public conversation—held in multiple spaces—democracy cannot measure up to the name.

When it comes to how to envision the public world, I come down with Fraser. But this book is not really another entry in the burgeoning theoretical field of deliberative democracy. This book is about the private world as much as the public. The first goal, I argue, needs to be the creation of a more pro-disagreement society, and this includes more argument in the world of friends, families, rock bands, camping trips, relationships, and the like. Change at that level is both more basic and easier to get started. Most anyone can open their mind and way of living to more disagreement, if they want. And such a shift would be valuable in its own right, in addition to laying groundwork for the creation of more democratic institutions.

## OBJECTIONS

When I ask my students if they think more people need to engage in the art of disagreement, they sometimes respond by saying, "that's a great idea in theory, but people don't want it, and they won't do it." To respond meaningfully to this claim it's necessary to turn it into its several constituent parts, to dig for the various reasons people might not "do it." One possibility is that participation in political disagreement and the opinion-forming process is inherently difficult and most people won't enjoy it enough to bother. Or it could be what people don't like—or assume they won't like—is the anger and confrontation they associate with disagreement. Maybe, on the other hand, it's about anticipated results: people could be reluctant to work hard at something they don't believe will do much good or, worse, they might see more political disagreement as something that will tear society apart.

On another note, a person could be uninterested in cross-border talk because they hate or look down on the people with whom they strongly disagree, perhaps to the point where they would feel immoral treating those others as if they were worth listening to. Similarly, a person might be inclined to stay away from disagreement because it *feels* immoral to them, as if it amounted to publically doubting the very existence of right and wrong. And, finally, they might believe that the basic rules of life have been laid down by God, so there's nothing to argue about.

To complicate the picture, a reluctance to engage with others might be based on beliefs about other people's reluctance or on doubts about their abilities. I might be ready to talk, but if my political or philosophical opponents are opposed to disagreement, maybe I won't stick my neck out. If I believe that "ordinary people" aren't capable of the sort of nonconspiratorial, generous, and principled thinking that healthy disagreement seeks to draw forth, maybe I won't bother to try engaging with them at that level. If I follow Zakaria and Huntington in believing that other people (not necessarily myself) are inherently prone to self-interest, where self-interest is a fixed star of economistic preferences, I may believe that democracy can never be anything other than the aggregation of those preferences and conclude that heightened levels of political talk and engagement would only serve to overload government with selfish demands.

Some of these obstacles are real. Disagreement is often hard work. In some situations the best that one will be able to say in its defense is that it *might* be very beneficial, and given the options is worth a try. And disagreement situations will include the pursuit of self-interests, and therein lies potential for abuse of the process, for manipulation of events in one way or another. In response, it has to be said, loud and clear, that there's nothing intrinsically wrong, and much that is admirable, about the pursuit of self-interest; it's not the same as the pursuit of evil or injustice. And people who engage each other in disagreement will, even as they pursue what they see as their interests, at times also end up reconsidering what's in their interest, based on what they learn from others. Still, some conceptions of self-interest are dangerous, in any given situation, the pursuit of which is hurtful to others or the common good. So the risk is real. And the benefits of disagreement—the improvements to life and society that would come with more regularized cross-border talk, even allowing for the failure of some individual attempts—are not easy to see in advance.

On the other hand, there are reasons to believe regularized disagreement would bring specific benefits that would do much to counter the above-discussed obstacles. The evidence (some of it provided farther ahead in this chapter and in Chapter 8) suggests that people usually have good experiences when engaging in facilitated cross-border discussions of community issues, and many more would have them if their communities seriously gave the process a try.[32] Also conceptions of self-interest and policy preferences can and do change, in part because of disagreement experiences. Dialogic encounters have been known to provide people with new, more positive windows on fellow humans. People do sometimes find that viewpoints different from their own don't result from self-interest or stupidity. People have emerged from debate feeling their own sense of right and wrong renewed and with an increased faith in the morality of those with whom they disagree. And people are sometimes pleasantly surprised, in such settings, by other people's abilities. In other words, some of the objections listed above add up only to the idea that change will be difficult, that people will need to be brave and imaginative and sometimes proceed in small steps, in order to go forward.

## STEALTH DEMOCRACY

Some other objections are more fundamental. What if, for example, most people are followers by nature, inherently prone to select leaders and then put trust in them? What if they are, in other words, fundamentally uninterested in the give and take of direct political participation? What if they will never want to parse the details of this or that policy or idea, preferring to leave such things to the wise and unbiased, if they can be found? These are among the conclusions put forward in 2002 by John R. Hibbing and Elizabeth Theiss-Morse in *Stealth Democracy*. Using focus group and national survey data, they argue that most people don't want to be more involved in politics, and for good reason, as increased participation in political decision making by ordinary voters would bring simplistic and dangerous ideas into government and would also result in chronic stalemate, frustration, and political alienation. The better arrangement, according to them, is the one most people now prefer: a government held accountable by the minimalist "stealth democracy" of elections and interest group competition, with empathetic, non-self-interested decision makers (ENSIDs) paying attention to public concerns and making decisions.

At the core of this argument is the claim that ordinary people assume that other ordinary people see the world as they do, and also that ENSIDs will, being above self-interest, likewise agree about what should be done on any given issue. Correspondingly, most people think policy disagreements are rooted in selfish forms of self-interest such as bias and excess ambition:

> They simply do not believe that debates and compromises are necessary, since we all want the same general things, since the best way of achieving those things will be readily apparent to those who study the problems in an unbiased way, and since the little details of policy are not that important anyway.[33]

This, say Hibbing and Theiss-Morse, is why the public has great respect for the Supreme Court. Even when they disagree about this or that Court decision, citizens tend to see the justices as ENSIDs, as not trying to "feather their own nests." Politicians, on the other hand, are seen as routinely biased, as making decisions to get reelected or to profit personally one way or another.

Ordinary people want democracy, the argument continues, not because they're interested in helping make decisions but because they accept their duty to hold these often selfish and always-tempted politicians accountable by means of elections.[34] True, when asked, Americans often say that they want to "increase the power of ordinary people," but, according to *Stealth Democracy*, what they mean is that they want to decrease the power of selfish politicians.[35] What they would *most* like is wise elites making the big decisions and "objective bureau-crats making their technical decisions."[36] The political reforms that garner the most public support are, accordingly, about process, not policy. The public wants money and self-interest taken out of politics; they want term limits, campaign contribution limits, lower pay for legislators, and the like.

*Stealth Democracy* is, however, more than an argument about what the people want. It's also a critique and is as such aimed in two directions: at deliberative democracy and at social capital theorists who call for more civic involvement. Unfortunately, the many schools of thought that fall under these two headings are misleadingly lumped together as if they were one. "The theorists" are said to tout "the glories of participatory democracy," going so far as to claim "that participation of any sort is good."[37] They try to "thrust" the public into politics against their wishes.[38] They try to "force" people to get politically involved.[39] Hibbing and Theiss-Morse, conversely, argue that "the solution to the problems of the political system is not as simple as just getting people involved."[40]

This is an appropriate response to the many naïve attempts to get people "in-volved," from patronizing get-out-the-vote efforts (as if not voting were never a politically informed choice) to proposals to make voting mandatory. Hibbing and Theiss-Morse are right to challenge the idea that more civic involvement will in and of itself reduce polarization and build new reservoirs of trust between citizens. As Cass R. Sunstein points out (as mentioned in Chapter 4) relatively homogeneous groups tend to silence internal critique and to move, by means of their group discussions, towards more extreme versions of the political positions they started with. It follows that more participation by the public in local, non-controversial, service-based, community groups will not necessarily move politics in the direction of greater rationality or more cross-border, overtly political forms of political participation. Even if such activities built social capital within the respective groups, it would not be the same as building border-crossing political trust (called "political capital" by Hibbing and Theiss-Morse), just as getting together socially is not the same as doing politics. Put another way, "bonding social capital" does not necessarily create "bridging social capital" and can even constitute an obstacle to the development of the latter (as seen in Chapter 2).[41] Thus, say Hibbing and Theiss-Morse, "voluntary community group activities all too often do nothing to help people learn how to come to a democratic solution on divisive issues of the day" and can even "diminish people's ability to appreciate the challenges and frustrations of democratic governance."[42] For example, people who volunteer more tend to bash "Washington" more, as they reason that, since their group succeeded in its (relatively noncontroversial) project, politicians who fail to solve public problems have no excuse.

## MORE SATISFACTION WITH GOVERNMENT SHOULDN'T BE THE GOAL

Hibbing and Theiss-Morse's argument as summarized thus far doesn't make a dent in the idea of deliberative democracy. Most theorists of the latter persuasion agree (who wouldn't?) with *Stealth Democracy*'s claim that "the solution to the problems of the political system is not as simple as just getting people involved."[43] The central notion of deliberative theory is that people can develop bridging social capital through *political*, rather than merely civil, involvement. Hibbing and Theiss-Morse have not, however, overlooked this claim, and once again they're not believers. They argue, for example, that "stronger political involvement will not make people more trusting, more other-regarding, or more supportive of government," and they also point out that "increased political interaction will not boost political capital at all and may very well do damage."[44]

Is this true? I turn to evidence farther on but first need to pay attention to the framing of the question. Whether or not political involvement will boost bridging social capital depends on what's meant by each term. On the subject of involvement, does it mean voting? Does it mean going to public policy hearings where much has already been decided before the citizens get to make statements, one at a time, without discussion? Or does it mean several days of well-facilitated deliberation by a cross section of citizens on a specific issue and with the benefit of expert testimony? Because they lump these things together, Hibbing and Theiss-Morse think they have shown that political involvement does not develop bridging social capital. They have not.

Why? Also, is it valid to fold the goal of developing more "support for government" into the concept of bridging social capital, along with the goals of making people "more trusting" and "more other-regarding"? Many theorists argue that increased deliberation will bring more legitimate (justifiable) governmental decisions, more justice, and/or better public policy but do not argue that it will make people approve more of government.[45] *Stealth Democracy*, on the other hand, speaks as if all "the theorists" agree that the problem to be solved is the decline in trust in government. This is, in fact, Hibbing and Theiss-Morse's concern, and it's not clear if it's the right one. They go on to confound this (dare I say "stealth") priority of theirs with the additional goals of making people "happier" (as in happy with government) and making them "like" politics more. They use these several terms more or less interchangeably. The success of public political deliberation and disagreement is, in other words, measured by a production of satisfaction standard, and not surprisingly, it comes up short. Yes, regular disagreement will sometimes make people *less* happy with government, as well as more critical of "the ways things are." The point is, however, that it might also increase their trust in political opponents, and even in many politicians, by redirecting attention and frustration in the direction of policies and processes and away from people as such. More disagreement might, in other words, reduce demonization and improve policy, even while it puts government on the hot seat.

Peter Muhlberger, a political scientist at Texas Tech University, hits the nail on the head on this subject, pointing out that *Stealth Democracy*'s "overarching concern is with insuring the stability and the legitimacy of the political system."[46] In this regard the book follows the sad social science tradition of treating political "legitimacy" as if it's the same thing as people *believing* the political system is legitimate. Perhaps social scientists go in this direction so often in part because "satisfaction" is measurable, and as such it seems like a nonnormative (scientific) concept. But the result is often the unreflective endorsement of the normative goal of political stability. This is what happens to Hibbing and Theiss-Morse; they proceed as if any government that people accept is thereby also one they *should* accept, or, to put it the other way around, they try to determine if deliberation will make government "better" by trying to measure if deliberative events lead participants to *feel* good about the government. They treat *seeming* to be just as identical to *being* just.

I nonetheless have to tip my hat to Hibbing and Theiss-Morse for highlighting the severity of the disagreement challenge. Their data make it clear: many citizens hanker unrealistically for rule by objective, selfless leaders, in part because the notion is that such people are the source of the best public policies. What society needs, the thinking goes, is expert saints and judges who ride into town and get it done. In reality, complex public policy decision making (unlike the up-or-down, what's-the-evidence decision making needed in a typical criminal case) is most likely to come out well if stakeholders and biased perspectives from many sides are involved in the process. Nonetheless, the vision of benevolent, Mount Olympus style wisdom is well established in American political culture and also is intrinsically tempting.

Hibbing and Theiss-Morse are right, then, that today's low levels of political participation are not simply the result of obstacles to voter registration or disgust with the way politicians argue in Congress. And *Stealth Democracy* is also correct when it asserts that merely creating more spaces for people to meet and talk will not bring them there or make them talk. Even if mixed groups of people do gather to converse there is no *guarantee* of good results. On the other hand, their concern for stability leads Hibbing and Theiss-Morse (in most parts of their book) to treat people's antipathy to politics as reality, once and for all, rather than as a challenge. It's one thing to say that people "do not like politics even in the best of circumstances" and "do not like the process of openly arriving at a decision in the face of diverse opinions."[47] It's another thing to say that *no* improvements to the political system could "generate significant long-term increases in meaningful participation on the part of the public." This makes the claim that low levels of participation are natural. "It is politics [that Americans] do not like, not a particular version of politics."[48]

Is it true that people, as such, dislike politics and disagreement? Again the framing of this question has to be considered. The dislike of a particular food might be simple, as in "I just don't like it," but even that could also be the result of an illness, an imbalance, or an old, negative association and therefore less than simple. The dislike of politics is surely also complicated. It might seem simple to Hibbing and Theiss-Morse's in part because they fall into survey research thinking about human nature. They rely on measured public opinion, gathered in a society that features low levels of political participation and doesn't celebrate feisty disagreement except as entertainment, and they treat this as a measure of what people inherently "are" and "are not"; they take people's statements of preference at face value, as valid measures of what they "want" in a deeper, more permanent sense. Why is such inference valid? No reasons are given.

In the meantime, other experts reach very different conclusions about the American distaste for politics, arguing that "the design of our current political institutions and practices turns citizens off."[49]

> If Americans find the presidential primary process long and boring, it is because that process is indeed longer than it should be . . . . If Americans find congressional elections dull, it may be because they are rarely competitive . . . . If Americans find partisan politics excessively ideological, nasty, and insufficiently focused on practical problem-solving, there is reason to think they are right.[50]

For what it's worth, no less than nineteen prominent social scientists jointly authored these words, or at least signed off on them, after completing a study chaired by Steven Macedo and sponsored by the American Political Science Association.

## CITIZENS NEED TO BE MORE SAVVY, NOT MORE VIRTUOUS

Hibbing and Theiss-Morse also falter by asking if political participation will make people into "better people."[51] First, who says people need to improve? That's not the language of many deliberative theorists. It's true that Rousseau, Jefferson, and other "republican civic virtue" theorists argue that public participation builds character, but some contemporary deliberative theories are not in that category, or not exactly. They depend instead on the notion that properly constructed (as opposed to manipulative, sham) disagreement events will, over time, change people's (quite reasonable) understandings of, and cost-benefit assessments of, political involvement. Politics will change its character, and people will become savvier and more disagreement-friendly, more open to participating in political conflict, seeing it as a potentially positive and necessary activity. True, this is a kind of self-transformation, but I wouldn't call it "improvement." The change is in one's worldview, not one's level of virtue.[52]

Second, Hibbing and Theiss-Morse answer their question about character improvement by saying that the gaining of a political voice "does not make people feel better about political processes," and this inappropriately makes the production of certain feelings and, more subtly, political stability the priority.[53] People feeling better becomes the measure, and what they should feel better about is the political system. Why? Does the political system deserve approval? I would say not yet. And even if and when "political" processes are all they should be, should people "feel good" about them? Not if that means losing their critical edge; not if it means failing to demand justice and good policy. A people can enjoy necessary levels of stability (meaning they can enjoy reasonable stability and safety in their lives, not the guaranteed persistence of government) even as, or because, they question and grumble about government.

Disagreement democracy anticipates endless disagreement and no end to at least some frustration with politics but hopes this will be combined with some good feelings about *conflict* and *other people*. This is in keeping with the tradition of participatory democracy, which argues that engagement in public talk can and will change what people want (not make them better). It trades on the easily observed fact that what people like is partly dependent on what they know and what they expect. Just as espresso is an acquired taste, so is public deliberation. But "taste" is, in a way, the wrong metaphor. If people acquire an appreciation of disagreement, it might be because they come to understand it as a duty or think it's beneficial to others rather than because it tastes good. Similarly, they might always dislike the process itself but come to see it as good for them anyway, as something that will make them feel better later, after they use it to rethink what they need or want. And it's possible that some will actually come to like it, not because of a change in "taste" so much as because their fears melt, their confidence grows, or they come to believe more in the ability of strangers to tell them things they don't already know.

Hibbing and Thiess-Morse are not unaware of this side of the deliberative argument. Their counterclaim is that disagreement encounters don't, in fact, make people more empathetic or supportive of conflict. "When people are confronted with diversity," they say, people "often withdraw from politics or fail to become more trusting."[54] This sounds final, but the study they cite actually found only that the presence of disagreement in people's "political networks" doesn't correlate with higher political participation. One has to ask: What kind of presence? Was it a facilitated discussion? Was it over time and in a setting where all are heard? Was it a yelling match? The authors don't say. Therefore, while it's inherently impossible to *prove* that a widespread embrace of disagreement *will* come to pass, it's also true that all Hibbing and Thiess-Morse prove is that movement in that direction will be difficult, take time, and depend on the *sort* of disagreement attempted.

Here again, the work of Muhlberger is important. He approaches the work of Hibbing and Thiess-Morse with a counterhypothesis: stealth democracy beliefs, while real, are not simply natural or given. Instead they arise in certain circumstances, in particular among people who lack exposure to the details of politics and policy. People who are so situated tend to develop a particular set of "socially problematic beliefs and orientations," including "reverence for authority, an incapacity to take other political perspectives, and low cognitive engagement."[55] Muhlberger names this combination a "parochial citizens worldview" and suggests that one of its root causes might be what Shawn R. Rosenberg calls "linear reasoning."[56] Linear thinkers (like conspiracy thinkers, as discussed in Chapter 4) have "simplistic conceptions of human agency."[57] Specifically, they "understand causality by focusing on an anchoring entity from which effects flow in a simple, direct manner" and so understand political action as the work of some leader's political "will."[58] To them, good policy results flow from good will and bad results come from someone's ill intent. Democracy therefore can only mean the rule of the monolithic (everyone-is-in-agreement, United We Stand) public will. "This will is then instantiated in a strong governmental leader or a small number of like-minded leaders, 'Deciders' with special knowledge of the public, who in turn direct the government to carry out the wishes of 'The Public.'"[59] This idea of democracy is what explains, by Muhlberger's reasoning, why so many Americans prefer the rule of ENSIDs to their own involvement in politics. It's not that they're politically uninterested or averse to conflict, as claimed (despite some occasional statements to the contrary) by Hibbing and Theiss-Morse. Instead parochial citizens are unable "to adequately conceptualize complex systems of governance" because they have not been exposed directly to the multiplicity of reasonable citizen viewpoints on a variety of issues.[60]

Muhlberger's hope is that the parochial approach to citizenship is just one of many possible ways of understanding, and being, a citizen. He therefore also hopes—and hypothesizes—that, far from being a fate rooted in natural reason or preference, stealth democracy beliefs "might be ameliorated through democratic deliberation."[61] Muhlberger sets out to test this theory by measuring the relevant beliefs and orientations of a group of Pittsburgh residents, both before and after they participated in a variety of activities. All participated in a daylong session on a local campus, during which they were given the means and opportunity to study four topics in a "library session" and to "deliberate" in one of three modes: "face-to-face, on-line, or individual contemplation."[62] Some received reminders of citizenship when they met; some did not. All the topics discussed connected to the issue of whether and how to consolidate public schools in Pittsburgh, in response to the decline in population. "The issue is contentious," says Muhlberger, "pitting parents against taxpayers and neighbors against the School Board. Fifty-four percent of participants reported that the issues directly affected them or their families."[63]

All the subjects of the study participated in phone and Internet surveys, and the variables measured were many. Did they think "individuals should suppress their wishes and goals on behalf of group-oriented roles" (vertical collectivism), have "punitive attitudes toward the disobedient," or believe that "some groups should dominate over others"?[64] Were they inclined toward political empathy and able to take the perspective of someone they disagreed with, or did they have a strong desire for certainty and order? Did they express little interest in thinking about ideas; did they report being conflict-averse; and did they know much about politics? And did they have a false impression of public consensus? Some variables were grouped together mathematically to form a measure of parochial citizen mentality. Others were grouped as stealth democracy beliefs, meaning the desire for rule by ENSIDs. And a few variables were brought together as an indicator of a "negative view of disagreement."[65]

One of Muhlberger's findings is that political uninterest "plays no role in explaining stealth democracy beliefs, while false consensus perceptions have 2.4 times the effect of aversion to conflict."[66] He also found that those who were more inclined to the authoritarianism of "vertical collectivism" and with low marks for "socio-political perspective taking" were more likely to possess stealth beliefs. These findings undermine Hibbing and Thiess-Morse's claim that "people don't want it" and instead support the contention that experience with deliberation might, by changing people's ideas about consensus and the sources of disagreement, move them away from political passivity and towards politics. And, in support of the latter idea, Muhlberger found that "deliberation helps ameliorate stealth democracy beliefs and some of the variables feeding into stealth beliefs."[67] Vertical collectivism went down among the subjects who deliberated. Many of those participants who entered the study with high expectations of conflict during the upcoming deliberations reported lower perceptions of conflict afterwards.[68] And there was no evidence that deliberation reduced participants' confidence in government. In sum, Muhlberger's data support the conclusion that cross-border citizen conversations on difficult issues are both possible and likely to be beneficial.

More evidence comes from the work of Vincent Price, Joseph N. Cappella, and Lilach Nir.[69] Using public opinion data gathered in February 2002, they examine "whether disagreement in political conversation contributes to opinion quality—specifically, whether it expands understanding of other's perspectives."[70] Their answer is in the affirmative. People who took part in more political conversations, and especially those who were exposed to more disagreement in their political conversations, were better able to (1) give reasons in support of their own opinions and (2) give reasons in support of opposing opinions. Specifically, they were able to list *more* reasons of each type. Those exposed to less political talk and less disagreement were, conversely, able to give fewer reasons, and also more likely not to be able to list *any* reasons of either kind. These associations were, moreover, not explained by other factors such as "education, political knowledge, interest, participation, and the like."[71]

The success of political argument depends heavily on people's ability to give reasons for what they want, believe, or favor (as well as name feelings, sing songs, hold up signs, and who knows what else). It also depends, as has been said, on the development of some degree of bridging social capital. And this virtue surely includes the ability to grasp something of the view of one's opponents. Thus the work of Price, Cappella, and Nir is heartening. It supports the claim that political participation may lead to the development of bridging social capital, and it therefore suggests that the deliberative democrats, or at least those of the pro-disagreement variety, do not live in a fantasyland of make-believe.

## WILL DISAGREEMENT IMPROVE GOVERNMENT?

Even if the development of political savvy turned the public toward participation, would that make for better policy? Hibbing and Theiss-Morse, not surprisingly, say no. They base this conclusion, however, on a look at situations that are either not deliberative or where it's not clear that much (or any) disagreement was present in the process. For example, they mention a jury that decides not to award punitive damages to a woman whose car was hit by a train. This is meant as evidence that the deliberating public is prone to irrationality, as the jury apparently made its decision on the grounds that the petitioner had had an affair and casually used drugs (though not on the day in question).[72] But what Hibbing and Thiess-Morse don't mention is if there was any forceful argument in the jury room for more than one side. What was the dynamic? Would what happened there also happen in a facilitated discussion among a heterogeneous group? Another supposed example of public irrationality is President Clinton's drop in popularity after it came out that he got a haircut while on Air Force One.[73] Presidential popularity is, however, an aggregate of surveyed public opinions; it's not even a decision, much less a deliberative one. Finally, they refer to other examples of group decision making and say they were marked by irrational ideological amplification (to use Sunstein's term); "[g]roup discussions affect collective outcomes, but not always for the best." There's no mention, however, of whether the members of the various groups were like-minded, if disagreement took place among them, or how the meetings were facilitated.[74] Thus the evidence may add up only to the claim that good policy making requires the presence of disagreement.

The public opinion research of R. Michael Alvarez and John Brehm supports the claim that Americans are capable of engaging in a democracy of conversation and thereby helping to produce quality public policy.[75] Alvarez and Brehm do confirm the oft-bemoaned fact that "Americans are generally unknowledgeable and uncertain about political issues," but they also find that "a profusion of core values and predispositions exists in the minds of Americans . . . [and these] provide important foundations for their opinions and survey responses."[76] Americans' variable responses to survey questions, say the authors, stem largely from a lack of information, uncertainty about how their values apply to the issue at hand or conflict among various beliefs rather than apathy, manipulation by others, or lack of cognitive ability. White Americans, for example, when exposed to new information and perspectives on race-related issues, become more consistent and logical in their response to questions about those issues, and less affected by question wording and order.[77] All in all, people's attitudes are not mindless or random, and neither are they so fixed or ideological that they're not subject to change. People can and do thoughtfully reconsider, or fortify, their opinions when an interchange of ideas brings new information, reveals new ways to apply their values to an issue, or suggests alternative ways to resolve value conflict.

Another way to approach the question of popular ability is to ask about expert ability. Are they better than nonexperts at making judgments on a given subject? A psychologist named Philip E. Tetlock approached this subject by studying the reliability of expert predictions (in the experts' respective fields of expertise) and comparing them to random guesses and the predictions of nonexperts who follow current events.[78] He also looked at how willing experts were to change their minds based on new developments and failed predictions and how willing they were to admit they were wrong. Admittedly, testing someone's ability to forecast the future is not the same as testing their ability to make political decisions or to disagree effectively, but it's certainly a relevant skill. And what Tetlock found is that experts are not, generally speaking, any better at forecasting than anyone else, and sometimes they're worse. Also, the experts who are more confident, specialized, and/or famous are worse at prediction (and less willing to admit mistakes) than those who are less so. Finally, "*what* experts think matters far less than *how* they think."

> We are better off turning to experts who embody the intellectual traits of Isaiah Berlin's prototypical fox—those who know "many little things," draw from an eclectic array of traditions, and accept ambiguity and contradiction as inevitable features of life—than we are turning to Berlin's hedgehogs—those who "know one big thing," toil devotedly within one tradition, and reach for formulaic solutions to ill-defined problems.[79]

I find Tetlock's work a ringing declaration of support for disagreement: first because it suggests that expert opinions need to be vetted by those of opposing experts and nonexperts, and second because the disagreement process is likely to teach people to be "foxes," to know at least a little bit about many things.

A final way one might respond to Hibbing and Theiss-Morse's argument about the quality of popular deliberation is to look at the history of decision making by elected representatives, presidential advisors, tyrants and their inner circles, and bureaucratic committees. As we have seen, all have also shown themselves very capable of falling into groupthink and ideological amplification. Many an elite has turned against his or her peers because of irrelevant factors such as where they had a haircut. In other words, to paraphrase Winston Churchill, disagreement democracy might be the worst of all political systems, except for all the others. Of course ordinary people will, if given the chance, make bad decisions. They will, however, also make good ones, and the presence of dissent and disagreement in their deliberations will move the odds in the right direction.

## STEALTH DISAGREEMENT?

Surprisingly, there are a few spots where *Stealth Democracy* seems to reverse course. Instead of speaking as if more public participation is a bad idea, the book gets downright pro-disagreement:

> We hasten to point out that there are situations in which participation can have the beneficial consequences advocates so badly want it to have.... [T]hese situations are likely to occur when the people involved recognize diversity in society and appreciate the frustrations inherent in democratic decision-making in the context of this diversity. The consequences of participation that result from this enlightened understanding are completely different from the consequences of untutored participation that is too often grudgingly and artificially induced.[80]

Many "advocates" could reasonably be insulted by these insinuations of naiveté, but, leaving that aside, where do Hibbing and Theiss-Morse go with their pro-disagreement observations? They advocate "education" to correct people's misunderstandings about politics. The average citizen, they believe, needs to be disabused of the notion that other citizens who are at all civic-minded must therefore think just like them; they need to unlearn the idea that "the source of disagreement cannot be ordinary people."[81] This means that they need to stop imagining all disagreement to be the product of self-interested elites and ugly interest-group politics. Hibbing and Theiss-Morse therefore recommend that "[I]nstead of pretending that all Americans are the same, the message needs to be communicated to people, probably through the educational community."[82] In other words, "[w]e must encourage involvement that is based on an appreciation of democracy and, heretical as it may seem, discourage involvement that is not."[83]

This argument contains a contradiction. "Artificially inducing" conversation is said to be bad, but "untutored" public participation is said to be unwise. While it's true that forcing people into badly facilitated conversations isn't a good idea (and for which of course no one is arguing), how far can "tutoring" go before it makes a conversation artificial? Not very far. Good facilitation is unlike tutoring; it does not seek to judge forms of participation except as needed to give all present a voice and encourage listening, and that's a good thing. Discouraging some forms of involvement because they're (supposedly) undemocratic, on the other hand, is likely to lead to overly managed conversations, to result in the exclusion of significant disagreement, perhaps even turning educational efforts into nothing more than a series of patronizing or ineffective public service announcements.

There's no reason to believe, moreover, that telling people, in school or elsewhere, that they should appreciate disagreement will in fact move them in that direction. The thing likely to so move them is disagreement itself. Nothing less than cross-border engagement with ordinary Americans is going to teach people that disagreement is inevitable even amongst people who are not evil or trying to feather their own nest.

## ON PARTISANSHIP

But, one might ask, aren't partisan feelings too fixed and intense to allow for more disagreement? To deal with this issue properly, it helps to start with the word itself, about which there is some confusion. Consider a 2004 election-year op-ed column by Alan Wolfe, a prominent scholar of American public opinion.[84] Wolfe cites the large amount of money raised by each of the major parties, along with the exceptional degree of unity on each side, to back his claim that "American politics are more partisan than ever." He further makes the case by noting, "[T]his is not Tweedledum and Tweedledee's election," that in other words significant policy differences are at stake. Thus far described, partisanship sounds like it could be a blessing. People are, it seems, responding to pressing issues in a healthy way by forming strong opinions and by getting involved. Wolfe, however, is complaining, not cheering. One can see why when he speaks of increased partisanship that goes beyond the taking of two sides to include the congressional flouting of long-standing traditions of across-the-aisle displays of respect. Opposing party leaders now appear to feel intense hostility for each other, and this is troubling.

The problem is that Wolfe, like many others, responds by lumping good and bad partisanship together. There's a difference between being politically passionate and being hateful or intolerant of others, but he pushes these two ideas together. One unfortunate result is that he leaves his readers unsure about just what is being asserted. Have both forms of political intensity increased? How many committed and ideological voters also disrespect their opponents? Wolfe's approach does not allow these questions to emerge. He apparently assumes that intense commitment goes hand in hand with the disrespect of others, as if unthinking, close-minded bias is an inevitable consequence of strong political conviction. This, however, is not so; it's just what people are used to.

Wolfe's idea is to increase voter turnout. His thought is that many voters are turned off ("disgusted"), and his hope is that a decline in partisanship could turn them back on and get them into the voting booth. But does this mean he thinks citizens could possibly get excited about politics without disagreeing much with others and without donating much money or otherwise getting in the partisan game? It's true that many citizens are disgusted by the flavor and quality of the partisanship they often witness, but a decline in public levels of political conviction is not what's needed to increase voter interest. And anyway what would be gained from an increase in the number of voters headed to the polls if they go there out of a sense of duty, without passionate (which means partisan) ideas in their heads? Very little, at least when it comes to giving government direction and/or holding elected officials clearly accountable. And there are circumstances where damage would be done as a result; citizens who dutifully turn out to vote sometimes give undeserved credibility to dictators and unjust political systems. Wolfe starts, then, with the wrong question. The problem is not how to get more people to vote, per se, but how to disentangle the three kinds of partisanship— loyalty to a political party, the demonizing of one's opponents, and having intense and informed political convictions. The first of these is neither good nor bad in and of itself. The third is, or can be, valuable. The second is the problem; it needs to be tamed by well-facilitated, humanizing disagreement experiences.

Party loyalty is certainly here to stay. As political scientists Donald Green, Bradley Palmquist, and Eric Shickler point out, the party identifications of Americans "form relatively early in childhood" and often persist. Also, they're right that "political events seldom affect partisan identities."[85] It just so happens, moreover, that the two major American political parties now line up more precisely with divisions in public opinion than they have in years. More Democrats see themselves as liberal, and more Republicans see themselves as conservative. And the leaders and activists in each political party are unusually united in outlook, compared to many times in the past, and thus square off against each other as two distinct groups.[86] In the face of all this, it's easy to conclude that America is intensely and stubbornly divided.

Again, however, this conclusion is based on the conflation of the many kinds of partisanship. The emergence of a clearer-than-usual divide between political parties, and even the rise of more overtly ideological forms of politics, does not mean that Americans are newly hateful, suspicious, or intolerant. There's considerable evidence, for example, from water cooler talk at work to chatter on basketball courts and at dinner tables, that many are now successfully combining passion and mutuality.

The passion is noted by the headline of a 2004 election-year newspaper story: "Bush vs. Kerry Ignites Battles over Dinner and the TV."[87] On the very same day, moreover, another newspaper used this heading: "As Political Debate Heats Up at [the] Office, Workers, Bosses Must Tread Lightly."[88] In the latter story a lawyer named Michael Stiegel is quoted as saying, "Politics has been occupying more lunch conversations than usual," and Tilden Katz, a media consultant for many firms, says that he's "surprised at how much more willing people are to talk about politics." Interestingly, this partisanship is treated by both headline and the story writers as if it were a problem—as if it will have potentially corrosive effects on morale and productivity—even though none of those interviewed reported a negative experience. "We debate a lot in my practice," said one man, speaking of his accounting firm, "I love talking politics." Perhaps many have tossed out that old maxim of polite company—"Don't talk about religion or politics"—with no harm done.

Some partisanship is, of course, not only a matter of identity but also a source of deep animosity and misunderstanding. Once a particular group of people has been subjected to a loss of moral or social status or an injustice (even an imagined one), it's all too easy for the resulting grievances to harden into badges of affirmation, such that the aggrieved experience their continued opposition to the perceived wrong-doers as essential. The grievance against them must be kept alive; new instances of victimization must be discovered; and the guilty party must be kept on the hook (to use Shelby Steele's phrase).[89] In this situation real communication, and thus the possibility of any cross-border learning and/or healing, are simply not on the table.

Tom De Luca and John Buell have an interesting take on this phenomenon. "The temptation to demonize can prove especially enticing under contemporary conditions of close electoral competition, a dwindling "middle," and extreme partisanship,"[90] but it's deeper driving force, they argue, is America's "moral paradox"—the way the realities of American life and culture persistently ask the question, "Why, in an affluent society that celebrates consumption and leisure, do we need to work so hard?"[91] The argument is, in other words, that people are not only upset; they're upset about a deep dilemma of our time. Capitalism is connected to a culture of hard work, but it also depends on the promise of rest and luxury as potential rewards. And, structurally speaking, capitalism is an edifice that requires continual economic growth and high levels of work and consumption to support that growth. This, say De Luca and Buell, is a moral paradox. Frustration and puzzlement at this situation leads to a variety of strong responses, including demonizing ones. It could all work, people sometimes seem to think, if it weren't for . . . (The demon of choice goes here: greedy conservatives, nihilistic liberals, radical feminists, lazy welfare recipients, etc.).

## DIFFERENT MORALITIES?

George Lakoff, in *Moral Politics: How Liberals and Conservatives Think*, offers a relevant theory. He argues that liberals and conservatives differ from each other significantly when it comes to the concepts they use to think about social problems, as well as about basic moral issues, such as how people ought to act in order to take care of themselves and others and what sort of behaviors bring success and deserve praise.[92] It's not that liberal and conservative ways of thinking fall neatly in line with any racial or ethnic identities, or somehow result from a person's class position. Nor are they separate "cultures" or "lifestyles" which one ought to preserve or which one ought to battle against. Instead they are two of the ways people react to a shared situation. These ways are then reinforced by group identifications, people's connections to various long-standing traditions of thinking about society, intentional efforts to propagandize, and the failure of those in each group to really talk to the "other side." The result, says Lakoff, is that liberals and conservatives use different "moral conceptual systems." Liberals believe in a "nurturant parent morality," while conservatives follow a "strict father morality."

The latter brand of thinking considers all morality to be properly modeled on a family headed by a "strict father" (who could be a woman acting as a strict father). This is someone who teaches self-reliance by enforcing the rules and by granting autonomy when earned. In the strict father moral system, strength takes the highest priority, where strength means self-discipline, self-denial, self-reliance, standing up against evil, taking responsibility for those naturally under one's authority, and obeying those naturally in authority over oneself. Thus citizens should, the thinking goes, pay their own way and also obey their commander-in chief. Thus, also, innocent fetuses should be saved, and guilty criminals should be resolutely punished.

Conversely, says Lakoff, the liberal view of morality is built on the idea of a "nurturant parent," meaning one who provides the support needed so that their children achieve full self-development. A nurturant parent is caring and empathetic and models this behavior so as to cultivate empathy in the next generation. Nurturance is a higher priority than strength, and the latter is in any case defined as the ability to be truly nurturing, meaning open-minded, unselfish, kind, and self-respecting. Interdependence is recognized. All are thought to be obligated to do their part to create the conditions for the proper self-development of themselves and others. Thus liberals believe that people ought to create the conditions necessary for women to have control over their bodies, for those who are poor to meet their needs, and for those who have turned to crime to have a chance at rehabilitation.

Lakoff's analysis is too neat. He seems determined, for example, to connect every single contemporary political position back to one of the two basic ideas of family, no matter how big the stretch. This carries the unfortunate suggestion that humans are naturally given to approach politics by applying family metaphors, that most people have always done so—and always will. To make matters worse, he also suggests that the way out of the current impasse of polarization (and away from what he sees as the mistaken morality of conservatives) is to have social scientists provide citizens and politicians with objective facts. This is a highly elitist vision: Leaders, says Lakoff, need to choose the right metaphors to communicate "truth" to the subjectivist masses. More specifically, liberals need to find a way to make their nuanced truths about morality make sense to those who yearn for an authoritarian parent.[93]

On the other hand, Lakoff usefully describes both liberals and conservatives as consistent and principled, given their respective starting points. He is right to point out that one reason people often appear contradictory and immoral to their political opponents is that their respective metaphorical foundations are not objects of their reflection; instead they feel them at a gut level. Thus it is that people often see others as farther from them, philosophically speaking, than they really are. Thus it is also—though this is not the conclusion Lakoff draws—that cross-border conversations will tend to reveal commonalities to opponents; the participants will tend to discover mutual concern with morality, despite different ways of coming at the subject.

Lakoff, then, helps to make sense of today's polarization, and one can take his argument and improve it by noting that the approaches to life and politics that currently divide many communities are actually at least threefold: the liberal, the libertarian, and the moral conservative. These positions differ from each other about what is proper to discuss in public, the respective roles that reason and faith ought to play in deciding what's moral or best, and the appropriate concepts to use to define problems. And each position comes with characteristic flaws: liberals are at risk of being condescending; libertarians are prone to dismissing all political argument as pointless; and conservatives have a tendency to fall into moralism. Each flaw, when in action, puts obstacles in the way of cross-border conversation and contributes to disagreement failure.

Consider liberals first. They tend to make claims by demanding that people's rights be honored, whether they're of the "negative" variety (e.g., the right not to have one's privacy violated) or "positive" in nature (e.g., the right to be provided a decent education). Liberals are less likely to put things in terms of moral obligation. This is one reason why many of their battles end up in the realm of rights claims, meaning in court, where the sphere of disagreement is confined to the jury room or appellate briefs and to consideration of narrowly defined legal questions. The rights approach to justice leads many liberals, for example, to staunchly defend free speech without saying much of anything about why anyone should actually bother to speak, much less why anyone should listen. And rights thinking leads many liberals to neglect important moral issues on the grounds that they're private issues, inappropriate as public topics. This conclusion is based on the mistaken idea that the only properly public questions are legal questions, as if the public realm consisted only of the sphere of official government action.

Sometimes liberals discourage conversation in another (equally unintentional) way; they join their rights talk to the condescending and mistaken notion that reason leads to one plausible answer to every question and that reason is best cultivated through "education," by which they usually mean formal schooling. The condescension comes in when it is assumed that ordinary people who are conservatively inclined are somehow "ignorant" and need to get educated so they can see the light. (This is ironic, given that the most powerful forces in conservatism are well-educated, clever thinkers who write very well and often popularize their ideas much more effectively than liberals do.) It's not that liberals are any more likely than anyone else to be snobs or "elitist" in attitude. Instead the problem is philosophical. The assumption is that if people developed their powers of reason fully through education, they would never disagree, and no conversation would be necessary. This faith in pure reason is not simply a liberal belief it's more widely shared than that, but it nonetheless helps to explain why many liberals fail to grasp that today's conservatives raise many legitimately important moral questions (about, for example, birth control, abortion, sex education, condom use, stem cell research, and the depiction of sex on television) that are worthy of public discussion, no matter how the rights issues at stake are resolved.

Libertarian conservatives (sometimes called liberals, or classic liberals, by political philosophers) are also committed to rights thinking, but they define rights narrowly, as only of the negative type, meaning the right to be left alone. They do not believe in the existence of positive rights, meaning the right to enjoy whatever conditions the society is capable of providing and which are minimally necessary to allow a person to pursue a worthwhile life. Libertarians are deeply suspicious of all forms of collective action, especially government action. Their antipathy to government, and concomitant faith in the bounty provided by entirely unregulated markets, follows from their view of power, which to them only exists when there is physical coercion or the threat of it. This perspective typically generates serious antipathies to cross-border conversation. True, one might want to persuade one's opponents, but by libertarian assumptions such efforts are not likely to accomplish anything, since humans are thought to be more or less mentally autonomous, each replete with his own "preferences." It seems that, instead of exchanging ideas, then, one should simply bargain with, try to outvote, kill, or simply ignore one's opponents, letting them do their own thing, provided that one's own free choice is not thereby put in jeopardy. Certainly from a libertarian point of view there is no reason to work with one's opponents to craft better government programs, as the idea is that there ought to be no such programs in the first place. Finally, according to libertarians people are not in any way duty bound to talk with others, as one's only real duty (at least to adults) is not to interfere with the rights of others.

Of course most people who call themselves "conservatives" are not libertarian, at least not through and through. Most are more aptly called social or cultural conservatives and tend to think explicitly in terms of moral duty rather than rights. In theory this might lead them to push for more public talk, and in a way it does, as they dominate talk radio and other similar settings, but unfortunately they often seem hell-bent (or maybe heaven-bent) at preaching only to the converted. They do not condescend so much as cast their opponents as heretics or demons, as people who need smiting or conversion, not education. This pattern fits with Lakoff's idea that conservatives follow a "strict father morality," dividing the world into the forces of good and evil, understanding moral strength as standing against those who are evil, and emphasizing loyalty, obedience, and respect for authority and moral truth. To many conservatives there is one single and authoritative moral truth (e.g., the Ten Commandments) and this truth is not up for discussion. Liberals seem to them (sometimes) as people who have fallen into immorality by failing to show the proper loyalty to this truth. By this way of thinking, allowing the questioning of the truth in discussion would be opening the door to moral weakness. Also by its lights there isn't much point in listening to liberal arguments, since they must be wrong anyway, given the immorality of their source.

These ideological descriptions are designed in part to encourage liberals, conservatives, and libertarians to take note of their own dark side, to consider their characteristic flaws. The descriptions are also designed to encourage members of the different groups to talk to each other, to say, in effect, "Your opponents do engage in moral thinking, even if it's not your moral thinking; maybe you can find some common ground; maybe they can learn something from you; and maybe you can learn something from them."

## IS MORE REASON THE ANSWER?

Al Gore, in *The Assault on Reason*, launches a much-needed clarion call for a more "informed citizenry." As he puts it, if people aren't "armed with knowledge and the ability to communicate it, no reform measures will save American democracy," in part because of the decline of print media, which used to provide a foundation for the nation's political conversation.[94] Television and the Internet have, says Gore, become the dominant media, and this has brought a decline in the use of logic, reason, and ideas in political discourse.[95] "The print-based public sphere that had emerged from the books, pamphlets, and essays of the Enlightenment has, in the blinking eyes of a single generation, come to seem as remote as the horse and buggy."[96] In its place one finds "visual rhetoric and body language," "image-based advertising campaigns" that are used "to shape the perceptions of voters," and the dominance of the moneyed interests that can afford to deploy these techniques widely.[97] "Today's massive flows of information," says Gore, "are largely only in one direction . . . . Individuals receive, but they cannot send."[98]

Gore is especially concerned about the way that this one-way politics relies on the mobilization of fear. While the human brain is "hardwired" to produce empathy, fear tends to trump both empathy and reason.[99] "When an emotional reaction like fear is especially strong, it can completely overwhelm our reasoning process."[100] Gore cites the Bush administration as an example, saying that it "resorted to the language and politics of fear in order to short-circuit debate and drive the public agenda without regard to the evidence, the facts, or the public interest."[101] One reason this happened, according to Gore, is that Bush himself proceeded on the basis of ideological rigidity and absolute certainty, with disregard for, and uninterest in, inconvenient facts: "[H]e ignores the warnings of his own experts, forbids dissent, and often refuses to test his assumptions against the best available evidence."[102]

There is much to this analysis. It's true that the idea of absolute certainty poses a threat to civility and democracy. Also, it's true that the old game of the politics of fear is alive and well. And the dominance of Madison Avenue on K Street, meaning the integration of advertising science with politics, does, indeed, amount to nothing less than a crisis. Gore is right, then, that "[w]e must create new ways to engage in genuine and not manipulative conversation about our future."[103] On the other hand, his frequent invocation of "the Enlightenment" hints at a problem. He places his faith in Reason, spelled with a capital R. He wants Americans to reintroduce "reason to its proper role at the heart of the deliberative process of self-government."[104] This, he believes, is what the framers of the U.S. Constitution had in mind: public life based on rational, science-based conversation. This is what Americans must move toward, despite the challenges. "Americans in both parties should insist on the reestablishment of respect for the rule of reason."[105] They should, for example, "transcend ideologically based distortions" with regard to the climate crisis.[106]

The problem with calls for a return to "reasoned conversation" is that they are too likely to function in practice either to provide little guidance or to exclude voices that ought to be heard. If by "reason" one only means some sort of sense making, if one means thoughts based on reasons of whatever kind, then virtually all political arguments fall within its ambit, and the call for reason doesn't amount to much. If, on the other hand, "reason" means that people should make "good" arguments, without "excess" appeal to fear and other emotions, then the deployment of the idea as a political standard is likely to have an unintended, antireason effect. Granted, Gore means only that people should use logic, reason, and facts to think critically about specific claims made during political discourse. But his call for a discourse of Reason gives ammunition to the unthinking denunciation of unwelcome messages as "unreasonable." And it also tends to feed into people's tendency to define themselves as reasonable by imagining a group of people who are the opposite. It's not an accident, or a matter of simple error, that Enlightenment thinkers compared themselves favorably to defenders of aristocracy, Africans, Native American "savages," traditional Catholics, the superstitious monks of medieval times, and Aristotle and Plato, accusing them all of irrationality or an inability to be rational. Likewise, during the Cold War, Martin Luther King, Jr., was dismissed both as irrational and as a Communist—and these were interrelated categories of denunciation at the time. Also likewise, after 9/11 it was said to be obvious to anyone with any sense that "of course" Saddam Hussein had weapons of mass destruction in his possession.

The other problem with making Reason the clarion call for improved political discourse is that it's not clear how doing so will tap into the natural human tendency of empathy. Gore is right to emphasize empathy. Bonds of sympathetic feeling, and the recognition of the suffering of others, are major bulwarks against inhumanity and brutality. But empathy is most likely to emerge when people encounter each other without an insistence that they stick to logic and facts. Empathy is a feeling, not an argument, after all, and one can have empathy for a person even when their argument seems irrational.

Gore might, then, be better off sticking to one-at-a-time responses to the views he finds unreasonable while emphasizing a need for cross-border human encounter and civil disagreement. He wants political discourse to be "governed by an unspoken duty to search for general agreement."[107] Why not, however, also celebrate cross-border talk where people are not bound in that way? Participants might, in fact, discover common ground, without having made it their goal. And they would in any case be less likely to put each other down before they listen to each other. This means they would be more likely to experience empathy, and it's empathy, more than reason, that stands as the *first* antidote to manipulation and fear.

## CONCLUSION

One reason that people often define themselves as reasonable by imagining a group of people who are the opposite is the need to strive *against* something, not just *for* something. It's well and good to ask people to be against manipulation and fear, but what, more specifically, is the enemy? To what is the disagreement ideal an antidote? If not unreason, what? I see disagreement as a counter to the impersonal forces of society and the unrelenting pressure of bureaucratic imperatives. Disagreement is a way to counter "the system" by means of messy humanity. Granted, any given system is actually many interconnected systems, each with changing and competing (partly discursive) elements, but taken together they still constitute a force that's under nobody's control, that pursues thoughtless goals such as predictability and the endless growth of whatever happens to be counted. Disagreement among flesh and blood individuals offers a way for people to work together nontyrannically to shape the future more consciously and more in accord with human values.

I also see disagreement as an antidote to the idea of easy or final answers, in other words as an opposite for absolutism, where the latter refers not to a specific religion or culture but to any philosophy that opposes conversation with outsiders or promises to end the need for conversation once and for all.

Disagreement can, finally, be positively compared to an untamed world of random fate and anarchy. While disagreement is not the opposite of unreason, it is akin to reason in that it does offer a democratic way for humans to make (and then remake) order. It's a form of *reasoning* that's open to all comers, at least as long as they play by the simple rules of the talk itself, if they abide by the rules of the democracy of conversation.

# CHAPTER 7

# Multiculturalism with Principle

[I]f we all waited until we knew we were right before opening our mouths, allowing ourselves zero risk of misunderstanding or overstatement, then nothing worthwhile would ever get said.[1]

—Bruce A. Jacobs

[T]he self is intrinsically dialogical: its viability depends on the quality of its responses to the environment. It cannot be understood or expressed except in relation to an audience whose real or imagined responses continually shape the way in which we define ourselves.[2]

—Mikhail Bakhtin

Multiculturalism is both a fact of life and a badly needed form of public action. Unfortunately, some fly its banner atop kitschy, patronizing, and/or manipulative celebrations of "difference." Meanwhile, social conservatives often misuse the word to name an imaginary enemy; they conjure up the idea of a hedonist, power-hungry "liberal elite" so as to have a foil for their "back-to-values" politics.[3] To further confuse matters, each of these errors occurs as part of legitimate effort to respond to difficult questions. What's truly different and what isn't, and how should one deal with the former? What's the right (principled) way to recognize the humanity of others? What are the ultimate, nonnegotiable rules of right and wrong, and how should they be put into action in the day-to-day world? What does it means to be loyal to one's culture and nation, and how important are such loyalties, relative to other values? Because people approach these important questions with very different (to some degree mutually demonizing) worldviews, the political scene now features the disagreement failure so often called the "culture war." In other words, the multiculturalism that's reality and the needed response of multicultural practice have both come to be overshadowed by a deployment of "multiculturalism" in an ongoing (and at times willful) set of misunderstandings. The term has come to be a political football and an obstacle to communication.

Despite these problems, principled cross-cultural sharing happens every day. People, in diverse settings, overcome obstacles and find ways to facilitate learning that crosses cultural, political, and ideological lines. They interact in ways that creatively combine principled position taking with listening and open-mindedness. The best of these efforts confound the idea that "cultures" are separate, autonomous, or homogeneous things in the first place while simultaneously respecting people's different histories and backgrounds. They demonstrate that multiculturalism, when well-conceived, can be a means to counter greeting-card naiveté, unprincipled relativism, fundamentalist narrowness, and untrammeled elite domination.

Such efforts are imperative. The United States, like many countries, is home to an astonishingly diverse array of people. Americans are also increasingly connected to the rest of the world, to the point where it's harder than ever to demarcate any U.S. "national interest" as a separate entity that might be pursued or, perhaps, compromised in the light of other values such as universal human rights. This means that the "Western culture" (never entirely "Western" in the first place) some defend has increasingly merged with other elements, to the point where one can speak of a conglomerate Western/Eastern/Internet-facilitated/considerably commercialized culture of the globe. In the meantime, in the face of this edifice, powerful differences between groups persist but don't always line up into coherent "cultures" that can be clearly distinguished from each another. People still have and need particular local identities, but these come in many flavors. And these flavors include different ideas about what counts as right and wrong—or at least different interpretations and applications of the same basic ideas. How, then, amidst such complexity, can people hang on to principle while also learning from each other? Should they adjust their ideas of nation and personal identity? What's the right way to do that? What's the right way to square national membership with being a human being?

This chapter responds to these issues by calling for "principled listening"—along with disagreement patriotism—as a way to break the logjam between people's desire to be generous to the views of others and their understanding of the need for absolute principles, for right and wrong. I begin by outlining the many variations of "live-and-let-live" multiculturalism.

## LIVE AND LET LIVE AS KITSCH

Often one of my students will defend a point of view by announcing that it's simply their point of view, that it's right because it's right for them. The views of others are, correspondingly, "just their opinions." This "live-and-let-live" approach to culture and morality sometimes takes the form of what Shelby Steele, in *A Dream Deferred: The Second Betrayal of Black Freedom in America*, aptly calls "kitsch."[4] By kitsch he means images that paper over the suffering, complexities, and irreconcilable beliefs of the world by inserting a vision of differences as nothing more than so many leaves growing on the same tree. People from around the world smiling and holding hands, multiethnic campers canoeing in bliss, singing UNICEF children: these are wonderful images in and of themselves, but the way they're typically packaged sends the false message that the peoples of the world can live together harmoniously merely by relaxing and thinking positively—and perhaps also by sending a check or buying Coke. The suggestion is that cultural harmony can be had without hard work and without personal or collective cultural change. If each person respects the cultures of others, all will join together and still retain their own culture. They will live and let live *and* melt together, happily simmering in a melting pot that's heated by smiles (rather than American ideals).

This can't work, for one because some cultural elements are not compatible with others. For example, the appearance of things as commodities to be bought and sold tends to destroy other ways of looking at the same items. One can understand gender equality and gender justice in many ways, and they're not all compatible. And the world is now witness to a rapid decline in the number of spoken languages, and each lost language means the permanent loss of perspectives on the world. These are situations of dilemma, contradiction, and potential tragedy. They reveal complexity. The tradeoffs and difficulties cannot be melted away.

One reason culture is complex is that often much is gained by the same processes that destroy. Much has been gained as a result of the increase in cross-global forms of communication, sometimes even for those who've lost touch forever with a language spoken in their family for generations. It's also complex because those changed by the world "outside" have always already been shaped by it beforehand. Cultures are never *entirely* "other" from other cultures, at least by the time they are encountered by someone who sees them as such. Many perspectives and practices were taken from, and/or imposed by, outsiders. They were adopted and adapted; they became local and they changed the locals. Is cricket a Pakistani game? It is now. But this means that Pakistan doesn't exist as a truly separate entity whose culture can be clearly demarcated from that of others. And this holds for every other country as well.

Even if cultures were autonomous entities, they would still contain their own internal contradictions. They would still have good and bad points of their own. They would still support the mistreatment or exploitation of some members of their very own societies. In the United States today some say husbands can and should "discipline" their wives. Others name the practice as domestic abuse. Whose views should the outsider respect?

Kitsch multiculturalism doesn't exactly deny the existence of these complexities, but it skirts the issue by acting as if all the beliefs of the world can fit with all the others, in one big happy family. This is more than patronizing; it also stands in the way of needed public action on many issues. It tells people that there's no need to make difficult decisions about this or that cultural element or social practice, that there's no need to keep parts of one's culture alive by, say, rejecting others.

## OF COURSE YOU AGREE WITH ME

One force that animates the more patronizing forms of multiculturalism is the subtle pull of unity. It can feel good to be all of one mind, and it can seem ahead of time *as if* it would feel good to reside in such a place. The pull of unity can seduce even those who most want to be "open-minded." Under its spell, multicultural programming easily morphs into loaded and manipulative "dialogues."

It's hard to bring this up without inadvertently feeding scare stories that conjure up images of power-hungry, fanatical, and ideologically rigid liberal professors brainwashing the nation's youth. Liberals and leftists have not, in fact, taken over American universities. Also, the typical college curriculum includes plenty of exposure to conservative ideas, many of which are hard to see because they're understood as mere fact or as apolitical, objective theory. Granted, liberal teachers (like their conservative counterparts) sometimes push ideas on their students and are sometimes unfair. But this is bad teaching or a personal foible. It's certainly not the result of a unified plot to brainwash and seize power. Neither is it the result of professors "going too far," as if whatever intellectual stance currently lies "in the middle" in a given discipline is thereby better, truer, or more objective.

Where liberals often err is in equating rational dialogue with the reaching of a certain result; they often assume that a genuine conversation, held in good faith, will of necessity lead to certain conclusions. Thus, for example, some assume that a genuine open-minded discussion about the claims of different groups will lead to the celebration of the lives of the historically oppressed. There's nothing wrong, and much good, about such celebration, at least if it's not dirt-denying and romanticized. But much is wrong with entering such conversations with the assumption that celebration is *the* only acceptable conclusion. To do the latter is to denigrate, by omission, the lives of those not designated as "historically oppressed." It is also, perhaps, to label people as "oppressors" simply because they reaped some relative benefit from oppression, never mind what it costs them, or how little power they have. Don't those people have a past that includes suffering? Don't others owe celebratory remembrance to their ancestors?[5]

There are other reasons, besides the pull of unity, that multiculturalism sometimes goes astray. It often labors under the influence of bureaucratic imperatives, some more edifying than others. In the university setting, for example, professors often worry about the approval of their bosses, the institution is often desirous of higher minority enrollments, and there's a constant need (especially in the humanities and social sciences) to raise money. Under the influence of such pressures, multicultural initiatives are sometimes tailored to fit with preexisting, already-accepted models. Perhaps they're used by competing schools or favored by grant providers, for example. And the program designs favored by granting agencies are not themselves free from the influence of bureaucratic imperative. Much of the funding comes from large corporations or government agencies that work closely with corporations. Many corporations are eager to craft a positive, minority-friendly public image as well as to get access, through the work of higher education, to a skilled but compliant work force and therefore may be most comfortable funding educational designs that are just as patronizing and manipulative as their own in-house employee programming.

To see how honest efforts to create open-minded dialogue can have mind-closing effects, consider the following hypothetical example. A college professor is convinced that all white Americans, including himself, unknowingly harbor racist assumptions or perceptions while also enjoying tremendous privilege thanks to their white status in society. The professor therefore designs a workshop designed to sensitize the students to these often-subtle forms of privilege and bring out any residual racism. The professor does not grade based on the points of view expressed, and encourages the participants to speak freely. Students are told, in good faith, that "there are no wrong answers."

Despite the good intentions, the assumptions governing the event make leading questions all too likely. Students might be asked, "In what ways does racism find expression in our society?" or "How do you feel when approached at night in the street by a group of black, male strangers? And white students might be asked, "Do you have any thoughts about the privileges that you enjoy as a white person in America?" These flow from, and the answers can only confirm, the assumption that white Americans enjoy certain privileges by virtue of being white.

It's not that I disagree with the last idea. In fact it strikes me as descriptive of an important reality. But what if it were also a reality that most whites are not privileged and quite sensibly do not feel privileged? What if they enjoy some privileges *relative* to others, but aren't thereby "privileged?" And what if, correspondingly, the participants assumed to be "of color" don't see their color in terms of membership in an underprivileged group? In that case a workshop like the one imagined above would probably leave some white participants unable to give voice to experiences of relative powerlessness and disenfranchisement and also leave some blacks with an alien public identity imposed on them.

These problems are not hypothetical. Bruce A. Jacobs, for example, in *Race Manners*, describes a cultural diversity seminar attended by his sister. It turned out that she—an African-American—possessed none of the cultural "attributes" of "African-Americans" that were listed by the facilitator, in an effort to "educate" the whites in the group.[6] This is not what happens in every workshop—some workshops provide wonderful, pro-disagreement learning experiences—but neither is it rare. Gatherings honestly meant to openly address racial issues too often end up guilt tripping and alienating many whites and imposing an artificial unity on blacks. Problems arguably shared by many whites and blacks—such as relative powerlessness—often receive little, or no, consideration.

It's not a big step from the pull of unity to the posing of moral relativism, meaning the position my students lean on when they say, "It's right for me," and thereby avoid thinking what might be difficult or threatening. These may seem opposite—with unity being on one side and relativism on the other—but both avoid actual engagement in difficult, not completely predictable, truly inclusive, risky conversations. But I will speak more on that subject shortly.

## THE SUBTLE ABSOLUTISM OF MODERATION

Another version of live-and-let-live multiculturalism is the melting pot idea. Arthur M. Schlesinger, Jr., in *The Disuniting of America*, offers a moderate version of this point of view. Membership in "America" is, he says, not about adherence to a particular vision of family or economy so much as about endorsement of democratic ideals and practice.[7] People can and should choose their own ways, with one exception: they should endorse the live-and-let-live tradition; they should support the great American ideas of inclusion and mutual respect. To Schlesinger this does not mean denying any shortcomings in that respect. The nation must do its part by finally living up to its democratic ideals, Americans should acknowledge the crimes of their country's history and injustices of its present, and the United States should honor the many different cultural traditions that are woven into the national tapestry. But, says Schlesinger, this brand of multiculturalism has become excessive, and the result is an erosion of a sense of common purpose, something vital to all societies, lest they fall into vicious "tribal antagonisms." Americans must, therefore, defend the melting pot ideal.

But why should anyone believe this, one might ask, rather than the obverse? Maybe America falls into tribal antagonisms because it doesn't have *enough* multiculturalism, meaning multiculturalism of the disagreement sort. This is not Schlesinger's line of thought. By his lights, America needs more universal endorsement of the ideals of freedom, democracy, and human rights. Without these America cannot be a nation; "democratic principles provide both the philosophical bond of union and practical experience in civic participation."[8]

> [W]hat has held the American people together in the absence of a common ethnic origin has been precisely a common adherence to ideals of democracy and human rights that, too often transgressed in practice, forever goad us to narrow the gap between practice and principle.[9]

This vision is either not as helpful or not as moderate as it seems. As stated, it's too vague to be of much use to ground peoples' identities or undergird shared practices. "Democracy" means different things to different people, for example. Also the model celebrates endorsement, and it celebrates abstract principle rather than specific activities. The thought seems to be that democratic "practice" will somehow flow from such endorsement.

A related problem is that the apparent moderate character of the approach comes from its vagueness. Thus, while Schlesinger's position appears to be "halfway" between total tolerance and an insistence on one way of living, it garners this appearance only as long as it's nothing more than a clarion call in favor of general principles. When Schlesinger gets more specific about what might provide national identity amidst difference his argument takes the same turn that every melting pot theory eventually takes. It turns away from tolerance of criticism. It demands too much melting.

This happens for Schlesinger when he insists that nationhood requires a commitment to America as *in fact* a place where freedom, democracy, and human rights *are* substantially realized. He says that this is a belief people must have if they are to have a shared sense of nationality, and he thereby contradicts his acknowledgment of the gap between values and practice. How, after all, can people open their ears to the claims made by some that the nation has serious flaws, if the very existence of a sense of nationality depends on the idea that there are no (serious) flaws? Schlesinger's approach is, then, less disagreement-friendly than it seems. It's a melting pot idea, not a taste-each-other's-dishes-to-check-them-out idea. The big risk with melting pot ideas is that the heat that does the melting is likely to be generated by an identity politics that cooks up scapegoats. This has long been the sad side of the celebration of America's national creed. Groups have always been denigrated for failing to live up to the standard, because they're (supposedly) "Communists," "filthy immigrants," "illegals," and so on.

Schlesinger himself does not engage in the politics of denigration; indeed he opposes it. He is, however, naive to think that racism, the stereotyping of welfare recipients, and the accusations of treason so often leveled against those who have questioned the status quo are all simply instances of a failure to live up to American ideals. They are instances of such failure, but they are also an expression of the downside (the absolutism) of the way those ideals have been defined and lived. This problem is inherent in all efforts to create nationality, and is especially at issue in a country like the United States that purports to be based on a creed rather than membership in a linguistic group, in ancient traditions of dress or cuisine, or in a shared history that predates the present-day government.

Schlesinger is right, then, when he says that the ideals of democracy and human rights are "too often transgressed in practice," but one needs to also realize that in some ways these very ideals, as they have been formulated and engaged in the practice of living, have not always goaded "us to narrow the gap between practice and principle." Sometimes the principles have instead let people pat themselves on the back even as they violate them. Such behavior is at one level simply the result of the inherent insecurity of human identity. But the melting pot American idea feeds the problem, in part because freedom and democracy can never be *fully* and *finally* realized, and therefore scapegoats will remain useful to redeem the idea of the nation. People know their country is not all it should be, but they nonetheless feel a need to believe in it, so they define some people as less than true members (e.g., as un-American) and then blame them.

What is to be done? Schlesinger points in the right direction when he says that "democratic principles provide both the philosophical bond of union and practical experience in civic participation."[10] What he seems to means is that democratic principles provide the "bond of union" *because* they lead people to experiences of civic participation. And when he speaks of such experience he seems to mean *shared* experience. If he does, he's right. Shared activities can indeed shore up identities and thereby help to create a sense of community. But what sort of shared experiences will do the job? As I said above, the sharing of national self-congratulation isn't the right answer, and Schlesinger doesn't offer a specific, concrete alternative. Since much of the current shared activity in the United States is nonpolitical and the current realm of the political is dominated by the consumption of political advertising, benign attempts to join people together by means of shared "democratic principles" are likely to do little more than bring some people to the voting booth and fill advertising space. And voting, while often treated as the exemplary form of political participation, can't possibly do the job of creating a sense of togetherness across difference, at least not without help. It does nothing, in and of itself, to build bonds between voters, and sometimes it does the opposite. Also many people now turn out to vote, and still Schlesinger speaks of a disunited America. And, finally, those who don't turn out to vote aren't likely to be newly moved in that direction by a call to democratic principles.

The answer is to reach beyond Schlesinger's approach and consider disagreement. Sustained disagreement practices could provide shared experience in civic life while also helping to tame the impulse to a single identity formed at someone's expense.

## RELATIVISM, ABSOLUTISM, AND GENEROSITY

America can be described as divided into absolutists (whether conservative, liberal, radical, or what-have-you), would-be relativists, and experimenters or believers in dialogue and disagreement. I use the term "absolutists" rather than "fundamentalists" to make it clear that I'm not referring to religious believers, per se. An absolutist is anyone with excessive pride and a righteous insistence on adherence to some sort of political correctness. The opposite of absolutism is humble acceptance, not atheism. It's the simple recognition that every human belief system comes up short in the face of the basic worthiness of all life, no matter how valuable they are otherwise. Such acceptance, if taken beyond mere lip service, means affirming the singular value of the life, the voice, and the perspective, of all opponents. It means being a radical when it comes to including people. And that means including, if possible, the protestors outside a meeting, the homeless folks who make commuters uncomfortable, and the terrorists who just killed someone's neighbor. All have a perspective that deserves a place in the conversation of the community, even if they refuse to peacefully take that place and even though it's not always the right time to try to initiate a discussion.

But this philosophy is a demanding one. When it comes to discomfort with disagreement, sympathy is in order. The risks are real. Any effort to grasp the point of view of an opponent has the potential to rock one's world, to change things forever, with at least some negative results. One's family might not approve of the new ideas. Friends might turn away. The listener might emerge uncertain about how to proceed in life, and find herself depressed as a result. Thus it's fair to ask, "Is engaged disagreement worth it?" In the end that's up to each person, but I firmly believe that the benefits, while hard to see until one takes a few steps on the risky road, far outweigh the costs. The hard work of listening and countering can, and usually does, give rise to a new appreciation of one's fellow human beings, a higher level of moral commitment and certainty about whatever beliefs one ends up with, and greater personal fulfillment. Unfortunately, most people have little contact with the practices and notions which would make for such productive exchange.

Sympathy for all points of view is also in order because everyone has to deal, in one way or another, with the challenges of their time. The current challenges include intense uncertainty. What is the future? Will inherited meanings make sense in the future? Will global warming or peak oil change everything? Will humanity have enough water to drink? Can the economy keep on growing? Will hard work pay off? Is a given community enough of a sure thing to justify putting some effort into it? Another contemporary challenge is the visibility of a great deal of suffering that all seem to agree is wrong but which continues unabated. Sex slavery and the selling of sexuality are among the world's more profitable business enterprises. Millions of children die of preventable diseases. School shootings make no sense. And so on.

Uncertainty and visible, undeserved suffering put great pressure on cultural beliefs, which are after all varied methods of formulating basic ideas of right and wrong in keeping with the challenges of the time. One common response to this situation is to bail out somehow, to take refuge in a live-and-let-live strategy, or refuse to think at all, perhaps looking for pleasure day by day in the world of the immediate senses. Absolutism is the other common response, whereby some move away from significant philosophical difference and against moral disagreement. Whether overwhelmed, anxious, or simply outraged by what they see around them, they define the community they want to live in as one of philosophical sameness. Whether they demand that everyone "celebrate difference" in a certain way or insist that to be truly moral one must pray to one true God, they hanker for a world of full agreement.

I see this dynamic at work in the college classroom. As I said above, my students often defend their point of view by announcing that it's "right for them" and that, accordingly, the viewpoints of others are right also but for those others. This is what Philip E. Tetlock calls strong relativism. "Strong relativism stipulates an obligation to judge each worldview within the framework of its own assumptions about the world."[11] Needless to say, when it comes to disagreement, this is a conversation stopper. If everything is just a matter of opinion, what's there to talk about? When I press, asking if there is anything at all in this world that's inherently good or bad, regardless of what people think about it, some say, "Yes," but then hasten to add that they are, once again, just giving their opinion! Such assertions of relativism are most likely to emerge in discussions of other societies; i.e., just because something is "wrong for us," doesn't mean that it's "wrong for them."

Other students firmly reject such thinking, often on the basis of religious conviction. I thank my lucky stars when they speak up, as they so often lead us into worthwhile discussion, pushing us to dig deeper and think about what we believe and why. Also I am thankful for their commitment to something. On the

other hand, I find myself disturbed because they often don't seem to be able to
hear ideas which are contrary to their point of view. It's not that they are impolite
or unfriendly; quite the contrary. And it's not that I expect, or even want, them
to change their minds about anything. It's just that so often they can't begin to
fairly summarize ideas they don't agree with, this despite their genuine (at times
even overdone) desire to please me, the teacher. I say to them, speaking of a view
they oppose, "You don't have to agree with it. Summarize it well; then tear it
apart if you want." I point out that if they truly grasp other arguments, they will be
better armed against them. They listen and nod their heads with good intention
but can't seem to go from there.

To some, this situation is a reminder of the fact that societies and individuals
must now be brave enough to choose moral principle over the dangerous relativism
too often championed by liberals. To others, however, it is equally obvious that
what one must choose is the health of individual freedom rather than the self-
righteous dogmatism too often pushed on us by social conservatives. True, there
are those who hope for some sort of middle way. But if the options are as described,
there is no coherent middle way, and the nation is stuck with culture war.
Fortunately, the options are not as described, for one because the reality of what
people believe is not as it seems. First, most of those who seem dogmatic don't
actually place dogma in the first rank of their values. Second, virtually all of those
who seem relativist are in fact acting on the basis of various moral beliefs. On
each side of the issue are individuals who have, as Lakoff might say, chosen a
moral language in their search for a philosophical anchor in this world. On each
side people act so as to dwell in what feels to them like a moral place. And many
are also simply seeking to avoid the discomfort of disagreement.

I can, for example, tell that my morally unassertive students do, in fact, have
beliefs, but one of them is that generosity toward others' and *their* beliefs is of
great value. It's also clear that some of their hesitancy comes from being uncertain
about how to proceed when it comes to the world of ideas and how to argue with
others. Add to this a normal dose of natural human laziness, a desire to get along,
and the insecurity of youth, and the result is the "just your opinion" response
to political claims. Thus, all of my students say that female genital mutilation is
wrong (if the subject comes up), but most have no idea how to defend this belief
in a way that does not simply put down someone who believes something else.
If they were more reflective and articulate about the reasons behind their own
beliefs, perhaps they would say that they believe in the inherent sanctity of the
individual, or in the right of every person to control their own bodily space. It
may seem to them, however, that their belief is just a "feeling" that they happen
to have and, being generous, they don't want to label someone else "wrong" just
for the feeling that *they* happen to have. Add to this the fact that finding another
path to understand and explain oneself is a lot of work, with no certain payoff,
and the conclusion is, apparently, clear to some: don't judge others, and don't
defend your own view either.

This critique of relativism also applies outside of the classroom. No one *really*
believes that everything is "just a matter of opinion." There are, it's true, various

coherent ideas of relativism that fall short of this extreme. And relativism of different kinds is implied or asserted in some texts, presentations, and discussions that aim to be multicultural. But nobody can consistently take a strong relativist position in the way he lives. Whether they're aware of it or not, people have beliefs they take to be true, not simply true "for them." Everyone, for example, has at some point in his or her life become angry, or experienced a similar emotion, because they have been treated "badly" by someone. It's not that they don't "like" the way they were treated; they feel *wronged*.

My more absolutist students do not squirm in the attempt to avoid moral thinking. They know what's true because truth comes from God and because God (whether by revelation, grace, or the gift of reason) has spoken. They can, thanks to this idea, provide a reason for their beliefs, but again their way of speaking is a conversation stopper. I sometimes respond by asking them if there are also any *other* reasons for the beliefs at issue. And they do, it turns out, have other reasons. They not only find God's injunctions to be right because they issue from God; they also find them convincing. What God says *sounds* right to them. Why? They have trouble answering. One reason they have trouble might be that their religious tradition encourages conversion talk rather than persuasion talk, where the latter means the offering of earthly reasons. A more fundamental reason, however, is that most of my social conservative students are like their more liberal or libertarian counterparts; they're unsure about how to use reasons in a discussion. And they, too, aren't particularly comfortable with disagreement. They don't want to tell the other students (or their professor) what to think. They just believe in God; that's all. Like so many people, they're generous, and they're argument-shy.

## SOCIAL CONSERVATISM

Many social conservatives are, of course, anything but argument-shy. Tammy Bruce calls multiculturalism an "assault" by the left on decency, freedom, and individual liberty. Touted by liberals as about tolerance and diversity, multiculturalism is, says Bruce, actually a means for imposing the "liberal agenda" of moral relativism onto the rest of society. As such, it threatens humanity with "the death of right and wrong."[12] Dinesh D'Souza similarly presents decency and freedom as Western and American values and contrasts them with multiculturalism, which is said to embody the assumption that Western civilization—and America in particular—is inherently criminal, with no redeeming qualities. And William J. Bennett weighs in with the same message, saying that liberals have imposed a course of study in the nation's schools that somehow manages to be both anti-Western and relativist at the same time. Students, argues Bennett, need to learn that "western civilization is good."[13] To teach otherwise is to undermine the very idea of right and wrong.

Liberals, the argument continues, are undermining right and wrong on numerous fronts. By extending "victim status" to numerous groups, they disrespect those who are not in those groups. By expanding government social programs and inventing special rights for supposed "victims" of discrimination and disadvantage, they morally ruin people who they claim to be helping. Government protection and subsidy, by this argument, breed dependency and "victim thinking." They destroy recipients' sense of personal responsibility and personal achievement, these being virtues and satisfactions that can only come to those who have a chance to fail if they don't make a personal effort. Multiculturalism is, by this argument, divisive, despite a welcoming appearance. It calls for recognition of some but at the expense of others. It declares some Americans special—as deserving of affirmative action, for example—while declaring others to be in need of "education" (sometimes called "brainwashing").

One can, however, turn the accusation around. All of the above-named conservatives present liberals as alien to, or somehow other than, "Americans." Bennett, for example, consistently places the words "liberal elite" opposite "the American People" and "Americans." The word "elite" functions, in other words, as an epithet in his work. By its use he rhetorically places some people outside of the "true" nation.[14] And with this move he trades on the inclination of many Americans to think of elites as the opposite of "the people," as both in power and a problem. He trades, in other words, on the tendency of the word elite to invoke conspiracy thinking (as seen in Chapter 4): to be in the category of elite is bad; to be of the people is good. This is essentially populism, a classical American political strategy that dates back to Andrew Jackson in the 1820s.

Bennett does, however, suggest that the elites of yesteryear deserve praise instead of blame. They were "traditional." They came from the world of business, not the media and the arts. They had "values," and they "led." Liberals, on the other hand, "manipulate" and "impose."[15] Here Bennett follows the work of Martin Diamond and the other antimulticultural foreign policy hawks who bolted from the Democratic Party during the Vietnam War. They (the original "neoconservatives") complained of the rise of a "new class," who they said were selling America up the river in many ways. Likewise Bennett claims that a distinct shift took place during the 1960s, dubbed by him the devaluing of America (also the title of his book): "The traditional elites of America used to be the repository of the bourgeois values of family, community, and self-restraint,"[16] whereas "Elite and Mainstream America now adhere to profoundly different sets of beliefs and values."[17] Liberals have, according to this narrative, taken over by virtue of their influence over the media, the arts, and academia. Bennett cites Rothman and the Lichters (as seen in Chapter 5) in claiming that liberal elites are "secular, liberal and cosmopolitan," as well as rejecting of work, sexual restraint, and self-control.[18] They're supposedly also "skeptical and distrustful of American society," and "[t]heir starting point is not evidence but ideology."[19] They harbor "outright hostility toward the middle class."[20] They're engaged in a politics of "radical nihilism."[21] And they have contempt for traditional art.

Someone who doesn't already agree with this argument might take note of the fact that Bennett, D'Souza, Bruce, and their colleagues rarely quote liberals, much less quote them in defense of the above-named positions. Apparently, no one will own up to being a "nihilist." No one has been caught yet on tape saying that they oppose right and wrong. No memos have surfaced describing a plan to fool ordinary Americans into opposing right and wrong. No one has, as far as I can tell, presented evidence of secret meetings attended by top liberals, though one would think such meetings might be needed to craft an "agenda" and coordinate a campaign of imposition. The social conservative argument is, in fact, radically short on evidence, to the point where the skeptic might come to doubt if the liberal elite actually exist as such. The most skeptical of skeptics might even notice that the conservative talk of liberal elites resembles traditional talk of the Devil and as such imports a religious idea—one that by definition has no connection to evidence—into an argument about flesh and blood fellow humans. But one need not go there in order to doubt that liberals are, in fact, a monolithic group with a plan or in possession of the lion's share of the nation's cultural or political power.

To say this is not to call into question the entire conservative critique of multiculturalism. Diversity workshops are, as has been seen, not always what they should be. Likewise, values do matter, and some cultural beliefs are better than others. But there's more than what first meets the eye in the social conservative argument. Its antimulticulturalism is at heart not about right over wrong so much as about branding some people wrong and then using this to build a politics, to pursue an "agenda." The lack of evidence it marshals in support of its "us-them" drama is, then, not an error and in any case doesn't matter. If the liberal Devil doesn't exist per se then it must be invented. As William E. Connolly points out, social conservatism needs the liberal "foil" in order to gather a constituency around its own agenda:

> Bennett's strategy is to draw members of the white working and middle classes, street cops, suburban dwellers, veterans, the military, conservative politicians, conservative religious believers, and working black urban dwellers plagued by street drugs and violence into a bellicose cultural coalition. That coalition is mobilized and animated through hostilities to university intellectuals, liberal journalists and politicians, moderate school administrators, disaffected residents of the inner city, illicit drug users, drug dealers, welfare recipients, philosophical police chiefs and convicted felons. . . .The battle lines are clean: the "American people" value America; the losers and amoral elements de-value it.[22]

The elements of the social conservative agenda vary somewhat, while coalescing around a core. Generally speaking, the conservatives who criticize multiculturalism are also against welfare and regulatory protection of worker rights or product safety. To one degree or another, they assert or imply that the road to economic success is to take one's chances in the sink-or-swim world of market competition. And this notion is supported by the claim that all failures to "make it" are the product of some kind of lack of "will." Thus their opposition to multiculturalism is animated by what they see as its connection to affirmative action, welfare, public housing, and the like. It all comes together as "special treatment" and "coddling." It seems to them to favor some over others, and it's thought to undermine the ethic of personal responsibility. Can't afford an apartment? Work harder instead of asking for rent control and subsidized housing. Don't make enough money? Push the government to abolish the minimum wage and increase overall profit levels, and then work hard to move up.

For social conservatives, then, "Western civilization" and "freedom" turn out to mean specific policies and philosophies of government. Connolly brings them together as one under the heading of "the conventional code of the nation." The code includes:

> individual responsibility for your own fate, faith in the capitalist market, belief in a moral god, commitment to the opportunity society, opposition to the welfare state, support for family values, identification with the military as guarantor of the nation in the last resort, and commitment to normal sexuality.[23]

In sum, the conservatives have an agenda, just like everybody else.

## HUMILITY VERSUS HUMILITY

As we have seen both sides in the American culture war have at least a degree of divisiveness in their thinking. Liberals sometimes guilt trip certain Americans as "privileged," but the latter often label those who oppose their particular ideas un-American. To frame the issue in terms of divisiveness is, however, to remain wedded to the idea that "having an agenda" is a bad thing. It's to cling to the notion that Americans should stand up for America in general rather than for this or that policy. And it assumes that people "should all just get along," that is, there's something inherently wrong with division. Once these assumptions are made then various unproductive, misleading accusations will be thrown back and forth. This or that proposal may thereby succeed, and this or that person may thereby get elected, but disagreement failure will remain the order of the day.

Perhaps one should ask other questions. What's the nature of oppression? How should people deal with different beliefs and also live together? How different are people's beliefs, really? What is personal responsibility? How obligated are people to help themselves, and how obligated are they to help others? Can people help others without hurting them? In what ways can people help themselves, and when is collective help necessary?

I personally see these questions as an improvement, but so what? They might not be the right questions. People can and should argue even about questions. Where, then, does argument stop? It stops with the ethic of generosity needed to undergird productive argument. The point is to avoid questions that are *inherently* demonizing. Granted, it's not easy to take a stand without inventing totally evil opponents. It's not easy, for that matter, to design a workshop that doesn't impose assumptions on the participants. Doing so requires a pro-disagreement perspective. Conservatives are right to bring up questions of value and personal character, but too often they do so in an antidisagreement way. Multiculturalists are right to insist on cross-cultural learning and recognition of suppressed perspectives, but they sometimes proceed in an antidisagreement way. The heart of the multicultural problem is, then, not relativism but absolutism. All cultures contain absolutism, meaning claims by someone that some beliefs are so clearly true that any questioning of them takes the questioner out of the realm of dialogue and into that of the irrational and wicked. Principled multiculturalism rejects such claims. Instead it asserts an ethic of generosity.

More specifically, principled multiculturalism calls for (and tends to cultivate) a "pro-disagreement sensibility," as discussed in Chapter 5. This sensibility includes a degree of epistemological humility. By this I don't mean humility as modesty about one's self-worth or modesty in relation to God or some other higher reality. And I also don't mean to name humility as one of the beliefs that make some cultures better than others. To do that would be to set in motion the process whereby some dismiss their critics as less than humble, as "arrogant," simply because they don't agree. "We are the humble ones," some say, "therefore we're better than you." Epistemological humility is more specific. It's modesty about one's own beliefs. It's bringing that modesty to others, especially to one's fiercest opponents. It's what Connolly calls "relational modesty" and "presumptive generosity" (as seen in Chapter 5).[24] It finds its realization in principled listening.

## BRAVERY AND LOYALTY

But before I turn to that subject, what about patriotism? To some, patriotism requires refraining from criticizing one's government or country, especially when it comes to foreign policy and whenever armed conflict with another government is looming or underway. To some, in other words, patriotism requires putting a substantive limit on principled listening. Is this the right position to take?

Patriotism combines emotion, idea, and commitment in a powerful package. Its appeal through the centuries makes it clear that many people—perhaps all in one way or another—need or want to believe that they're part of something moral. Patriotism can be such a belief, helping to ground a person's existence, in part by means of the recognition it brings. Apparently, some find a fuller sense of reality by putting themselves at risk of dying for their country. Certainly patriotism functions to help many people feel as if they have transcended mere self-interest. And, paradoxically, that seems to be something every person needs. Even the most brutal dictators need to see themselves as something more than a brutal dictator.

Patriotism is especially suited to help a self become a connected self because it provides something specific to be loyal to, as in "*my* country." John Bodnar, a scholar of American patriotism, puts it this way: it's "easier for people to feel self-respect in belonging to a group of heroic soldiers, proud blacks, or chosen Protestants than to a larger, unspecified community of equals."[25] These words also make it clear that there are possible forms, or ways to understand, patriotism. There are many ideas and collectivities one could be loyal to; there are many ways to define loyalty. The general ideas—sacrifice for the sake of something bigger, loyalty to specific others, and self-respect and morality through service—admit of many applications.

Bodnar emphasizes two historical currents of American patriotism. One is essentially "a dream of a powerful nation rooted in the desires of powerful men and women who supported it for order and moral certainty at home and in the world."[26] This idea, "heavily influenced by the more aggressive sentiments of nationalism and the quest for domination of others, both inside and outside the United States," has taken a leading role in the nation's history. It usually represents "true patriots" as warriors or, alternatively, as those acting in support of warriors and their military campaigns.[27] I call this idea of patriotism "Giving One's Life for the Country."

The other American current identified by Bodnar has the idea of the rule of law at its center. It grounds patriotism "in the hope of fair treatment for all citizens."[28] This is a classic liberal notion, in the spirit of James Madison writing in *The Federalist Papers*. Its demands less of the patriot than the first idea, but it does call for more than merely abiding by the law. A patriot is one who tries to make their way without dependence on others, and who in turn allows others to do likewise. I call this the "Play by the Rules" idea.

I would like to suggest two more conceptions of patriotism, each of which has currency (followers) around the world. One is essentially the same as the multiculturalism of Arthur M. Schlesinger, Jr. As we saw earlier, Schlesinger sees the endorsement of democratic principles as a way Americans might undo "the disuniting of America" and find a new sense of national purpose.[29] His theory is, then, a theory of patriotism. By its lights a patriot is someone who supports the great ideals of inclusion and mutual respect. He speaks of the United States, but the notion finds loyalists elsewhere as well. I call it "Celebrate Our Rights" patriotism.

The fourth idea I have to offer is that patriotism is nothing other than engaging in dialogue and disagreement wherever one lives, in service to that local community, to one's country, and to the wider world. I call this idea "Do Disagreement."

These four ideas are not exhaustive. People could be, and are, loyal to nation and group in other ways. Also the ideas are not necessarily mutually exclusive. Depending on how they're interpreted, they can be combined, at least to some extent. The point is that patriotism is not inherently antidisagreement. Patriotism does not necessarily set limits on the multiculturalism of principled listening. It depends.

Consider "Giving One's Life for the Country." Can one take this idea on without also adopting the notion that there's something better about one's country, compared to other countries? That seems like a difficult juggling act. Most warrior patriots don't serve "country" as an abstract concept. They serve *their* country. And in doing so they brace themselves to kill others who belong to, or represent, something from outside the country: "the enemy." True, soldiers have at times held their enemy in respect. In World War I, the story goes, men from the two sides left the trenches on certain holidays and broke bread together before resuming their positions and shooting. But respecting other soldiers as individuals is not the same as treating their country as morally equivalent to one's own. And to do otherwise, to look at other nations as lesser, is in keeping with patriotism's need for specifics.

This means that "Giving One's Life for the Country" has, then, an antidisagreement tendency. It's not easy to believe one's country is the best and also welcome any and all criticism of that country. On the other hand, it's possible. And it's also possible, if one so chooses, to stick with "Giving One's Life" patriotism while rejecting United We Stand. The two modes of thought typically go together, but they can be separated. So I ask warrior patriots to look back at Chapter 4 where that concept is critiqued, where I argue that internal disagreement and dissent do not, in fact, make a country weaker in the face of an enemy.

The "Play by the Rules" and "Celebrate our Rights" concepts are much alike. And they too, like the warrior idea, lean away from disagreement. To see how this is so one need only apply the same criticism applied earlier to Schlesinger's work. Like his idea of multiculturalism, each of these concepts can be interpreted in a way that's too vague and too abstract to generate much sense of national feeling. In that case the ideas demand too little and fail to offer a specific locus for loyalty. So they either don't wash as ideas of patriotism or do so by slipping into a form of United We Stand. They become, in other words, the demand that one brook no criticism of "the rules," of how "the rights" are defined, or of whether or not people really have rights.

In defense of the fourth concept, "Do Disagreement," I have a few points. First, there's nothing abstract about meeting real people one disagrees with, getting down to it, and then maybe breaking some bread together. Members of a community can find some togetherness even amidst profound disagreement, if they communicate those differences in ways that inform each other of their mutual humanity, if, that is, they thereby get to know each other. This is a tall order, I admit, especially given how often people move, how little rooted they sometimes are in the places they reside. But it is possible, and so it's possible for disagreement to provide the specific loyalties needed for patriotism.

Second, the specific loyalties nurtured by "Do Disagreement" don't push patriots to see their nation as the best or right so much as worth serving because it's where they live and where they find community in disagreement. This approach makes patriotism compatible with accepting criticism of the country, and it encourages widening the circle of argument, from community to nation and from nation to world. It has the potential, in other words, of supporting a nonabsolutist national identity that builds community without silencing alternative voices, new ideas, or hard to hear messages and thereby doing violence to humanity's multiplicity of needs, perspectives, and identities. People can, perhaps, all be patriots, without being enemies.

Someone might reasonably object that this discussion reveals a higher loyalty to disagreement than to country. They would be right. "Do Disagreement" is a mode of patriotism that puts patriotism in its proper place. Patriotism is a value, but it's not the highest value. Nations are locations of loyalty, and that can be good. And nations can be a means to justice, and people should try to make them so. But loyalty to nation should never come before, or simply stand in for, loyalty to justice. People, life, and justice come before country, in the moral scale of things.

## PRINCIPLED LISTENING

Seyla Benhabib, in *The Claims of Culture: Equality and Diversity in the Global Era*, offers a vision of multiculturalism akin to principled listening. On the one hand, she celebrates encounter between profoundly different experiences, perspectives, and identities. The need for such encounter is, by her lights, more obvious and more pressing now that humanity abides in the "global era." The difficulties are great, thanks not only to the intensity of difference but also to the multitude of injustices that interweave with and shape that difference. But the opportunity is great also. The different persons of the world have much to offer.

On the other hand, for Benhabib multiculturalism comes second to discursive, deliberative democracy. The latter is the mode of living and encounter within which respect for culture must find its measure. In part this is because there are no coherent, static "cultures" that can be either preserved or destroyed. Cultures are instead marked by "internal complexity and essential contestability."[30] Multiculturalism also comes second because every individual is always more than a member of various groups. A person's interests and ideas do not simply flow, and can't be deduced, from, their social and cultural location. No list of characteristics, not even their ethnicity, race, class, and gender, can exhaust who they are.[31] Thus it is that Benhabib rejects "mosaic multiculturalism," according to which each "culture" constitutes a distinct piece of the world tapestry.

One might say, then, that multiculturalism has no *intrinsic* value. It's the individual who has such value. On the other hand, to respect individuals one must also respect them as bearers of the diverse meanings by which they make sense of the world. Multiculturalism, of the right kind, is therefore essential. And the right kind is, according to Benhabib, agonistic and questioning. This is what she means when she quotes Bonnie Honig's injunction to "take difference seriously." And that's what I mean when I call for the rejection of the pull of unity. As Honig says, one must "give up on the dream of home." Or, rather, one must do so if they imagine "home" to be "a place free of power, conflict, and struggle."[32] There can be no such place.

The right sort of multiculturalism is, then, not neutral. It's not equally welcoming to all visions of human possibility. Instead it's implicitly critical of, and threatening to, those cultural beliefs that insist on the dream of a univocal home. It insists, after all, that democracy come first and that difference has intrinsic value. This means that it challenges all forms of absolutism, even as (and by virtue of the fact that) it invites them into conversation. Benhabib makes this clear: "If one must choose, I value the expansion of democratic inclusion and equality over the preservation of cultural distinctiveness."[33]

Fortunately, says Benhabib, one does not always have to choose; "sensitivity to the politics of culture and a strong universalist position are not incompatible."[34] While "democratic inclusion and equality" are mandatory, they can be combined with cultural sensitivity by means of democracy. Specifically, Benhabib calls for "deliberative and discursive democratic multiculturalism" held under conditions of "legal pluralism," where the latter means "egalitarian reciprocity, voluntary self-ascription, and freedom of exit and association."[35]

As I said, this vision is akin to principled listening. The idea is that people don't need a "home" that's free of power, conflict, and struggle in order to thrive or to live within the bounds of the moral. People can instead dream of, and I believe create, a humbler, more pro-disagreement home. This would be a democracy of conversation and as such would include "power, conflict, and struggle" while also giving each generation the opportunity to address this trio peacefully, by means of generous encounter.

I do not speak first and foremost of a form of government. Granted, legal pluralism does imply certain institutions, but what's most important is principled listening as an ethic and sensibility. To wit:

- Each person should make an effort to periodically engage in cross-border disagreement or exchange, within the limits posed by their need for personal space and personal integrity.
- Each person should make an effort to come to encounters bearing some epistemological humility, some generosity of interpretation, and some faith in the equal worth of all involved.
- There are no such things as discrete cultures that can be preserved or rejected in their entirety.
- All people have culture, and all cultural beliefs are imperfect adaptations that arise out of older beliefs, in response to specific situations. Every cultural belief helps (or at one time did help) specific peoples to live in specific realities—in part by providing them with identity.
- People have much in common; cultures always overlap.
- Every culture has elements worth preserving and elements worth rejecting.
- Patriotism is seeing one's country as one's own and therefore as the specific place where one can serve humanity in general. And patriotism requires principled listening and disagreement, not United We Stand.

## CONCLUSION

If multiculturalism means according rights to cultures as such, it's a problem. If it means putting the sanctity of cultural beliefs on par with the sanctity of the individual, then it's wrong. And if it means treating all beliefs as inherently equal, with no conversation about their validity possible, then it should be rejected. But if multiculturalism means that there are many beliefs about how to live that are fundamentally at odds with each other, at least in some ways, but also worth listening to and not evil or irrational, then multiculturalism is reality. And if multiculturalism means principled listening, then it's a badly needed form of public action.

CHAPTER 8

# Disagreement Practice

By the public sphere we mean first of all a realm of our social life in which something approaching public opinion can be formed.... [A] portion of the public sphere comes into being in every conversation in which private individuals assemble to form a public body.[1]

—Jürgen Habermas

How extraordinary to presume that having been elected, our governing representatives should magically know the answers to all the contentious, complex problems that are facing us today. The time has come to re-think what sort of democracy we want.[2]

—Janette Hartz-Karp

I have, throughout this book, done my best to explain and defend disagreement, rather than catalogue its many manifestations. The idea is that people will find their own best ways to bring disagreement into their lives, if that's what they want. They might attend a large formal gathering to discuss a neighborhood issue. They might initiate a conversation with fellow workers who seem different. They might change the way they make decisions at work. They might gather friends from a house of worship and go to lunch with devotees of a different religion. Or they might develop cross-border civil talk in their own family—often the hardest task of all. People can and will figure out what sort of disagreement activities make sense for them.

In keeping with this idea, this chapter tackles four tasks. It provides enough examples of disagreement practice to provide a sense of the possibilities. It considers race and terrorism as examples of issue areas best approached by means of disagreement. It uses a pro-disagreement lens to look at the "civic education" movement currently underway in higher education. And it offers principles and ground rules meant to be useful in guiding disagreement activity.

The variables are many. How big is the group? Is there a specific issue, and how contentious is it? Do the potential participants share an affiliation (e.g., are they students at the same school or people working at the same company)? Do they share a goal (e.g., do they all want to go to the protest but disagree about whether or not to engage in civil disobedience)? Will the talk be open to the public or a select few? Will it be inside or outside of government and with or without a decision at the end? Are there reasons to keep remarks anonymous? Are people participating as official representatives of others or as more as "themselves?" As situations vary, so should the plans of action. Some meetings need to be facilitated. Sometime people are too angry to make a decision but need to get to know one another. Sometimes a special role for "experts" is more appropriate than at other times. And so on.

Those goaded to learn more about what's going on in the world of disagreement might start with a visit to the Web site of the National Coalition on Dialogue and Deliberation. They might also read Matt Leighninger's *The Next Form of Democracy: How Expert Rule Is Giving Way to Shared Governance—And Why Politics Will Never Be the Same* [3] or Frances Moore Lappé's *Democracy's Edge: Choosing to Save Our Country by Bringing Democracy to Life*.[4] And they might search for information about the Wisdom Council, the National Issues Forum, and the World Café. What they will discover is a groundswell of grassroots, bottom-up, democratic activity, quite of bit of which is disagreement-friendly.

## STUDY CIRCLES IN IDAHO

Between 1990 and 2003 the population of Kuna, Idaho, quadrupled in size to almost 9,000, and the number is likely to double again in the next decade, in part because of an influx of residents who commute to nearby Boise. This growth has brought many benefits and possibly also done some damage. It has certainly created conflict. Where should new schools be put, and who should attend them? What about traffic and pollution? Will big box stores bring more costs than benefits, or vice-versa, and for whom? In 1998 a group of local residents, thinking that better communication between residents was needed, headed off to Kansas City to learn about study circles.[5] A study circle is a group of "8 to 12 people from different backgrounds and viewpoints" who meet for several two-hour sessions "to talk about a critical public issue."[6] Usually many circles are created on a given topic so as to accommodate all who are want to take part. Before the conversations begin the members of each circle are provided with information ("easy-to-use, fair-minded discussion materials," in the words of the Study Circle Resource Center) about the issue.[7] Each circle then meets, chooses its own ground rules, and sets out to increase mutual understanding, discover common ground, and contribute to the process of "social, political, and policy change."[8] The group discussions are "led by an impartial facilitator" whose job is to see to it that everyone gets an equal say (or at least an equal chance to speak) and encourage participants to try to understand each other's views—rather than to simply say their piece or, alternatively, try to agree just for agreement's sake.

When the group returned to Kuna they created an organization called Kuna ACT (Alliance for a Cohesive Community Team) and set about trying to put what they had learned into practice. In 1999 they came close to securing town funding for a study circle initiative. There was, however, too much opposition, in part because some thought that Kuna ACT was trying to use the study circles to help pass a controversial multimillion-dollar bond proposal for a new high school. The town had already purchased land for the new school, but there were doubts. As Julie Fanselow puts it, "there were fears that more urban problems—including drugs and teen pregnancy—were making their way to town"[9] and that the new school would contribute to this process. Before the year was out, the study circle initiative, the bond proposal, and two pro-Kuna ACT council members had all gone down to defeat.

As told thus far, the Kuna story is testimony to the difficulty of starting cross-border conversations. Such talk might, once underway, generate sufficient mutual trust to keep it going and make it worthwhile, but when the need to converse is first perceived, those calling for discussions are likely to be from one side or the other. Fortunately, Kuna ACT was undaunted, and two weeks after the bond proposal was defeated, the group succeeded in getting 80 people to attend a study circle on the growth issue. "During the next month, Kuna residents met five times and talked with one another as they never had before."[10] The discussions produced a series of rather general ideas—"improved communication between citizens and officials, public planning for growth, creating a community mission statement, boosting volunteerism, and much more."[11] More importantly, they laid a foundation for connected cross-border communication with action; they cultivated the realization on the part of many that they could put their heads together across disagreement and then get listened to by those in power. In the meantime, these initial conversations brought many Kuna politicians on board, presumably because of personal conviction and because it was relatively safe, politically speaking, to support ideas that emerged from study circles.

In April 2000, "education re-emerged as the monthly topic" of the study circle meetings, and "among those who attended were a number of people who had worked to defeat the school bond the previous fall."[12] In response, the school board delayed putting the final touches on a new bond proposal, the idea being to let citizens talk about it first, and the result was that "[i]n September 2000, just a year after the defeat of the previous bond issue, a vote on the $15.2 million bond measure easily surpassed the two-thirds majority Idaho requires to pass a school bond."[13] This process in turn helped put Kuna ACT firmly into the role of bringing people together to deal with community issues as they arose. Study circles have since been used to help the town craft a development and zoning plan and to better coordinate disaster planning across different emergency responders. "By 2002, city officials faced with any pressing issue were likely to say, 'Let's take it to study circles.'"[14]

## INSIDE THE CIA

On December 3, 2007 the Central Intelligence Agency declared, with "high confidence," that the Iranian government had halted its nuclear weapons program back in 2003 and hadn't restarted it.[15] This finding contradicted the agency's claim of just two years before and, more importantly, was at odds with long-standing insistence by the Bush White House that Tehran was a "rogue nation" run by irrational zealots bent on establishing an "Islamic kingdom" in the Middle East, even at the cost of their own lives and the destruction of the Iranian state. The new National Intelligence Estimate instead portrayed the Iranian leadership as "guided by a cost-benefit approach rather than a rush to a weapon irrespective of the political, economic and military costs." It portrayed them, in other words, as people who might be successfully approached with diplomacy and negotiation as opposed to military buildup and covert operations.

Congressional oversight seems to have played a role in this turnabout, first in bringing pressure on the CIA to issue an updated intelligence estimate, and second in pushing the sixteen intelligence agencies to share more information with each other and vet each other's claims. In addition, the Democratic majority in Congress may have made some inside the CIA feel freer to disagree with the Republican president. It's also clear that much of the impetus to reconsider came from a concern inside the agency to do its job well and salvage its reputation. Personnel were embarrassed about their 2003 failure to counter the Bush administration's insistence that Iraq possessed "weapons of mass destruction." One senior analyst, speaking anonymously, said, "We felt that we needed to scrub all the assessments and sources to make sure we weren't misleading ourselves." But the most important factor in the agency's shift, especially in the context of this discussion, is the *way* it scrubbed those assessments and sources. "The report was drafted after an extended internal debate," according to *The Washington Post*, and this debate "included 'Red Team' exercises in which groups of intelligence officers tried to punch holes in the new evidence."[16] Disagreement was, in other words, put to work.

## NATIONAL ISSUES FORUMS

One of the leading sponsors of public deliberation is the National Issues Forums Institute (NIFI). Chartered in 1989 and supported by the Kettering Foundation of Dayton, Ohio, NIFI is dedicated to the idea that "people need to come together to reason and talk—to deliberate about common problems."[17] NIFI provides support (materials, grant writing, etc.) for the forums, which are "locally organized, moderated, and financed."[18] Any group that utilizes NIFI support to organize a forum becomes part of the National Issues Forums (NIF) network. NIFI is flexible about the method used, but the general idea is to bring diverse community members together, offer them with brief summaries of opposing arguments on the issue at hand, and provide the structure and facilitation that will lead to an extended, inclusive discussion.

One NIF forum took place on January 31, 2006, when some seventy-five people gathered at Summerville High School in Dorchester County, South Carolina. Dorchester, like Kuna, had been experiencing rapid growth, both in population and in geographical spread, and faced the typical growth challenges, such as increased traffic, pollution, loss of green spaces, shifting housing values, and winner and loser businesses and neighborhoods. The organizer of the event, Clemson University's Laboratory for Deliberative Dialogue, asked the participants to approach the issues with three deliberative principles: seek understanding rather than winning, look beyond facts to consider what's of value to the community, and make choices together about desired actions.[19]

The session started with a ten-minute video presentation that (borrowing from an NIFI issue book), described three different points of view: "(1) Fulfill the Suburban American Dream, (2) Strengthen Cities, Stop Sprawl at its Source, and (3) Free Americans to Choose Life-styles."[20] The participants then split into three groups, went to separate rooms, and began to converse. As they talked, facilitators wrote their comments on flip charts. Almost three hours later they reconvened to share their many observations and ideas. Finally, forty-five of the discussants filled out a postforum questionnaire before they went home.

The official report of the event doesn't offer an analysis of what was learned or decided but instead lists the many comments made, as recorded on the flip charts. As might be expected, they read a lot like a conversation: comments come from every direction; people go on tangents; and there's a good deal of repetition. On the other hand, there's plenty of knowledge and wisdom on display. A town planner could certainly use the remarks to make a list of issues and competing values that ought to be taken into consideration. And one can guess that participants might have learned from each other, as many sides of the issues were represented. For example, one person's comment, "We need a tri-county plan," was followed by someone else's, "Do you want someone in Charleston County to make a decision about you in Dorchester County?"[21] And comments that emphasized the importance of planning, as in, "Planning should come from people on the ground and not developers,"[22] and, "Community choices should be incorporated into all plans," sat next to remarks that stressed a need to respect individual freedom, as in, "People leave out the owner of a property who has made and maintained an investment,"[23] and, "People have the right to use land as desired as long as it does not adversely impact neighbors."[24]

The flip charts also reveal an appreciation of trade-offs and knowledge of local government: "If you don't like density then you need to be prepared for sprawl and vice versa," "In many communities there are good plans but they needed to be followed," "Going to council meetings doesn't help because we get no feedback from council," "The general feeling is that development decisions are a done deal before the meeting," and "1990–2000 property values increased 20%, people living in poverty rose by 11%."[25]

More importantly, many participants expressed a willingness to sacrifice in order to achieve common values or do the right thing. For example, 69 percent of the participants who filled out the postforum questionnaire reported, "[We] favor the use of tax money to improve older communities, EVEN IF this slows down growth in other areas where many people want to live."[26] This suggests that face-to-face conversations about public issues can—if well-designed and facilitated—help to mitigate not-in-my-backyard thinking and, therefore, help communities to address difficult issues in a productive way.

## CIVIC EDUCATION

Can the values expressed by the NIF idea be taught in school? Many colleges and universities have, in recent years, launched programs aimed at teaching "civic engagement" and providing "citizenship education." The Carnegie Foundation for the Advancement of Teaching has helped lead the way with its "Political Engagement Project" and by touting a book, *Educating Citizens: Preparing America's Undergraduates for Lives of Moral and Civic Responsibility*, by Anne Colby, Thomas Ehrlich, Elizabeth Beaumont, and Jason Stephens.[27] The argument of *Educating Citizens* is that schools can and should teach moral character, motivate civic action, and provide skills that support the exercise of civic responsibility. "Colleges and universities ought," they say, "to educate for substantive values, ideals, and standards, at least in broad terms, and should not be content with what is sometimes referred to as values clarification."[28]

A central component of most civic education programs is "service learning," whereby students receive academic credit for going off campus to participate "in organized, sustained service activity that is related to classroom learning and meets identified community needs."[29] As with traditional internships, students are expected to try on professional roles, think about what they might do with their lives, and make needed job connections. Less traditionally, it is hoped that service learners will come to understand social and political issues in a new way while also realizing they can "make a difference." A student might, for example, study poverty in class and apply the ideas by working at a homeless shelter. The theory is that the empowerment that can come from taking action and seeing results might counterbalance the hopelessness that can come from exposure to social criticism.[30] According to *Educating Citizens*, this approach works: engagement by students in community service is "associated with gains in . . . civic responsibility (such as a sense of efficacy to change society), and life skills (including leadership, interpersonal, and conflict resolution skills)."[31]

There is, however, cause for concern. Specifically, the aimed-for civic participation is not always conceptualized in ways that adequately include disagreement, and when that's the case it's not clear why the programming should count as civic education. Consider, for example, the "National Dialogue Project: Journey towards Democracy: Power, Voice, and the Public Good," sponsored by the Association of American Colleges and Universities (AACU) in the spring of 2003. The project issued an invitation to colleges and universities "to sponsor robust and candid dialogues about how to put student learning about democracy and the public good at the center of academic inquiry."[32] But what, then, is democracy? The title suggests that democracy includes dialogue, but the invitation instead issues an injunction to have dialogues about *how to teach* democracy. Looking at the grant invitation in its entirety, one finds little to suggest that democracy itself requires the cultivation of dialogue skills among the citizenry. I suspect that this is because democracy was taken for granted by the project designers, that it was assumed to be already there in the form of constitutional structure and the right to vote. Whatever the ideas of the designers, the *effect* of their invitation can only be to reinforce the notion that the problem to be addressed by "civic education" is that people are failing to step up and join in, not that there's something missing in the world they're asked to join. This is a common problem in citizen education efforts. "Dialogue" is assumed to already reside in the world of voting and campaigning, and the so-called education amounts to proselytizing; students are urged to be "responsible" and vote.

I was happy to discover that one of the grantee schools, St. Lawrence University, went beyond what was explicitly called for and submitted a truly pro-disagreement proposal. An added bonus was that the school is only 10 miles from my house, and I was able to participate. I saw that public involvement was solicited when I spied a local newspaper ad that began with the headline "Tired of all the shouting?" and went on to say, "Let's try a better way to promote community understanding and involvement. We need your help!" Specifically, the idea was that students and community members would gather in small groups to "probe issues reported in its regional newspaper" (*The Watertown Daily Times*). So it was that I went every week, for several months, to the St. Lawrence campus to meet with four students, a town planner, a businessman, and a businesswoman.[33] We discussed the role of the local military base in the economy, possible trade-offs between development and the environment, the viability of tourism in the area, the odds of ever getting the "rooftop highway" leg of the Interstate in the North Country, and more. We disagreed and we agreed. In the end we issued a report, and more importantly, we learned from each other and made connections.

The other funded proposals stuck more closely to the cautious AACU language. Richard Stockton College of New Jersey, for example, proposed holding a series of dialogues. One would aim to "determine the most meaningful pedagogies for civic education and engagement." Another would aim to improve and augment "civic engagement courses" at the school and at area community colleges. A third dialogue would solicit ideas from active alumni to help "assess how well Stockton students . . . [were] prepared for civic engagement." And the fourth would include the community so as to enable "multiple stakeholders to express their views." Under the heading of the final dialogue, the College encouraged teachers to speak with their students "on engaging them with fundamental democratic questions through classroom discussions and practical experiences in local communities."[34]

Note that the planned subject of Stockton's community dialogue was not an actual issue facing the community. Neither was it left to the participants to determine. Instead the mandate was to discuss how to create "effective public participation in the public arena." The idea, in other words, mirrored the AACU language in calling for talk *about* participation. Notice also that when teachers are asked to get students involved in the community and "engaged" about "democratic questions," no mention is made of dialogue and disagreement as inherent or desirable aspects of community involvement or democracy. The definition of these crucial terms is, apparently, up to the individual professors. Students in a given class might, then, fit the bill by doing service work at a local soup kitchen and then reading about democracy (however defined) when back on campus. This might be good or even great, but it's not per se a dialogue initiative.

Most of AACU grant-winning proposals were similar to Stockton's. Discussions were to be held *about* dialogue (e.g., on how to expand dialogue in the future, or how to prepare students to have dialogue later in life, or what might lead society, someday, to more dialogue.) Or discussions were to be held on campus in order to better achieve predetermined goals. The University of Massachusetts, for example, aimed to create six "dialogue circles." The goal was to bring together the faculty, students, and communities of its three ethnic studies programs with its service learning programs, the idea being to then "explore the relationships between [them] that foster democratic relationships within communities." One circle, said the plan, would "consist of a one-day symposium to ensure that multiple community perspectives inform the public's learning, planning, and action" while another would "bring together an invited panel of nationally renowned faculty who represent best practices in linking ethnic studies and service learning with students, faculty, staff, and community members at UMASS Boston."[35]

This language makes it clear that some goals of the college had already been chosen. It was hoped, for example, that ethnic studies would collaborate with service learning, and the question was only how to go about it. Also one of the planned circles was asked to decide how, not whether, "global themes and perspectives intersect with both ethnic studies and service learning paradigms." Were these the right questions for UMASS Boston? Possibly they were. And probably the discussion sessions moved them forward in a good way. But, if the idea was to promote dialogue itself, the participants were going to have to make that happen without help from their official mandate.

Admittedly, this critique of the AACU initiative depends in part on a reading of stated goals and program descriptions. St. Lawrence went beyond what was required, and in practice other schools might have done so as well. But that would not be enough to negate the AACU's subtle antidisagreement message. Declarations of purpose are important in their own right; they count as a form of teaching in and of themselves; and the AACU language mirrors many democracy promotion efforts in celebrating conventional forms of participation in the existing political system as if they *are* democracy. Do the candidates running for political office, and who have a chance of winning, offer truly opposing analyses and plans of action? Is at least one of them worth choosing? Do any of them mean what they say? Even if they do, will those elected receive much in the way of real power once in office? The typical get-out-the-vote campaign takes affirmative answers for granted, and the National Dialogue Project is similar, perhaps thereby working against the development of new citizen power instead of for it. What students may learn, in other words, is to endorse the existing political ethos of voting-as-a-form-of-consumption and constituency building via cliché and demonization.

The argument of *Educating Citizens* also depends on readings of stated goals and program descriptions, and in a less warranted fashion. It's well and good, for example, to note that most leadership programs "include goals involving civic responsibility and engagement,"[36] but one still has to ask how civic responsibility is conceptualized, and what in the curriculum will actually inculcate it, if anything. Sometimes *Educating Citizens* defends a positive assessment of a civic education program without dealing with these questions. Sometimes it simply notes the promising name of a major (e.g. "Community Leadership and Development") or defends the positive assessment by repeating it, as in, "Many of the academic programs [at Alverno College] have a strong focus on moral and civic responsibility."[37] Is this "focus" more than a well-intentioned goal listed on the school Web site? If so, is civic responsibility understood in a pro-disagreement way? *Educating Citizens* doesn't say.

Similarly, while the book says that values should be taught, it seems at times oblivious to the potential problem of one-sided, politicized education, imparted with good intent and in the name of "civic education."[38] The reliance on service learning as a modality makes this problem very real. What organizations are the students going to work with or for? What is the political bent of those organizations? Well-meaning professors (meaning those who are not manipulative or have no intent to brainwash, in other words, the vast majority) might, simply by sending students off to work with a particular organization, send the problematic message that civic responsibility means being of a certain political persuasion. This is both unfair and likely to turn off students who feel they're being told what to think.

## DOING IT BETTER

Don't misunderstand. Civic responsibility and being of a political persuasion are perfectly compatible. Political affiliation should not, however, be linked in any way to grades. Also, students need first and foremost to be taught the "civic duty" of listening to views from every side, extremes included, and giving those points of view serious consideration. As a form of political participation, such listening is both more fundamental than voting and a good way to provide a foundation for thoughtful voting (or thoughtful nonvoting). It can and should be built into civic education programming. Disagreement should, in other words, be treated as the key "value" to be taught. Teachers and administrators who take this approach are more likely to (1) avoid imposing particular views without thereby resorting to relativist mush, (2) give students a wide range of choices about where they might do service work, (3) maintain a clear line between the grading process and the level of student enthusiasm for the work of this or that advocacy group, and (4) communicate this distinction clearly and convincingly to students.

The good news is that many college courses already teach disagreement values. One course cited by *Educating Citizens* (also listed as one of twenty-one

"Participating Courses and Programs" in the Carnegie Foundation for the Advancement of Teaching's "Political Engagement Project") is "Ancients and Moderns: Democratic Theory and Practice," taught at Providence College.[39] Professor Rick Battistoni starts the class by asking half of the students to "design and act out a thoroughly undemocratic discussion, and the other half to design and act out a perfectly undemocratic classroom."[40] The first reaction of many students is "their feeling that 'real' democracy is a good idea but utterly unrealistic, and at some level, undesirable."[41] Many change their minds, however, over the course of the semester, as they participate in democratic decision making with their classmates and also receive guidance in their efforts to collaborate. "Innovative pedagogical tools include . . . exercises using different democratic decision making devices (such as selection by lot, direct democracy, and representative democracy)."[42] They also include a course project where students can opt to work in groups, each of which is supposed to create a "democratic action." Each group has to organize itself "democratically," in whatever way the members define that term, and each group must create an event which exemplifies "the democratic ideals and theories the students have read about and discussed."[43] Battistoni doesn't tell the students what to be for or against when it comes to the action itself; instead they do have to defend what they do as somehow "democratic." The result is that students often emerge believing it's both desirable and possible for people to work across borders and make decisions together.

Courses like "Ancients and Moderns" are reminders that universities, for all their faults, now serve society as relative bastions of dialogue. There are, on the other hand, forces at work in higher education that push in less democratic directions. First, there are many constituencies at any given school who cleave to a notion of objectivity that underestimates the value and necessity of including different perspectives as a part of inquiry into any subject. Second, universities are large organizations that need to pay the bills and, as a corollary, honor the concerns of students' parents and prospective employers. As such they tend to play up their role as workforce training centers rather than as incubators for critical thinking. Third, universities compartmentalize (as they must, at least to a degree) by allocating different perspectives and approaches to separate spaces ("turf"). This creates incentives for programs to defend their respective budgets, spaces, and decisional autonomy, and this in turn inclines them to defend the autonomy of other programs (as in "I won't question yours, if you don't question mine"). The result is sometimes an avoidance of cross-program dialogue about curriculum and schoolwide issues.

How can civic education go forward successfully, in this context? First, when it comes to changing society, schools need help from the outside. Even a pro-disagreement college education requires the follow-up of disagreement outside academia: "[T]he percentages of students who rate as very important helping others in need, participating in community action, and influencing the political structure show temporary increases over the four years of college, but almost all of these increases disappear in the five years after college graduation."[44] Second, the civic education movement needs to become pro-disagreement at its core. That's the only way to avoid lapsing into programs that (1) do little besides serve up overly general clichés, thereby failing to motivate much new civic engagement or (2) function as advertisements for existing political systems rather than as genuine calls to further develop democracy.

## TALKING TERRORISM

Terrorism is one of the many contemporary issue areas best approached by means of disagreement. But what does this mean? Saudi Arabia's Crown Prince Abdullah provides a useful starting point. In June 2003, concerned about the millions of disenfranchised and unemployed young men in his country who he saw as a breeding ground for terrorism, Abdullah broached the possibility of allowing greater freedom of expression in the kingdom, as well as more political participation. Evan Osnos, in an op-ed piece in the *Watertown Daily Times*, responded as follows:

> "[T]o the young bearded men who pour out of the main Al Rajkhi mosque in Buraydah on a hot November afternoon, those efforts to engage the Saudi people are misguided. They want the government to speak directly to the militants, to discuss their grievances. Saudi leaders have publically dismissed that possibility out of hand, saying that they will handle militants 'with an iron fist.'"[45]

The Saudi position is in line with that taken by governments around the world. Supposedly it's both wrong and pointless to talk to terrorists: it's wrong because it would condone and reward immoral actions, thereby creating more of the same, and it's pointless because terrorists are so clearly in error—and once one knows someone else is a "terrorist" there's nothing else about them to understand. So it was that, in September 2007, "[a] group of about 40 elected officials and civic leaders gathered Sunday outside Columbia University" to protest the appearance there, as an invited speaker, of Iranian President Mahmoud Ahmadinejad, who was in town to visit the United Nations.[46] The protestors, some of whom bore signs that said, "Don't give a platform to hate," and, "Go to hell," saw Ahmadinejad as a Holocaust denier and a sponsor of terrorism and considered it wrong to even listen to him. New York State Assemblyman Dov Hikind said, "There is no excuse to invite this madman, this little Hitler.... This is immoral. This is outrageous. This is sick. Do we have to invite him into our community?... There is absolutely no justification." Significantly, there is no indication that protestors were mollified by the fact that Lee C. Bollinger, the president of the university, delivered a stinging rebuke of—in fact publically denounced—the Iranian president to his face *before* allowing him to so much as begin his public address. The event still marked him as a person who might have something to say worth hearing, and to some this amounted to an endorsement of evil itself.

Similar thinking was at work later that year when *New York Times* columnist Paul Krugman was accused by some of "tolerance for anti-Semitism" merely because he chose to wonder, in print, about why Malaysian Prime Minister Mahathir Mohamad included anti-Semitic remarks in a speech.[47] The implication of such criticism is that there's no need to try to understand anti-Semitism; it's just wrong, and the proper response is simple, absolute rejection. Krugman (who by the way is Jewish) responded by noting that President George W. Bush and his advisors seem at times to assume that the "war on terror" is going well simply because they know it's the right thing and are therefore surprised and mystified by the distrust directed at them by moderate Islamic leaders. They might do better, says Krugman, by trying to understand that distrust, just as he tried to understand the Malaysian prime minister's invocation of anti-Semitism. Unfortunately, he concludes, a "post 9/11 version of political correctness has made it difficult to even discuss their points of view."[48] Like Osnos, he suggests a need to understand and discuss the beliefs that motivate militants, no matter what one thinks of those beliefs or of the militants' actions.

One reason to use the word "militant" is the problem of who should count as a "terrorist." When Mark Juergensmeyer, author of *Terror in the Mind of God: The Global Rise of Religious Violence*, interviewed religiously inspired violent militants from around the world—"Christian, Jewish, Muslim, Hindu, Sikh, and Buddhist"[49] —he discovered the common belief that the world is *already* a violent place, that a war of good against evil is *already* underway, and that they are under a moral obligation to enter into that war and defend virtue and morality.[50] They are not "terrorists," then, from their own point of view. I don't mean to say that violent attacks on civilians (or on soldiers, for that matter) are justified just because someone thinks they are or that they're justified "for them." The point is that it's important to make a clear distinction between trying to understand someone's point of view and approval of their actions. All human actions, even the most heinous, are committed by real flesh and blood humans, not representatives of pure evil. Humans do things for reasons and because of feelings connected to reasons; humans act with ideas in mind.

When it comes to the acts that usually go by the name of terrorism, certain ideas play a role over and over: First, fellow human beings are dehumanized. They're placed into the abstract category of the enemy—be it "America," "the infidel," "world Jewry," or "the Palestinians." This is what makes it possible for the attackers to override their natural compassion and kill. To them the victims are either not innocent or simply disappear as real individuals so as to reappear as a mere part of a strategic picture. In this respect, terrorism is akin to war in general, as well as to genocide, torture, and other crimes of violence. Second, violent militants believe that the enemy is all around them and in possession of unbounded aims, bent on destroying the militant's religion, civilization, and way of life. Third, violent militants are alienated; they feel surrounded by a deeply immoral world that provides no place for meaningful, virtuous action and no legitimate public realm with a place for them.[51] Fourth, many violent militants believe in the immanent end of the world. This, often along with promises of reward in the afterlife, is what leads some to the desire to die for their cause.[52]

Fifth, and perhaps most significantly, many violent militants endorse an aggressive idea of masculinity and defend male power and male control over women as necessary aspects of a moral order, an order they believe is threatened by the individualism and secular discourse of Western-style modernization. Female suicide bombers are not unheard of, but they're in the minority, not usually in positions of leadership, and, says Juergensmeyer, "motivated by secular political ideologies or ethnic separatism" rather than by religion."[53] Most violent militants are not only male; they're virulently antihomosexual. And most of their organizations feature male bonding rituals and create intense forms of male camaraderie. As Juergensmeyer sees it, this is based in a need to create what seems like a virtuous order among manly men, and this is in turn connected to the above-mentioned feelings of alienation and loss of moral order.

> Because men have so frequently held the reins of public order as their gendered responsibility in society in the past, they have felt particularly vulnerable when the public world has fallen apart or has seemed beyond control. In this case, they have seen active women and gays not just as competition, but as symptoms of a world gone awry.[54]

The purposeful infliction of terrorizing violence is, then, made possible by ideas, not simply by "evil." To put it another way, the people who engage in such violence see it as a way to act morally, and this perception is based on ideas they endorse. Granted, these notions are sometimes so deeply rooted in a given person's identity that they're immune to challenge. On the other hand, only a few people are in that position. There are millions of others who consider violent activism the only plausible response to an untenable situation but whose minds might be changed by new understandings. For many, the abstraction and demonization that lead them to endorse violence can be undone, or at least countered, by humanizing understanding.

Indeed, the scourge that goes by the name of terrorism points uniquely to disagreement, for several reasons. First, the attackers and their organizations are not acting as representatives of a nation or government (though they may see themselves as defending the autonomy of a people or territory) and as such have no necessary location or inherently bounded membership. Terrorists affiliated with a given cause might not be organized into a single group that can be identified, and the various affiliations are in any case subject to change and rearrangement at any time. Second, terrorist attacks do not aim at conquering territory or vanquishing an army so much as at creating disruption, fear, and instability, perhaps also pressuring governments to change certain policies. Third, anyone can acquire methods and means of terrorism, if they really want to. Fourth, terrorism is now firmly established in the public mind as a possibility, role models and all. Fifth, the availability of food and water for billions of people now depends on the functioning of intricate, vulnerable systems of production and distribution.

The point is that, while particular terrorists might be jailed or killed and some might even mend their ways, terrorism as a tactic and view of the world can only be effectively countered by weakening the ideas that support the infliction of suffering or by otherwise addressing the alienation that can create a suicide bomber. This means, first of all, that the *total* defeat of terrorism is a tall order, requiring nothing less than the defeat of the long-standing human problem of us–them demonology. It also means that significantly reducing the risk and incidence of terrorism—a more realistic, near-term goal—is impossible by means of force alone. Instead, going forward requires dialogue and disagreement. It requires cross-cultural learning, even in situations of anger and tension. It requires the establishment of practices that keep people connected as fellow human beings, as part of one diverse human society, whatever their differences. Granted, increased cross-border understanding can't defeat terrorism on its own. Other measures are necessary, the two most obvious being police work and policy changes that address real grievances of marginalized populations. But disagreement can and must play a key role.

There are resources to draw upon. Many Islamic scholars, for example, stand firmly in opposition to terror in the name of Islam. Abdolkarim Soroush is an Iranian moderate Islamic theologian who argues that the Islamic faith should turn away from the pursuit of political power and rely instead on "moral suasion."[55] As Juergensmeyer reports it, Soroush understands the Islamic notion of "jihad" as an injunction to Muslims to enter into "the contestation of ideas rather than opposing political sides."[56] A disagreement approach to terrorism—especially to terrorism in the name of Islam—could draw upon voices like Soroush's as part of an effort to bring religious militants, victims of terrorist violence, those who sympathize with militant movements, and antiterrorists together in conversation. Topics to be covered might include the proper relationship of politics and religion, the meaning of the Koran, the ideal of an Islamic state, effects of Western-style economic development on Islam, the presence of U.S. troops around the world, the Palestinian-Israeli conflict, and more. The potential benefits are many

First, face-to-face, peaceful interactions between perceived enemies stand to undermine the terrorist-friendly vision of a world divided into absolutes of good and evil. Juergensmeyer tells of a symphony performed by musicians from opposing sides in Bosnia and of a cross-border rugby match in South Africa. According to him, these events created badly needed "neutral spaces" and cultivated a sense of community across borders, without thereby requiring unity.[57] Such events can, he argues, reduce violence. "It is difficult to belittle and kill a person whom one knows and for whom one has no personal antipathy."[58]

Second, alienated Muslim men might, by virtue of being included in conversations that give voice to their grievances, come to think of the existing world as one that offers them meaning and membership. And this might direct them away from the alternative communities offered by terrorist groups, by means of what Juergensmeyer calls "stages of symbolic empowerment."[59]

Third, such inclusion might benefit men and women all over the world by giving new impetus and direction to the gender revolution, now some 300 years old but also stalled and stymied in certain ways. The creation of more pro-disagreement public spaces could offer support to the assertion of peaceful, less gendered ideals of strength, bravery, valor, and public service, ideals which could then serve as alternatives to warrior ideals of masculinity. There is bravery, after all, in generous listening and in speaking up for oneself firmly but nonaggressively. Granted, it may be that warrior/princess notions of gender are poised for a world-wide resurgence, but I like to think of them as on their way out, with terrorism and the war on terror mere last-gasp attempts to keep those identities alive. What's most likely is that the future of these ideals has yet to be determined. If Muslim activists offer the peoples of the world a gentle, nonviolent concept of Jihad, one that's not based on putting men and women in traditional roles, and if angry, alienated Muslim men, otherwise drawn by visions of apocalyptic struggle and moral sacrifice, find a venue for moral action in settings of public disagreement, then maybe movies like *Gandhi* will become more common and those like *Rambo* less so.

Fourth, those who consider terrorists to be "snakes" that need to be exterminated, rather than people with real grievances or who address the real grievances of others, might—given a pro-disagreement format—discover that they can acknowledge the validity of grievances without even appearing to condone the terrorist response. And they might even find some of their views challenged. For example, according to Juergensmeyer many religious militants challenge "the notion that secular society and the modern nation-state can provide the moral fiber that unites national communities or the ideological strength to sustain states buffeted by ethical, economic, and military failures." And, he goes on to say, "Their message has been easy to believe and has been widely received because the failures of the secular state have been so apparent."[60]

Fifth, a disagreement approach to terrorism is likely to give nonviolent Islamic "moderates" (who are maybe the actual "radical" ones) more of a voice. They tend to disappear from view in the face of terrorism and antiterrorist responses. In disagreement-friendly conversational settings such leaders as Abdolkarim Soroush would be in a better position to step up and be heard.

And sixth, those who advocate terror in order to get publicity—a common motive, according to Juergensmeyer—could instead get publicity by virtue of participation in public conversations. They could find in those settings an alternative way to act on their vision of life as a struggle for virtue.[61] Some killers are, moreover, driven by a desire to be equal with their opponents, and disagreement sessions could confer some of this recognition. Keep in mind that in order to get such recognition the perpetrators of violence would have to likewise confer recognition on their enemies. That is what pro-disagreement dialogue does. The opportunity to be heard would not, then, amount to a reward for violent actions. Many violent activists will, in fact, decline to participate when asked. But some will say, "Yes," and the result can only be a weakening of the idea that the struggle for virtue is part of an end-game of the world, or that a battle is underway between those who are purely on the side of good and those who embody pure evil.[62]

## INCLUDING RELIGION

The problem of religiously inspired violence can't be dealt with without properly addressing the broader question of how to include religion in politics. Make no mistake: faith does play a role in politics and always will. In part this is because some religious perspectives are simply not compatible with privatized religious practice. They instead make demands on believers when it comes to shaping the public realm. Their vision of piety includes living in a certain kind of society; it cannot be enacted by one person at a time. It's also because all religious beliefs come with ideas about how one should live, and there's simply no way to act politically and leave such ideas to one side. And, finally, it's because faith goes well beyond religion. Many people are not religious, but everyone has faith in something. Being human is not, and never will be, entirely based on reason, emotion, and instinct. Faith will, then, always find its way into politics somehow, and the question is how. For those who want to avoid religiously inspired war and violence, the answer can only be disagreement. Religiously inspired political perspectives need to be argued about in public spaces.

I'll say more about faith shortly, but first I want to make the point, important for an American audience, that the involvement of religion in public political conversation is not a violation of the First Amendment to the U.S. Constitution. That impressive piece of writing imposes two prohibitions: First, the government may not interfere with religious exercise. This is generally interpreted to mean that rules that interfere with a religious activity have to have a strong secular justification and also be applied to people regardless of their religion (e.g., no man can have several wives, whether he is Mormon or not). Second, the amendment prohibits the establishment of a government-sponsored religion—at least by the *federal* government. (There are those who believe the authors of the amendment aimed to preserve the right of each state government to impose its own religion.) As far as I know, no legal scholar has ever interpreted either part of the Amendment to mean that religion can't play a part in people's political thinking, expression, or decision making. Nor is such prohibition possible.

This doesn't mean it's right, wise, or even good strategy for religions, as such, to take part in party politics, endorse candidates, raise campaign funds, or affiliate themselves with this or that idea of government. Stephen L. Carter, in *God's Name in Vain: The Wrongs and Rights of Religion in Politics*, argues that religions "will almost always lose their best, most spiritual selves when they choose to be involved in the partisan, electoral side of American politics."[63] This is not, however, a legal argument or a once-and-for-all claim. Carter says "*almost* always [italics added]" rather than "always." And, writing as someone "inspired by . . . [his] love of God and love of . . . [his] country," he also argues "there's nothing wrong, and much right, with the robust participation of the nation's many religious voices in debates over matters of public moment."[64] I agree, as long as the many nonreligious voices—with their faiths and their ethics—are included as equals.

But, one might ask, since faith is by definition a set of beliefs that are absolute in some way, why would anyone of faith be willing to embrace permanent dialogue with opposing faiths, religious or otherwise? One reason is mutual respect for faith itself. As I said earlier, every point of view rests on faith of some kind. Even science rests on faith. Granted, the theory of evolution is not a faith belief *in the same way* as the notion of the Bible as revelation. The former, for example, declares itself subject to the standard of squaring with continually discovered empirical "facts," while the latter self-consciously does not. Both are, however, inclusive of faith: science cannot prove that the universe itself is real, or fake, or that the "evidence" it uses is not the result of some god's dream. And neither can religions prove the existence of God, at least not using the scientific-type standards of evidence. That's the whole point of faith.

The pro-disagreement sensibility has faith of a kind. My own not-so-religious faith tells me, for example, that religions are ways by which people tackle the ethical imperative of human existence. It tells me that religions are ways to grasp and make sense of the mysteries of existence. My version of a pro-disagreement sensibility therefore calls upon me to respect religion and religiosity. And it calls upon me to welcome religion and religiously inspired perspectives into my conversations. Will all come to the table? No. But I can and should invite everyone nonetheless.

## PALESTINIAN-ISRAELI DIALOGUE

Inspiring examples of such talk can be found in the small Palestinian-Israeli dialogue movement. Nowhere is the connection between allowing religious conviction into politics and dealing with terrorism more apparent than in the Middle East, where two groups—closely related by language, culture, and the roots of their respective religions—each make exclusive claims to the same territory and even claim some of the same sites as their exclusive sacred religious ground. There are few places in the world where the creation of cross-border talk faces more obstacles. Yet such talk is underway.

For example, in 1992 Len and Libby Traubman began inviting people to their home in San Mateo, California, to take part in a weekly Jewish-Palestinian dialogue. "The meetings became hugely popular; articles were written on the couple, and several groups sprouted in imitation across the country. The idea was to create a respectful atmosphere in which people could discuss their fears and concerns without threat of violent reactions."[65]

Another example is the Seeds of Peace camp, a nonprofit enterprise begun in 1993 in Otisfield, Maine. The camp has, over the years, "brought together more than 2,000 teens from regions in turmoil worldwide" using the vehicle of "sports and other outdoor activities," along with "group discussions designed to get young people out of their own skins."[66] Many of the campers are Israeli or Palestinian. One of them, a seventeen-year-old Palestinian named Tamer Shabaneh, described his experience this way: "You see the human side of your so-called enemy and nothing looks the same again."[67] David Shoolman, a seventeen-year-old Israeli, made a similar point: "I'll tell people that I have a Palestinian friend, and he's a great person. That's how I measure progress."[68]

Shana Kirsch, who grew up in a Jewish household in California, learned about the Seeds for Peace camp in 2000, and this inspired her to join forces with three of her fellow New York University students—Sarah Hoffman, Liz Aakhus, and Kellen Kaiser—to form an Israeli-Palestinian dialogue group at the University.[69] Hoffman was the secretary of the Arab Student Union; Aakhus grew up in Damascus, Syria; and Kellen Kaiser was a left-wing, pro-Israeli activist, and together they hosted several cross-border conversations. "People on both sides of this issue are incredibly passionate, and we're not trying to diminish their passion," said Kirsch. "We want to create a place where people can talk about their passions but also learn to listen, to accept that we all have our own truths and learn to respect them. . . . I understand that it's personal for people. People have families there and religious beliefs. But . . . [w]e should be able to talk."[70]

One more example: in 2003 Adrienne Dessel, inspired by a three-day training session organized by the Public Conversations Project (PCP), joined "two other community members, an Israeli man and a Palestinian man," to create an "Israel/Palestine Community Dialogue" in Knoxville, Tennessee.[71] One advantage they had was precedent. Residents from local Israeli and Palestinian communities had recently started gathering "once a year for socializing and conversation." Perhaps that's why Dessel and her partners were able to gather fifteen participants, "two from the local Arab/Palestinian community and 13 from the local Jewish/Israeli community." Another advantage was the use of a disagreement-friendly process, conceptualized under the guidance of the PCP. The members of the group set their own ground rules—one of which was to avoid criticism—and they and the cofacilitators gently reminded each other of those rules as the session unfolded. A third advantage was that "there were clearly . . . differences even within the Jewish/Israeli community." I can imagine this fact acting to protect the two Arab/Palestinian participants from feeling outnumbered. And, finally, the questions posed to each participant in turn, as they sat in a circle, were well designed and in keeping with the agreed-upon ground rules: (1) "Which of my life experiences might best help the others understand my perspective on this issue?" and (2) "What is at the heart of the matter for me? What values, hopes, concerns and assumptions shape my perspective?" The result of this thoughtful preparation was a dialogue that lasted almost two hours and an agreement by all to meet again, in one month's time.

Admittedly, these various disagreement experiences, taken together, reached only a tiny fraction of those who feel strongly about the issues that divide the Middle East. They do, however, make it clear that much more is possible. One of the obstacles to further change in the right direction is that those who seek to advance the cause of peace so often turn to political leaders and ask them to negotiate. While such talk does have an essential role to play, leaders by definition have turfs to defend and constituents to represent. They therefore need support from below; they need support—and pressure—from the results of person-to-person dialogues where less is at stake and there is room to cultivate cross-border understandings.

## RACE TALK

Another issue area that calls for a disagreement approach is race. On the one hand, there's plenty of agreement that might serve as the foundation for productive discussions. For example, many people know that, when it comes to health, infant mortality, and rates of employment, income, and wealth, there are considerable differences between so-called racial groups. And an overwhelming majority of citizens now reject biological theories of racial hierarchy. On the other hand, people differ widely when it comes to how open they are to neighborhood integration, who they'll approve loans for, whether or not they think nonwhites are currently being subjected to significant amounts of discrimination, whether or not they think affirmative action is a good thing, and more.[72] If there's so much to talk about and enough common ground to get started, why is the subject so often avoided or treated gingerly?

One reason is the fear of being labeled or considered racist. Accusations of racism are in some contexts very damaging and can even cost people their jobs. Also people widely abhor racism and don't want to give it any hint of approval. They may not understand that in parts of the United States slavery was reality long after if was abolished by law, even well into the 1960s. They may not know how high the barriers were for American blacks when it came to reaping the benefits of the economic boom that came after World War II. They may not understand the effects of urban renewal, highway construction, real estate exclusions based on making money, and the rest. But they know that racism is terrible and wrong, and they don't want to appear to have any truck with it whatsoever.

The problem, however, is that once racism is treated as an all-or-nothing attitude rather than a complex historical phenomenon of people adapting to economic structures and doing so at each other's expense, then (as with the issue of terrorism) there can seem to be nothing worth talking about. Or, rather, the talk about race that does take place is likely to be dominated by signals of allegiance, rather than by the consideration of views, experiences, issues, feelings, and so on. As Shelby Steele puts it, some say things to keep whites "on the hook," while others say things to show that they're ashamed of the racist past or thoroughly reject it.[73] Those who step outside of the pattern—whites who question affirmative action, sports commentators who bring up the role of race in sports achievement—often don't even get the chance to say what they meant. By speaking they have signaled their endorsement of the racist past, and so others rush in to denounce them, thereby making clear that *they* do not endorse it.

The clear rejection of racism and the racist past *is* essential. The deployment of racial brutality and the race idea over the years, as a means to shore up some people's identities and make money, is indeed abhorrent. Ironically, however, the assertion of absolute opposition to racism tends to make subtler, but nonetheless powerful, racial barriers and inequalities disappear from view. People are busy proving themselves when it comes to the past, and what's going on in the present is missed. Or, worse, once it's assumed that racism as a structure is over and done with, and all that's left are a few racists who should be fired, there's no way to make sense of today's glaring racial inequalities of wealth and health, except by means of a new racism, this time of the nonbiological kind. Nonwhites *do* have a problem, some say: it's their "culture," supposedly, or their "marriage patterns." Perhaps it's "welfare dependence" and thus the fault of government. In any case it can't be "racism," the thinking goes, because that notion has been reduced to one of its many variations: brutal prejudice.

Not long ago I heard a radio talk show caller declare racism a crime on par with child molestation. On the one hand, this assertion makes a certain amount of sense to me. Some forms of racism are not only brutal and cruel beyond words but have also served as a foundation for equally brutal systems of economic exploitation and control. And the caller might have meant mostly to signal her degree of outrage about racism. She was, perhaps, making the claim that racism has, in the aggregate, done as much harm as child molestation and not asserting that those who have a racist view deserve the same punishment as those who molest a child.

On the other hand, the caller's comparison is a conversation stopper when it comes to exactly the things that most need to be talked about. There are subtle habits of mind and ways of speaking, for example, that contribute to the world's unfair treatment of groups of people. Take group thinking, when the actions or attitudes of individuals are perceived as somehow speaking for, or representative of, the entire group they belong to (or are thought to belong to). To think this way is to treat a group as a kind of organism, as one being, and of the individual members as so many appendages or representatives. Such thinking can be quite convenient at times, making the world more quickly comprehensible and even making many sentences shorter. It's helpful to speak about nations as singular actors, saying that "China" did this or "Israel" did that. Often what's meant, however, is that the Chinese or Israeli *government* did something, and usually what actually happened is that some members of a government acted, despite the misgiving or opposition of others. In the world of race, this way of thinking is racism or at least lends crucial support to racist actions. Should such turns of mind be considered criminal? Not if talking about them and loosening their grip is the goal.

Bruce A. Jacobs provides an example of groupthink about race when he speaks of how black and white commuters sometimes make an effort to avoid sitting next to each other on the train. Many black Americans are, he points out, understandably on the defensive: "The 'home turf' nastiness some black passengers may show a white commuter can best be understood as a sort of revenge. From the standpoint of many blacks, whites have done all but beg to be disliked."[74] True, but on the other hand there it is—group thinking. It is not that many, or even most, whites have begged to be disliked. It is "whites" who have done so, and thus it seems as if the group as a whole deserves to be held accountable. Granted, it makes sense to want someone held accountable, and all whites have, as whites, been exempt from the particular suffering that's been handed out to blacks, as blacks. But the group thinking that piles whites together is nonetheless more exactly what the world needs less of.

The group thinking just described is analogous to that which is done, and has long been done, to blacks. The U.S. national history is one of telling millions of people, by means of countless words and actions, that they're "black," different, and inferior. It would be a miracle, then, if most American blacks did not lead towards thinking of whites as a unit and as potentially dangerous. It would likewise be a miracle if American blacks did not think of themselves as somehow at one with all other blacks, if they did not think of blacks as a group that must stick together at all costs. It follows that it's both unfair and unrealistic to ask people to forget about race, to move directly to being race-blind. Instead people have to work at undoing the idea of race, and this requires cross-border conversations about race matters, without undue fear of saying the wrong thing.

One reason there isn't more engagement in disagreement about race is that many people apply a legal idea of responsibility to the issue and decide it's not their problem. In the courtroom the defendant is either guilty or not guilty, and there's no sharing of guilt by the community. When it comes to limiting and guiding the punitive power of the state, this all-or-nothing thinking makes some sense, even if it also poses problems. It is, however, deeply misleading as a way of comprehending the crimes perpetrated by culture, system, economy, and history. Similarly, it doesn't make much sense to leave the tasks of social repair to the people who "did it." Who are they? This is, however, a common mode of thought: "It wasn't me who perpetrated racism, so why should I fix it?" "I never owned slaves, so why should I take second place in a job search?" And, "Racism is white people's fault, so they should be the ones to address it." Bruce A. Jacobs' response is to the point: "Sure, and it was the shipbuilders job to rescue people from the Titanic."[75]

Unlike the problem of the sinking Titanic, race-related problems are deeply connected to cycles of mind and culture. Fortunately, vicious cycles can often be countered by virtuous cycles—one can, that is, intervene to disrupt a cycle and turn things in a different, better direction. When it comes to race, people can positively influence the future by intervening in the present and bringing a generous attitude to cross-race conversations. As Jacobs says, speaking to an imagined white audience, "Okay, so black Americans can be touchy sometimes. So can you. Disagree anyway. I mean, who came up with the fainthearted idea that blacks and whites will break out in hives when they disagree."[76]

## WHAT MIGHT ONE LEARN IN RACE TALK?

One problem that might be productively addressed by disagreement is discrimination in the workplace. Glenn C. Loury, using his training as an economist, has grasped some of the relevant dynamics by engaging in a series of "thought experiments."[77] He asks his readers to start with the eminently plausible assumption that many white employers and supervisors have, in the not-so-distant past, expected less from blacks on the job. Assume also, says Loury, that many workplace tasks, especially those in the professional realm, are such that one has to use trial and error to become good at them. In this situation it stands to reason that many blacks, having been treated unfairly by an employer more than once or knowing of such mistreatment of other blacks, might act in a guarded manner when it comes to performing those workplace tasks. They may hesitate to make the extra effort that risks temporary failure on the way to learning. They will be,

after all, aware that others may have low expectations of them and might therefore be concerned to avoid confirming those expectations by passing through the
failure stage. And if they do hesitate in this way, concludes Loury, their employers
may take it as confirmation of stereotypes, concluding that black employees aren't
smart enough to work independently, committed, and so on.

In other words, job discrimination sometimes gets support from a vicious circle.
Understandable actions of black employees, caught in binds created by history,
shape white perceptions in the wrong direction. And some white employers
become hardened, cynical, or unwilling to lend a hand, thinking, "I told you
so" or "I tried, and look what happened." They become, to put a point on it,
a kind of racist, even if inadvertently and despite the fact that they personally
oppose biological theories of racial inequality. Fortunately, this negative cycle can
be countered by communication. Employers who become aware of the dynamics
that are at work can take the simple step of explicitly encouraging their employees
to use trial and error, while also making an effort to communicate clearly that the
error part is expected and not a problem. And black employees might, if more
aware of the pitfalls of hesitation and more able to see employer misjudgment as
a correctable human foible, steel themselves to dive in and sometimes fail, on the
way to success.

What else might people learn from cross-border race talk? Here are some ideas:

- Most white men don't have much power, except relative to others and of
  a sort that they—the white men—can't easily see. As Jacobs says, "[The
  fact that] African-Americans have suffered, arguably more than any other
  group except for the American Indians, does not entitle us as blacks to
  ignore the suffering of others. If anything, it should help us to understand
  others' suffering, and even to see how it might connect with our own."[78]
- Thousands of white Americans have risked their careers and even their
  lives in the fight against racism, ever since the enslavement of blacks
  began.
- Despite the decline in the incidence and power of traditional racism and
  despite the important gains in the area of legal equality, there is still
  reason for moral outrage in the realm of racial inequality, for example, in
  the area of racial profiling by police.
- The police are often put in tough spots, thanks to the world's racial and
  ethnic tensions: white and nonwhite police officers all have something
  to say worth hearing.
- History leaves a mark on people in the present. Personal will is not enough
  to overcome the past.

This last point deserves some elaboration. *How* does history make a mark on
the present, when it comes to race and thinking about race? First, every generation
inherits a distribution of jobs, places of residence, education levels, skills, savings
held by family members, level of health in the family, and so on from the past,
and these then shape the present, for example, by shaping the degree to which
people have role models, have the "connections" that can help procure a good

job, or have the ability to survive a temporary crisis without becoming homeless or destitute. This differential distribution has hurt minorities, along with most people in the lower economic third of society. Second, history hands the people of the present various misunderstandings about each other. And third, history also hands out identity commitments that can make moving away from inherited understandings—even misunderstandings—costly, painful, or even unacceptable. This in turn means that some will turn away from cross-border conversations, no matter what. Others, however, will find themselves less a slave of history and more a beneficiary of its mixed legacy, if they're given a chance to reconsider their identities and loyalties in a pro-disagreement context, where they can test new identities without being unduly pressured to change who they are.

Even under such conditions, healthy cross-race communication won't be easy, at least most of the time, but guidelines can help. Consider, for example, Jacobs' ideas about how to approach discussions of affirmative action: "(1) Talk about issues, not individuals; (2) don't start off on the defensive; (3) bring up the topic only when it is relevant; (4) if you don't want to be stereotyped, don't buy stereotypes; and (5) don't assume who is 'for' and who is 'against.'"[79] These rules provide a pro-disagreement foundation. Add them to real people sharing space and being heard, and it's amazing what can happen.

## AN EXAMPLE

It was 1995. The "Multipurpose Room" at SUNY Potsdam was almost full, so there must have been at least 500 students present. It was a great turnout, seeing as how about 3,000 undergraduates were enrolled at the time, and many of them lived off campus. The point was to have an open-ended conversation about the escalating racial tension on campus. After several opening statements by administrators and such, students came forward, one by one, to the microphone, to vent their concerns, tell a story about what happened to them, or react to something that had just been said by another student. The discussion was frank and heated, but also careful and respectful. Every speaker went out of their way to make sure they weren't misunderstood, to reassure those potentially perceived as the "other side" (all the white students to some, all the nonwhite students to others) that they did not mean to belittle them or their concerns. It was obvious that they knew how easy it is to say the "wrong thing" when it comes to race, but they didn't pull any punches. All this, despite (or because) little had been done by way of preparation, and the meeting facilitation was minimal.

What was accomplished? There had been no edict as to expected results and, correspondingly, nothing was voted on or otherwise decided at the meeting. Also, the group had not reached the point of agreement when, after several hours had passed, it became obvious that everyone still in the room was tired, and it was time to quit. On the other hand, a college task force was created, and it went on to form a "bias response team." Also, some participants gathered afterwards and organized a "World in Potsdam" diversity festival, now an annual event in the town. In my view, however, the most important results of the meeting were the good feelings and the connecting that happened in the room while people were talking. There was a sense of importance in the air and one could feel the spirits of speakers rise as they felt themselves heard. Certainly many students saw the forum as a big success. They knew it hadn't put an end to racial problems on campus, but many reported learning something, and many spoke also of an improved racial atmosphere at the college, an observation that was corroborated by the staff that provides supportive services for students and oversees the residence halls. How, one might ask, could a few hours of exchanging views have this result? It could do so by giving students the experience of being listened to and taken seriously by fellow students from across the racial divide. It could do so by giving each participant an opportunity to be considerate towards others who they don't normally talk to and to see those others be considerate towards them. And it could do so by allowing people to show other people something of what they are, thereby revealing all of them as much alike, despite differences. A few hours of the right kind of conversation can, in some situations, weaken a chain of mistrust and perhaps even contribute to its eventual destruction.

## WITH OR WITHOUT DECISION-MAKING

I now turn to questions of process. One thing deliberative democrats disagree about is whether the deliberation aimed for should be decisional or not. Must it be a part of government and lawmaking, as in a series of referendums with discussions attached, or should it be independent of authoritative decision making, more along the lines of opinion formation and space for people to get to know one another? Ethan J. Leib, as we have seen, argues for the former. On the other hand, most of the disagreement examples mentioned above are of the latter variety, and the same thing is true of most of the activity in the nascent dialogue and deliberation movement. In part this is because it's difficult to get the powers-that-be to create new decision-making opportunities for the general public, but it's also because there are advantages to disagreement with no decisions at stake.

One advantage is that those who talk with each other are free of the pressure to agree that's created by the need to make a decision. True, such pressure can be valuable; people sometimes make concessions or accept compromises in order to get something or get something done. And the need to find at least some common ground can give people an incentive to listen to those whom they might otherwise dismiss or ignore. On the other hand, the pressure to agree can work in opposing directions, leading people to harden their position or negotiate without taking the chance of listening. The goal becomes trying to get something rather than learning from and educating each other. Also, negotiations in that context will often lead groups in a strong position—with many followers or lots of clout— to work exclusively with those who are similarly situated and ignore those they consider minor players, who perhaps possess views that are on the edge rather then near the center.

In this context it's worth revisiting an idea presented in Chapter 1: *Disagreement failure exists when ideas and experiences that are playing an important role in a given situation are not brought to the surface in cross-border, public conversations and when that omission leads to serious harm or injustice or to a failure to realize worthwhile goals that would otherwise be within reach.* There are situations in which a reliance on discussions held in official decisional spaces, without the benefit of extensive cross-border discussions held elsewhere, will lead to disagreement failure as just defined. A law might be passed, or a decision made, at the expense of what's really needed or best.

Consider the immigration issue in the United States. Thousands of people live in the country illegally, with more arriving each day. Most work for a living, pay taxes, and provide needed and affordable labor for various businesses. Some start businesses of their own and hire others. But all of them use resources, perhaps needing affordable housing or seats for their children in school. And some are poor and must rely on the government for health care services. There are those who say that they take jobs away from legal residents, are lawbreakers, and deserve to be deported. Others argue that illegal immigrants have a right to try to provide food and shelter for themselves and their families and also that the jobs most of them perform are typically rejected by residents with legal status.

Disagreement can't reach anything like its full potential on this issue, in my view, if it's restricted to official decision-making settings. What about the perspectives of illegal aliens? They're not citizens, so they would have no right to take part in such decision-making (though some might manage to do so anyway). And many U.S. citizens would surely oppose giving them official decision-making powers, as in the right to vote, for example. On the other hand, some of those same citizens might be willing to take part in *dialogues* that included those without legal status, if this meant that no decision hung in the balance. If such talks were held and if they were well conceptualized and facilitated (with respect shown for all views in the room), they would surely result in an increase in mutual understanding, and that could only redound to the good. The benefits might be as basic as a reduction in tension and anger. Or, more ambitiously, a new dynamic might be set in motion, one that, over time, leads to the emergence of something like a national consensus on the issue.

## PRINCIPLES AND GROUND RULES

I conclude this chapter with two lists. The first is called "philosophy," as it offers attitudes and ideas that, if brought to political conversations, will lead in the direction of disagreement success. The second is called "process," as it suggests ways to organize conversations and how one might best behave once those conversations are underway.

### Philosophy

- Value the extreme: extreme ideas are not necessarily worse, or better, than middle-of-the-road ones; also one way to shrink the sphere of violence is to move anger and alienation into the realm of discussion.

- Expect to find underlying commonalities across borders: considerable common ground can often be found, despite the persistence of intense disagreement.
- Expect irreconcilable differences: they're there, even within groups that seem as one, and even among one's own.
- Put time in now, and save it later: time and energy spent on the front end is often repaid, with interest.
- Think to combine certainty with uncertainty: remember that speaking and acting with principle does not require absolute certainty; people can be both sure of themselves and open to other points of view.

## Process

- Show respect: listen; try to create a process or a structure that gives all a chance to have their say; avoid labeling.
- Question: emphasize thinking critically about what people say rather than demanding "balance" in the views involved or the number of views presented.
- Be pro-bias: avoid reliance on experts, and treat bias as a good thing, something to be tested by encounter with other biases.
- Let be: let disagreement be, don't demand resolution.
- Create safe spaces: be concerned for the comfort of others, without shirking from the clash of ideas; don't use violence or threaten to use violence.
- Don't team up against others: seek encounters that are relatively even matched; don't confront an individual with a mob of antagonists.
- Use facilitators for group discussions: as a general rule facilitators should not take a side in the discussion.
- Frame discussions in nonjudgmental ways: if possible, start with a topic or question that doesn't assert or accuse.
- Include, without pressure: use a procedure that invites all those present to take part while also allowing each person control over how much they get involved.
- Cross borders: work hard to invite people who might disagree and get them talking to each other. Recruit leaders from different organized sides—if there are any—to help to plan and facilitate the event.
- Consider including a joint task for the participants: it might be setting up and cleaning up.
- Don't let experts dominate the discussion: it's often best to bring in experts afterwards or as consultants, if at all; politicians might call for similar treatment.

## CONCLUSION

Are these the right principles and guidelines? What if someone's faith tells them it's wrong to place the false or sinful beliefs of others in a place of respect by inviting their proponents to a conversation? What if they also see such talk as potentially a threat to morality and therefore as a threat to their children and others to whom they have a responsibility? And, what if they think that respect for authority would be undermined by placing the messages of authority figures in doubt in open-ended cross-border discussions?

Here's a response: One need not show disrespect when one disagrees, whether with elders, those in positions of leadership, one's parents, or the learned. Also, while respect and authority are important values, so is disagreement. Or, to put it another way, these values connect to each other. The celebration of disagreement is based on the idea that all people deserve respect, not just those who have earned special respect because of the position they occupy in someone's life or belief system. And this form of respect calls for principled listening. It calls upon people to enter conversations with generosity and an open ear, regardless of their position on the issues at hand.

The pro-disagreement response also argues that there's no reason to think that respectful conversation, even with one's enemies, will encourage relativism. One does not commit to agreement with others by agreeing to talk to them or by committing oneself to the idea that all points of view have some sense to them and are adopted for understandable reasons. Granted, endorsement of this latter idea must, perforce, open a person up to engagement with others, but such engagement is just as likely to strengthen their convictions as to weaken them. And if it leads them to change their mind, so be it. Changing one's mind is compatible not only with respect but with freedom as well.

# CHAPTER 9

# Freedom and Disagreement

[T]he self is intrinsically dialogical: its viability depends on the quality of its responses to the environment. It cannot be understood or expressed except in relation to an audience whose real or imagined responses continually shape the way in which we define ourselves."[1]

—Mikhail Bakhtin

Michael Sandel, in an essay called "The Politics of Public Identity," takes note of a dilemma. On the one hand, humans need community and civic engagement. They need to feel a sense of belonging and connectedness. On the other hand, they're attracted to the idea that no one has the right to tell anyone else what to think. This idea of moral freedom—to use Alan Wolfe's phrase—is especially influential in the United States.[2] Thus the dilemma: how can people combine community and moral freedom? How can one have duty to one's group and also have freedom from the tyranny of that group? How can people be civically engaged and yet avoid the absolutist response?[3] The answer offered by this book is the embrace of disagreement, both in theory and in daily life.

To put it another way, humans can avoid the absolutist response by redefining community to include disagreement as one of its essential features. Yes, people need community, but that doesn't mean they need agreement. An ideal community is not a melting pot. Nor is it a smorgasbord of differences that simply coexist or are "celebrated" in an easy, superficial way. Community is instead a coexistence of different individuals who make life together by regularly hammering out differences and learning from each other and by working together on needed tasks.

The fact that one ought not to aim for moral unity does not mean that people have no obligations when they communicate. Conservatives are right to speak of duties as well as rights, and in this respect they share common ground with those leftists who, like Nicholas Garnham, call for a more participatory, radically democratic society; "while the rights to free expression inherent in democratic theory have been continually stressed, what has been lost is any sense of the reciprocal duties inherent in a communicative space that is physically shared."[4] Garnham speaks of two such duties: the obligation to listen and to accept some responsibility for the effects of what one says. These are pro-disagreement virtues.

One might counter by making the assertion that people can coexist *without* hammering out differences, instead going their separate ways and relying on a minimal state, individual rights, and free markets to adjudicate their relationships and maximize their individual freedom. To assume, however, that such lack of restraint is all there is to freedom is to make two false assumptions. First, it's to assume that people's opinions are always truly their own, that they always fully know their own best interest, and that a "public" realm of freedom will, therefore, flower automatically, as long as there's no state censorship or overt political repression. Second, it's to assume that the individual is not intrinsically bound up in relationships with other individuals, that relationships are things that are chosen by an autonomous person.

There is, however, nothing automatic about being in possession of one's own mind, and thus there's nothing automatic about freedom. To be free a person needs to take the space provided by the absence of restraint and *use* it. And this must often mean acting with other people and freely accepting certain restraints, based on ideas about what ought to be done. Freedom therefore requires thinking and deciding, and these in turn require disagreement. Also, while it's true that many relationships are chosen, it's also true that human beings can only discover and rediscover themselves as thinking beings—as one who can change their mind about something and therefore can choose—by already being in relationships. Specifically, the individual needs the experience of disagreement in relationships to be able to disagree with themselves, to reflect. And it's only by means of such self-disagreement and reflection that people have the chance to change their views on a subject. Without disagreement experience, then, people can't act on choices that are fully their own; they're not autonomous; they're not fully free. In *On Dialogue* Dmitri Nikulin says it this way:

> [I]t is important to recognize the worth and goodness of a non-antagonistic conflict, or the ability not to agree, which is of value both for human relationships and for the very constitution of the human qua person. Such disagreement . . . permits the restoration of a dialogue over and over again by recognizing the value of the other's objections, including one's own objections to oneself, and it allows one to remain and continue to be in dialogue with the other. It is only in this way . . . that personal autonomy can be realized and established.[5]

In sum, people need disagreement both because dissent brings information and ideas and because the experience of considering objections is necessary to be a thinking, free being.

Freedom therefore requires respect for views at the "vital edge" (as seen in Chapter 3), meaning at the extremes of left, right, and wherever. After all, every view now in the "center" was at some point on that edge. The political center should not, in other words, be confused with the sort of moderation recommended by Aristotle or the Dalai Llama. They mean the middle points of character, feeling, and behavior. They mean that it's wise for a person to chart a moderate course between courage and caution, undereating and overeating, dependence and independence, passion and calm, commitment and distance, working and playing, and public life and private life. They don't mean that the most popular viewpoint, or the one that seems partway between opposites, is the best. The best ideas are often at the edge.

## LIMITS AND WARNINGS

Disagreement is not a panacea:

- Better disagreement will not in and of itself eliminate racism, racial enmity, terrorist threats, the commodification of sexuality, or global warming. It can, at best, point the way and build support for what's best or right. And it can reduce the number and power of the hate responses that so often come when problems are not solved.
- All efforts to disagree, no matter how well designed and carried out, will bear the marks of the divisions and injustices of the larger society. This is, however, no reason to wait. Injustice will not go away first and will never go away completely.
- There is a danger of excessive seriousness. Disagreement needs to be what Oliver Wendell Holmes called "electrical," a force field of positive and negative charges, with plenty of wit and humor thrown in to temper seriousness and make ambivalence safe enough to take seriously.
- There is the danger of poorly designed and/or poorly carried out forms of disagreement that leave participants angry, hardened, or feeling unheard. There is likewise the danger of faux dialogue that masquerades as the real thing. On the other hand, these problems exist now, and must be dealt with one way or another.

## STARTING NOW

One way to make the creation of a healthy disagreement practice less of a challenge would be to somehow reduce economic inequality. I don't mean zero inequality, just less. When economic differences are extreme, as they are now in the United States and elsewhere, those struggling to make ends meet are often too busy and stressed to take the time and energy to engage in political life, and sometimes they're also too dependent on the wealthy to risk sticking their necks out in a public gathering. On the other end of the economic ladder are people who can afford to ignore public talk because they can afford private solutions to public problems; they can build a gate around their houses, hire security guards, buy bottled water, etc. Moreover, some of the very rich are likely to find cross-border talk threatening to their interests, and they might—understandably—try to use their political clout to curtail it. Another problem is that those who occupy key roles in the system of allocating investment—a relative few, in today's world—are often deferred to, sometimes unconsciously. And this means that their perspectives on what's worth discussing and what's needed might dominate the agenda setting and talk of disagreement events.

Despite these limitations, people can and should push ahead to create new forms of cross-border talk. Lower levels of inequality may never arrive, for one thing. Also public conversations will never be entirely free of power differentials, no matter what. And more importantly, the distortions of power that exist now are not total enough to make such talk pointless. This is for at least two reasons: First, cross-border disagreement sessions will give ordinary people more clout by giving them opportunities to be heard, new ideas about how the world works, and opportunities for coalition building. Second, the class divide is simply not that wide. People from all different walks of life stand to find fulfillment and freedom by accepting disagreement into their lives.

It's also important to point out that class difference is one of the subjects people can and should disagree about in the first place, as is the more general question of exactly what conditions are most likely to make cross-border encounter both plentiful and productive. These conditions will vary from situation to situation. On the other hand, some conditions are not negotiable. One of them is the creation of a tradition of openness as to who participates and what can be brought up. It's also necessary to go beyond endorsement of openness and make an active effort to include whoever is not currently included. One must go outside and invite the protestors and those who are angry—even those who are violent—to peacefully come inside. There's no alternative, when it comes to effectively addressing the urgent issues of our time. And there's no better way to remain fully in touch with one's humanity while those issues are addressed. We need to hear from a wide range of people on every subject. We must hazard the event.

# Notes

## Preface

1. Erica Goode, "Home Alone," *The New York Times Magazine*, June 17, 2007, 1, http://www.nytimes.com/2007/06/17/magazine (accessed August 4, 2007); see also Robert D. Putnam, "Pluribus Unum: Diversity and Community in the Twenty-first Century: The 2006 Johan Skytte Prize Lecture," *Scandinavian Political Studies* 30(2). (June 2007): 137–174.

2. Erica Goode, "Home Alone," 2.

3. Ibid., 3.

4. David Brooks, "The End of Integration," *The New York Times*, July 6, 2007, http://select.nytimes.com/2007/07/06/opinion/06brooks.html (accessed August 30, 2007).

## Chapter 1: Disagreement Today

1. John Rawls, quoted in Seyla Benhabib, ed., *Democracy and Difference: Contesting the Boundaries of the Political* (Princeton, NJ: Princeton University Press, 1996), 111.

2. Michael S. Rosenwald, "Old and Young Honor Veterans in Parade: Peace Group Calls for Iraq War's End," *The Boston Globe*, November 12, 2003.

3. David Brooks, "Age of Political Segregation," *The New York Times*, June 29, 2004.

4. Deborah Tannen, *The Argument Culture: Stopping America's War of Words* (New York: Ballantine Books, 1998), 1.

5. Ibid., 6.

6. Ibid., 25.

7. Ibid., 26.

8. Ibid., 10.

9. Albert Camus, quoted in *Familiar Quotations*, 16th ed. (Boston, MA: Little, Brown and Company, 1992).

10. Francis Moore Lappé, "Voice," in *Democracy's Edge: Choosing to Save Our Country by Bringing Democracy to Life* (San Francisco, CA: Jossey-Bass, 2006), 220, 230.

11. Alan Wolfe, *Moral Freedom: The Search for Virtue in a World of Choice* (New York: W. W. Norton, 2001), 195.

12. Laura Chasin, Anne Fowler, Frances Hogan, Melisa Kogut, and Madeline Mc-Comish, "Interview: Members of the Public Conversations Project Discuss Their Group's Series of Confidential Conversations about the Issue of Abortion," interview by Margot Adler, *All Things Considered*, National Public Radio, January 19, 2003.

13. Nicki Nichols Gamble and Madeline McComish, "Analysis: Dialogue on Abortion," interview by Neil Conan, *Talk of the Nation*, National Public Radio, January 21, 2003.

14. Ibid.

15. Laura Chasin, Anne Fowler, Frances Hogan, Melisa Kogut, and Madeline Mc-Comish, "Interview: Members of the Public Conversations Project."

16. Nicki Nichols Gamble and Madeline McComish, "Analysis: Dialogue on Abortion."

17. Ibid.

18. Ibid.

19. Ibid.

20. The Southern Poverty Law Center, "First Mix It Up Day Is Hit from Coast to Coast," *SPLC Report* 32(4) (December 2002): 1. Mix It Up at Lunch Day was a joint initiative of Tolerance.org and Teaching Tolerance.

21. Daniel Yankelovich, *The Magic of Dialogue: Transforming Conflict into Cooperation* (New York: Simon & Schuster, 1999).

22. Ibid., 15.

23. Ibid.

24. Ibid., 45.

25. Sheldon Wolin, "Fugitive Democracy," in *Democracy and Difference: Contesting the Boundaries of the Political*, edited by Seyla Benhabib (Princeton: Princeton University Press, 1996), 31.

## Chapter 2: A Mixed Disagreement Legacy

1. The Master, a character in Oliver Wendell Holmes' *The Poet at the Breakfast Table*, quoted in Peter Gibian, *Oliver Wendell Holmes and the Culture of Conversation* (Cambridge, MA: Cambridge University Press, 2001), 131; see *The Writings of Oliver Wendell Holmes*, 13 vols. (Boston: Houghton Mifflin, 1892).

2. Mireya Navarro, "Bricks, Mortar, and Coalition Building," in *How Race Is Lived in America: Pulling Together, Pulling Apart*, by correspondents of *The New York Times*, introduction by Joseph Lelyveld (New York: Henry Holt and Company, 2001), 266.

3. James Farr, "Social Capital: A Conceptual History," *Political Theory* 32(1) (February 2004): 6–33.

4. Robert D. Putnam, *Bowling Alone: The Collapse and Revival of American Community* (New York: Touchstone, 2000), 21.

5. Ibid, 19.

6. James Farr, "Social Capital," 9.

7. Ibid.

8. Daniel Kemmis, "Barn Raising," in *Rooted in the Land: Essays on Community and Place*, eds. Bill Vitek and Wes Jackson (New Haven, CT: Yale University Press, 1996), 170–71, 174.

9. Robert D. Putnam, *Bowling Alone*, 23.

10. Anne Colby, Thomas Ehrlich, Elizabeth Beaumont, and Jason Stephens, *Educating Citizens: Preparing America's Undergraduates for Lives of Moral and Civic Responsibility* (San Francisco: Jossey-Bass, 2003), 3.

11. Studs Terkel, "C. P. Ellis," in *Race, Class, and Gender in the United States: An Integrated Study*, 5th edition, ed. Paula S. Rothenberg (New York: Worth Publishers, 2001), 641.

12. Ibid., 645.

13. Jürgen Habermas, *The Structural Transformation of the Public Sphere*, trans. Thomas Burger (Cambridge, MA: Polity Press, 1989).

14. Harry C. Boyte and Sara Margaret Evans, *Free Spaces: The Sources of Democratic Change in America* (Chicago, IL: University of Chicago, 1992), 342.

15. Mary P. Ryan, "Gender and Public Access," in *Habermas and the Public Sphere*, ed. Craig Calhoun (Cambridge, MA: MIT Press, 1992), 271.

16. Ibid., 269.

17. Ibid.

18. Ibid.

19. Kevin Mattson, *Creating a Democratic Republic: The Struggle for Urban Participatory Democracy during the Progressive Era* (University Park, PA: Penn State University Press, 1998), 77–78.

20. Michael Schudson, "Was There Ever a Public Sphere?" in *Habermas and the Public Sphere*, ed. Craig Calhoun (Cambridge, MA: MIT Press, 1992), 148.

21. Ibid., 164.

22. Ibid., 146.

23. *The Autocrat at the Breakfast Table* (1858) can be found in *The Writings of Oliver Wendell Holmes*, 13 vols. (Boston: Houghton Mifflin, 1892).

24. Peter Gibian, *Oliver Wendell Holmes and the Culture of Conversation*, 315.

25. On William James and truth, see William E. Connolly, *Pluralism* (Duke University, 2005), chap. 3; see also Richard Rorty, *Philosophy and the Mirror of Nature* (Princeton, NJ: Princeton University Press, 1979), 11–12, 317–318, 373, 390.

26. Mikhail Bakhtin, *Problems of Dostoevsky's Poetics*, trans. R.W. Rostel (New York: Ardis, 1973), 90, 103.

27. Oliver Wendell Holmes, *The Autocrat at the Breakfast Table*, quoted in Peter Gibian, *Oliver Wendell Holmes and the Culture of Conversation*, 127.

28. Peter Gibian, *Oliver Wendell Holmes and the Culture of Conversation*, 128.

29. Ibid., 129.

30. Jon Sterngrass, *First Resorts: Pursuing Pleasure at Saratoga Springs, Newport & Coney Island* (Baltimore, MD: Johns Hopkins University Press, 2001), 4.

31. Ibid., 2.

32. Paul Kleppner, *The Third Electoral System 1853–1892: Parties, Voters, and Political Cultures* (Chapel Hill, NC: University of North Carolina Press, 1979).

33. Michael Schudson, "Was There Ever a Public Sphere?" 155.

34. Ibid., 144–145.

35. Ibid., 155.

36. Michael McGerr, *A Fierce Discontent: The Rise and Fall of the Progressive Movement in America, 1870–1920* (New York: Free Press, 2003), 54.

37. Daniel J. Boorstin, *The Americans: The Democratic Experience* (New York: Random House, 1973).

38. Henry Curtis, quoted in Kevin Mattson, *Creating a Democratic Republic: The Struggle for Urban Participatory Democracy during the Progressive Era* (University Park, PA: Penn State University Press, 1998), 84.

39. Michael McGerr, *A Fierce Discontent*, 73.

40. Ibid., 79.

41. Ibid., 65.

42. Ibid., 66.

43. Ibid.

44. John Dewey, *The Public and Its Problems* (Denver, CO: Swallow Press, 1927), 208.

45. Kevin Mattson, *Creating a Democratic Republic: The Struggle for Urban Participatory Democracy during the Progressive Era* (University Park, PA: Penn State University Press, 1998), 45; see also note 30 on p. 146.

46. Ibid., 33.

47. Ibid., 38.

48. Ibid., 41.

49. Ibid., 42.

50. Ibid.

51. Ibid., 52.

52. Ibid., 53.

53. Ibid., 65–66.

54. Ibid., 61.

55. Ibid.

56. Ibid., 53–54.

57. Ibid., 64.

58. Ibid., 46.

59. Frederic Howe, *The Confessions of a Reformer* (New York: Quadrangle Books, 1925), 245; quoted in Kevin Mattson, *Creating a Democratic Republic*, 46.

60. Kevin Mattson, *Creating a Democratic Republic*, 46.

61. Ibid., 63–64.

62. Ethan J. Leib, *Deliberative Democracy in America: A Proposal for a Popular Branch of Government* (University Park, PA: Pennsylvania State University Press, 2004), 57.

63. Ibid., 4.

64. One such historian is Edward Stevens, "Social Centers, Politics, and Social Efficiency in the Progressive Era," *History of Education Quarterly* 12 (1972): 18, 28–30.

65. Michael Mattson, *Creating a Democratic Republic*, 40.

66. Michael McGerr, *A Fierce Discontent*, 196, 215.

67. Ibid., 282.

68. Ibid., 291.

69. Ibid., 282.

70. Michael Mattson, *Creating a Democratic Republic*, 11.

71. Michael McGerr, *A Fierce Discontent*, 289.

72. Ibid., 290.

73. Ibid.

74. Michael Mattson, *Creating a Democratic Republic*, 112–113.

75. Michael McGerr, *A Fierce Discontent*, 307–308.

76. Michael Mattson, *Creating a Democratic Republic*, 108.

77. Ibid., 109.

78. Ibid., 116–120.

79. Harry Truman, quoted in E. J. Dionne, Jr., *Why Americans Hate Politics* (New York: Touchstone, 1991), 172.

80. Barry Goldwater, quoted in E. J. Dionne, Jr., *Why Americans Hate Politics*, 173.

81. Grant McConnell, *Private Power & American Democracy* (New York: Alfred A. Knopf, 1966).

82. Theodore J. Lowi, *The End of Liberalism: The Second Republic of the United States* (New York: W. W. Norton & Company, 1979).

83. Ibid., 57.

84. Ibid., 75.

85. Ibid., 57.

86. Ibid., 58.

87. Ibid., 57.

88. Ibid., 80.

89. Sheldon Wolin, *The Presence of the Past: Essays on the State and the Constitution* (Baltimore, MD: Johns Hopkins, 1989), 41–42.

90. Carter A. Wilson, *Racism: From Slavery to Advanced Capitalism* (Thousand Oaks, CA: Sage Publications, 1996), 176–193.

91. Barbara Hinckley, *The Symbolic Presidency* (New York: Routledge, 1990).

92. Quoted in E. J. Dionne, Jr., *Why Americans Hate Politics*, 179.

## Chapter 3: Argument after World War II

1. E. J. Dionne, Jr., *Why Americans Hate Politics* (New York: Touchstone, 1991), 74.

2. Thomas Byrne Edsall and Mary D. Edsall, *Chain Reaction: The Impact of Race, Rights, and Taxes on American Politics* (New York: W. W. Norton & Company, 1992).

3. E. J. Dionne, Jr., *Why Americans Hate Politics*, 78.

4. Ibid.

5. Jennifer L. Hochschild, *Facing Up to the American Dream: Race, Class, and the Soul of the Nation* (Princeton, NJ: Princeton University Press, 1995), 58–59.

6. Ibid., 60.

7. Ibid., 64–65.

8. Ibid., 63.

9. Ibid., xii.

10. See, for example, Eduardo Bonilla-Silva, *Racism without Racists: Color-Blind Racism and the Persistence of Racial Inequality in the United States* (Lanham, MD: Rowman & Littlefield, 2006), 13.

11. Ibid., 66; A People for the American Way poll.

12. Jack Ludwig, "Is America Divided into 'Haves' and 'Have-Nots?'" Gallup News Service, April 29, 2003, http://www.gallup.com/poll/8275/America-Divided-Into-Haves-HaveNots.aspx (accessed July 22, 2007).

13. Lydia Saad, "A Downturn in Black Perceptions of Racial Harmony: Two-Thirds of Blacks Are Dissatisfied with Society's Treatment of Blacks," Gallup News Service, July 6, 2007, http://www.gallup.com/poll/28072/Downturn-Black-Perceptions-Racial-Harmony.aspx (accessed July 24, 2007).

14. Jennifer L. Hochschild, *Facing Up to the American Dream*, 68.

15. Ibid., xvii.

16. Ibid., 68.

17. Carter A. Wilson, *Racism: From Slavery to Advanced Capitalism* (Thousand Oaks, CA: Sage, 1996), 129–131.

18. Shelby Steele, *A Dream Deferred: The Second Betrayal of Black Freedom in America* (New York: HarperCollins, 1998).

19. Joshua Green, "A 'Great Society' Conservative," *The New York Times*, August 14, 2007, http://www.nytimes.com/2007/08/14/opinion/14green.html?_r=1&oref=slogin (accessed September 25, 2007).

20. Bennett Harrison and Barry Bluestone, "Zapping Labor" and "The Crisis of the American Dream," in *The Great U-Turn: Corporate Restructuring and the Polarization of America* (New York: Basic Books, 1990).

21. E. J. Dionne, Jr., *Why Americans Hate Politics*, 75.

22. Wikipedia contributors, "Head Start," http://en.wikipedia.org/wiki/Head_Start (accessed August 7, 2007).

23. Thomas J. Sugrue, *The Origins of the Urban Crisis: Race and Inequality in Postwar Detroit* (Princeton, NJ: Princeton University Press, 1996), 7.

24. E. J. Dionne, Jr., *Why Americans Hate Politics*, 74.

25. Wikipedia contributors, "NASA Budget," http://en.wikipedia.org/wiki/NAS_Budget#Annual_budget_breakdown_through_the_years_1958-2007 (accessed September 25, 2007).

26. Wikipedia contributors, "Social Security," http://en.wikipedia.org/wiki/Social_Security_%28United_States%29#Expansion (accessed September 27, 2007).

27. Carter A. Wilson, *Racism*, 10.

28. Ibid., 177.

29. Thomas J. Sugrue, *The Origins of the Urban Crisis*, 119.

30. Ibid., 269.

31. E. J. Dionne, Jr., *Why Americans Hate Politics*, 80.

32. Mindy Thompson Fullilove, *Root Shock: How Tearing Up City Neighborhoods Hurts America* (New York: Ballantine, 2004), 4.

33. Thomas J. Sugrue, *The Origins of the Urban Crisis*, 49.

34. Ibid., 50.

35. Ibid., 47.

36. Mindy Thompson Fullilove, *Root Shock*, 144.

37. Thomas J. Sugrue, *The Origins of the Urban Crisis*, 51.

38. Ibid., 48.

39. Ibid.

40. Ibid., 42.

41. Ibid., 26.

42. Ibid., 43.

43. Ibid., 62.

44. Ibid., 95.

45. Ibid., 34.

46. The Detroit Council on Better Housing, quoted in Thomas J. Sugrue, *The Origins of the Urban Crisis*, 50.

47. Thomas J. Sugrue, *The Origins of the Urban Crisis*, 9.

48. Paul Johnson, Betty Jean Fields, Patricia Mathis, and Ted Swisher, "Analysis: Upper-Income Neighborhood Rejects Habitat for Humanity Building Houses There,"

interview by Phillip Davis, with Bob Edwards as host, *Morning Edition*, National Public Radio, 7/1/2003.

49. Ibid.

50. E. J. Dionne, Jr., *Why Americans Hate Politics*, 105.

51. Ibid., 107.

52. Arthur M. Schlesinger, Jr., "Not Right, Not Left, but a Vital Center," *The New York Times Magazine*, April 4, 1948, Section 6.

53. E. J. Dionne, Jr., *Why Americans Hate Politics*, 116–118.

54. Ibid., 336; see also 335–338.

55. Friedrich Hayek, "Is Democracy Special?" in *Democracy: Theory and Practice*, ed. John Arthur (Belmont, CA: Wadsworth, 1992), 101–102.

## Chapter 4: United We Stand and Conspiracy Thinking

1. Daniel Hellinger, "Paranoia, Conspiracy, and Hegemony in American Politics," in *Transparency and Conspiracy: Ethnographies of Suspicion in the New World Order*, ed. Harry G. West and Todd Sanders (Durham, NC, and London, UK: Duke University Press, 2003), 227.

2. Samuel P. Huntington, *The Clash of Civilizations* (New York: Free Press, 2002).

3. *Morning Edition*, National Public Radio, July 9, 2007.

4. *On Point*, National Public Radio, July 9, 2007, 10 A.M. (EST) session.

5. Mark Juergensmeyer, *Terror in the Mind of God: The Global Rise of Religious Violence* (Berkeley, CA: University of California Press, 2000), 174.

6. Ibid.

7. Cass R. Sunstein, *Why Societies Need Dissent* (Cambridge, MA: Harvard University Press, 2003).

8. Ibid., 11.

9. Ibid., 58.

10. Ibid., 112.

11. Ibid., 113–114.

12. Ibid., 5.

13. In addition to the above-cited book, see also Cass R. Sunstein, "Deliberative Trouble? Why Groups Go to Extremes," *Yale Law Journal* 110 (October 2000): 71–119.

14. Cass R. Sunstein, *Why Societies Need Dissent*, 112.

15. Robert Elegant, quoted in Edward S. Herman and Noam Chomsky, *Manufacturing Consent: The Political Economy of the Mass Media* (New York: Pantheon, 1988), 170.

16. Edward S. Herman and Noam Chomsky, *Manufacturing Consent*, 170–171.

17. Ibid.

18. Ibid., 193.

19. Peter Braestrup, *Big Story: How the American Press and Television Reported and Interpreted the Crisis of Tet 1968 in Vietnam and Washington*, 2 vols. (Boulder, CO: Westview, in cooperation with Freedom House, 1977).

20. Michael Beschloss, *Reaching for Glory: Lyndon Johnson's Secret White House Tapes, 1964–1965* (New York: Simon & Schuster, 2002).

21. Daniel Hallin, speaking at the American Media and War-Time Challenges Conference sponsored by the Triangle Institute for Security Studies, Chapel Hill, NC, March 21–22, 2003, 3, http://pubpol.duke.edu/centers/tiss/pubs/documents/Hallin.pdf (accessed September 12, 2007).

22. Ibid., 4–5.

23. David Garrow, "Reaching for Glory: Lyndon Johnson's Secret White House Tapes, 1964–65. Listening to Lyndon: the Private Agony of a President No Way Out," *Washington Monthly*, March 2002, review of Beschloss, *Reaching for Glory*, http://findarticles.com/p/articles/mi_m1316/is_200006/ai_83794465 (accessed September 22, 2007).

24. Leslie Gelb, "The Essential Domino: American Politics and Vietnam," *Foreign Affairs*, (April 1972), http://www.foreignaffairs.org (accessed October 2, 2007).

25. Walter Isaacson, *Kissinger: A Biography* (New York, NY: Simon & Schuster, 1993), Chapter 12.

26. Quoted by Glenn Greenwald, in "Terry Moran, Michael Gordon and the Mark Halperin Syndrome," Salon.com, February 11, 2007, http://www.salon.com/opinion/greenwald/2007/02/11/halperinsyndrome/ (accessed April 12, 2008); also partially quoted by Hugh Hewitt at his Townhall.com blog site, "That Was a Slander; That Wasn't an Apology," October 31, 2006, http://hughhewitt.townhall.com/blog/g/3330c64e-5520-4c8b-aa18-2cfbc24525d1 (accessed April 12, 2008).

27. Stephen Kinzer, *Overthrow: America's Century of Regime Change, from Hawaii to Iraq* (New York: Times Books, 2006), 148–165, especially 165.

28. John Prados, ed., "Introduction," *The White House Tapes: Eavesdropping on the Presidents* (New York: New Press, 2003), quoted in Stephen Kinzer, *Overthrow*, 165.

29. Stephen Kinzer, *Overthrow*, 163.

30. Luther Gulick, *Administrative Reflections from World War II* (Tuscaloosa, AL: University of Alabama Press, 1948), quotations from 124, 126, and 125 respectively.

31. Stephen T. McCarthy, October 7, 2005, customer review of Tale Brooke, *One World* (End Run Publishing, 2000), http://www.amazon.com (accessed September 17, 2007).

32. Robert Alan Goldberg, *Enemies Within: The Culture of Conspiracy in Modern America* (New Haven, CT: Yale University Press, 2001), ix.

33. Mark Fenster, *Conspiracy Theories: Secrecy and Power in American Culture* (Minneapolis, MN: University of Minnesota Press, 1999), 80.

34. G. William Domhoff, *Who Rules America*, 5th ed., (New York: McGraw-Hill, 2006).

35. Ibid., 200.

36. Daniel Hellinger, "Paranoia, Conspiracy, and Hegemony in American Politics," in *Transparency and Conspiracy*, ed. Harry G. West and Todd Sanders, 207.

37. Ibid.

38. Ibid.

39. Ibid., 211.

40. Mark Fenster, *Conspiracy Theories*, 108–117.

41. Ibid., 63–68.

42. Steven Lukes, "Power: A Radical View," in *Power: A Reader*, ed. Mark Haugaard (Manchester, UK: Manchester University Press, 2002); Michel Foucault, "Right of Death and Power Over Life," *The History of Sexuality, Volume 1: An Introduction* (New York: Vintage Books, 1980); Wendy Brown, *States of Injury: Power and Freedom in Late Modernity* (Princeton, NJ: Princeton University Press, 1995); Eric A. Schutz, *Markets and Power: The 21st Century Command Economy* (Armonk, NY: M. E. Sharpe, 2001).

43. Michel Foucault, "Right of Death and Power over Life."

44. Robert Alan Goldberg, *Enemies Within: The Culture of Conspiracy in Modern America* (New Haven, CT: Yale University Press, 2001), 260.

45. Mark Fenster, *Conspiracy Theories*, 93.

46. Ibid., 108–117.

47. Charles Murray, *What It Means to Be a Libertarian: A Personal Interpretation* (New York: Broadway Books, 1997), 59.

48. Democratic National Committee, *2004 Democratic Party Platform: Strong at Home, Respected in the World*, a9.g.akamai.net/7/9/8082/v2002/www.democrats.org/pdfs/2004 platform.pdf (accessed March 31, 2007) 13, 14, and 4 respectively; Republican National Committee, *2004 Republican Party Platform: A Safer World and a More Hopeful America*, http://www.gop.com/media/2004platform.pdf (accessed March 31, 2007), 39, 10, 5, and 7 respectively.

49. Beverly Daniel Tatum, Public Address at a "People of Color Conference," December 6, 2001, accessed through the National Association of Independent Schools (NAIS), http://www.nais.org/about/eventdoc.cfm?ItemNumber=144651 (accessed January 14, 2007). Tatum is the author of *Why Are All the Black Kids Sitting Together in the Cafeteria? A Psychologist Explains the Development of Racial Identity*, 5th ed. (New York: Basic Books, 2003).

50. Pluralism is rarely asserted by democratic theorists these days, mostly appearing as an assumption in other contexts, such as American government textbooks. One contemporary pluralist argument is that of John R. Hibbing and Elizabeth Theiss-Morse, *Stealth Democracy: Americans' Beliefs about How Government Should Work* (Cambridge, UK, New York: Cambridge University Press, 2002).

51. Mark Fenster, *Conspiracy Theories*, 69–70; Mike Davis, *City of Quartz* (London, UK: Verso, 1990), 224–260.

52. John R. Hibbing and Elizabeth Theiss-Morse, *Stealth Democracy*.

## Chapter 5: The Strange Case of the Mass Media

1. G. William Domhoff, *Who Rules America*, 5th ed., (New York, NY: McGraw-Hill, 2006), 128, 127.

2. Ibid., xvi.

3. Ibid., 123–24.

4. "Americans See Liberal Bias on TV News," *Rasmussen Reports*, July 13, 2007, http://www.rasmussenreports.com/public_content/politics/current_events/general_current_events/media/americans_see_liberal_media_bias_on_tv_news (accessed October 29, 2007).

5. Stanley Rothman and S. Robert Lichter, "Personality, Ideology and World View: A Comparison of Media and Business Elites," *British Journal of Political Science* 15(1) (January 1985): 40; see also Robert S. Lichter, Stanley Rothman, and Linda S. Lichter, *The Media Elite: America's New Power Brokers* (Bethesda, MD: Adler and Adler, 1986).

6. Stanley Rothman and S. Robert Lichter, "Personality, Ideology and World View," 47.

7. Austan Goolsbee, "Lean Left? Lean Right? News Media May Take Their Cues from Customers," *The New York Times*, December 7, 2006, http://www.nytimes.com (accessed October, 29, 2007).

8. According to one survey of the subject, some ninety corporations who spend lots of money on advertising told radio networks they worked with to not put their commercials on any of the programs of the avowedly liberal "Air America" radio production company; FAIR, "Air America Blackout," October 25 and 31, 2006, http://www.fair.org/images/BCmemo.pdf (accessed April 29, 2007).

9. For evidence in this direction, see G. William Domhoff, *Who Rules America*, and Edward S. Herman and Noam Chomsky, *Manufacturing Consent: The Political Economy of the Mass Media* (New York: Pantheon, 1988).

10. G. William Domhoff, *Who Rules America*, 127–128.

11. Matthew Gentzkow and Jesse M. Shapiro, "What Drives Media Slant? Evidence from U.S. Daily Newspapers," National Bureau of Economic Research, November 2006 http://www.nber.org/papers/w12707.pdf (accessed January 28, 2007).

12. "Americans See Liberal Bias on TV News," http://www.rasmussenreports.com (accessed October 29, 2007).

13. Bernard Goldberg, *Bias: A CBS Insider Exposes How the Media Distort the News* (New York: Harper Paperbacks, 2003).

14. Marke D. Watts, David Domke, Dhavan V. Shah, and David P. Pan, "Elite Cues and Media Bias in Presidential Campaigns: Explaining Public Perceptions of a Liberal Press," *Communications Research* 26(2) (1999): 144.

15. G. William Domhoff, *Who Rules America*, 128.

16. William E. Connolly, *Pluralism* (Durham, NC: Duke University Press, 2005), 25.

17. Ibid., 26.

18. Ibid., 4.

19. Ibid., 4, 64, and 81 respectively.

20. Laura Chasin, Anne Fowler, Frances Hogan, Melisa Kogut, and Madeline McComish, "Interview: Members of the Public Conversations Project Discuss Their Group's Series of Confidential Conversations about the Issue of Abortion," interview by Margot Adler, *All Things Considered*, National Public Radio, January 19, 2003.

21. All the quotations in this paragraph are from Thomas E. Patterson, *Out of Order* (New York: Alfred A. Knopf, 1993), 180.

22. Ibid., 176.

23. Ibid., 180 and 181.

24. Ibid., 17.

25. Ibid., 181.

26. "President Discusses the Economy in Kentucky," February 26, 2004, http://www.whitehouse.gov/news/releases/2004/02/20040226-3.html (accessed October 20, 2007). Also, on March 4th Bush sat in a high chair "alongside five small-business workers" and likewise communicated with the people; "Bush, on 'Talk Show,' Discusses Jobs," *Watertown Daily Times*, March 5, 2004, A1.

27. "Bush, on 'Talk Show,' Discusses Jobs," *Watertown Daily Times*, March 5, 2004, A1.

28. Craig Calhoun, "Introduction: Habermas and the Public Sphere," *Habermas and the Public Sphere*, ed. Craig Calhoun (Cambridge, MA: MIT Press, 1992), 29.

29. Michael Warner, 1992, "The Mass Public and the Mass Subject," *Habermas and the Public Sphere*, ed. Craig Calhoun, 379.

30. Foreign Policy Association, *Great Decisions*, brochure (New York: Foreign Policy Association, 2003); see also http://www.fpa.org (accessed November 23, 2003).

31. See http://www.fpa.org/newsletter_info2496/newsletter_info.htm (accessed November 23, 2003).

32. See http://www.fpa.org, from a January 30, 2003 interview with Dr. Milhollin (accessed November 23, 2003).

33. http://www.fpa.org, from a January 30, 2003 interview with Dr. Kupchan (accessed November 23, 2003).

34. http://www.jointhedebate.org/ (accessed November 23, 2003).

35. http://www.jointhedebate.org/ (accessed November 23, 2003).

36. http://www.afsc.org. (accessed November 23, 2003).

37. Deborah Tannen, *The Argument Culture: Stopping America's War of Words* (New York: Ballantine Books, 1998), 5.

38. Al Gore, *The Assault on Reason* (New York: Penguin, 2007), 260.

39. Daniel Yankelovich, *The Magic of Dialogue: Transforming Conflict into Cooperation* (New York: Simon & Schuster, 1999), 43.

## Chapter 6: Democracy as Conversation

1. John Dewey, *The Public and Its Problems* (Denver, CO: Swallow Press, 1927), 216.

2. Dmitri Nikulin, *On Dialogue* (Lanham, MD: Lexington Books, 2005), xi.

3. Bruce Ackerman and James Fishkin, *Deliberation Day* (New Haven, CT: Yale University Press, 2004), 3.

4. Bruce Ackerman and James S. Fishkin, "Deliberation Day," in *Debating Deliberative Democracy*, eds. James S. Fishkin and Peter Laslett (Hoboken, NJ: Wiley, 2003), 7, 11–12.

5. Ibid.

6. John Rawls, *A Theory of Justice* (Boston, MA: Belknap Press, 2005).

7. Jürgen Habermas, *The Structural Transformation of the Public Sphere*, trans. Thomas Burger (Cambridge, MA: Polity Press, 1989); see also *Between Facts and Norms: Contributions to a Discourse Theory of Law and Democracy*, trans. William Rehg(Cambridge, MA: MIT Press, 1996) and "The Public Sphere," *New German Critique* 3 (1974): 49.

8. Amy Gutmann and Dennis Thompson, *Why Deliberative Democracy?* (Princeton, NJ: Princeton University Press, 2004), 141.

9. Ibid., 13–17.

10. Fareed Zakaria, *The Future of Freedom: Illiberal Democracy at Home and Abroad* (W. W. Norton & Company, 2004).

11. Ibid., Chapter 5, "Too Much of a Good Thing," and throughout.

12. Ibid., 169.

13. Ibid., Chapter 5, "Too Much of a Good Thing."

14. See Theda Skocpol, *Diminished Democracy: From Membership to Management in American Civic Life* (Norman, OK: University of Oklahoma Press, 2003), 13; William E. Hudson, *American Democracy in Peril: Eight Challenges to America's Future* (Washington, DC: CQ Press, 2004).

15. John Dryzeck, *Deliberative Democracy and Beyond: Liberals, Critics, Contestations* (New York: Oxford University Press, 2002), 1, 2, respectively.

16. Amy Gutmann and Dennis Thompson, *Why Deliberative Democracy?*, 11.

17. Ibid., 33.

18. Ibid., 7.

19. Ethan J. Leib, *Deliberative Democracy in America: A Proposal for a Popular Branch of Government* (University Park, PA: Penn State University Press, 2004), 4.

20. Ibid., 39.

21. John Dryzeck, *Deliberative Democracy and Beyond*, 171.

22. Amy Gutmann and Dennis Thompson, *Why Deliberative Democracy?*, 26–28.

23. Michael Sandel, *Democracy's Discontent*, (Cambridge, MA: Harvard University Press, 1996).

24. Amy Gutmann and Dennis Thompson, *Why Deliberative Democracy?*, 29.

25. Nancy Fraser, "Rethinking the Public Sphere," in *Justice Interruptus: Critical Reflections on the "Postsocialist" Condition* (New York: Routledge, 1997), 70.

26. For general discussion of the self-developmental potential of democracy, see Samuel Bowles and Herbert Gintis, *Democracy and Capitalism: Property, Community, and the Contradictions of Modern Social Thought* (New York: Basic Books, 1986); Mark Warren, "Democratic Theory and Self-Transformation," *American Political Science Review* 86 (1992): 8–23.

27. Nicholas Garnham, "The Media and the Public Sphere," in *Habermas and the Public Sphere*, ed. Craig Calhoun (Cambridge, MA: MIT Press, 1992), 371.

28. Harry C. Boyte, "The Pragmatic Ends of Popular Politics," in *Habermas and the Public Sphere*, ed. Craig Calhoun (Cambridge, MA: MIT Press, 1992), 351.

29. Lizabeth Cohen, *A Consumers' Republic: The Politics of Mass Consumption in Postwar America* (New York: Alfred. A. Knopf, 2003).

30. Craig Calhoun, "Introduction: Habermas and the Public Sphere," in *Habermas and the Public Sphere*, ed. Calhoun, Craig (Cambridge, MA: MIT Press, 1992), 30.

31. Matthew A. Crenson and Benjamin Ginsberg, *Downsizing Democracy: How America Sidelined Its Citizens and Privatized Its Public* (Baltimore, MD: Johns Hopkins University Press, 2002), 234.

32. See, for example, Peter Muhlberger, "Report to the Deliberative Democracy Consortium: Building a Deliberation Measurement Toolbox," Deliberative Democracy Consortium, 2006, Washington, DC, 1–51; National Coalition for Dialogue and Deliberation, http://thataway.org/exchange/resources.php?action=view&rid=2163 (accessed January 31, 2007).

33. John R. Hibbing and Elizabeth Theiss-Morse, *Stealth Democracy: Americans' Beliefs about How Government Should Work* (New York: Cambridge University Press, 2002), 157.

34. Ibid., 158.

35. Ibid., 105.

36. Ibid., 141.

37. Ibid., 5.

38. Ibid., 212.

39. Ibid., 225.

40. Ibid., 5.

41. On the other hand, bonding capital has, at times in American history, supported political participation. See Theda Skocpol, *Diminished Democracy*, 12.

42. John R. Hibbing and Elizabeth Theiss-Morse, *Stealth Democracy*, 186.

43. Ibid., 5.

44. Ibid., 184.

45. Nancy Fraser, "Rethinking the Public Sphere," *Justice Interruptus*.

46. Peter Muhlberger, "Stealth Democracy: Authoritarianism, Parochial Citizens and Deliberation," Draft, published in the ACM International Conference Proceedings 4 (2007), htpp://portal.acm.org/dl.cfm (accessed September 20, 2007).

47. John R. Hibbing and Elizabeth Theiss-Morse, *Stealth Democracy*, 3.

48. Ibid., 9.

49. Steven Macedo, *Democracy at Risk: How Political Choice Undermine Citizen Participation and What We Can Do About It* (Washington, DC: Brookings Institution Press, 2005), 2.

50. Ibid., 3.

51. John R. Hibbing and Elizabeth Theiss-Morse, *Stealth Democracy*, 201–207.

52. Mark Warren, "The Self in Discursive Democracy," in *The Cambridge Companion to Habermas*, ed. Stephen K. White (New York: Cambridge University Press, 1995).

53. John R. Hibbing and Elizabeth Theiss-Morse, *Stealth Democracy*, 199.

54. Ibid., 187.

55. Peter Muhlberger, "Stealth Democracy," 1.

56. Ibid., 6–9; Shawn W. Rosenberg, *Reason, Ideology, and Politics* (Princeton, NJ: Princeton University Press, 1988); Shawn W. Rosenberg, *The Not So Common Sense: Differences in How People Judge Social and Political Life* (New Haven, CT: Yale University Press, 2002).

57. Peter Muhlberger, "Stealth Democracy," 5.

58. Ibid., 7.

59. Ibid., 8.

60. Ibid., 5.

61. Ibid., 1.

62. Ibid., 19.

63. Ibid., 21.

64. Ibid., 10.

65. Ibid., 30.

66. Ibid., 30.

67. Ibid., 36.

68. Ibid., 39.

69. See, for example, Peter Muhlberger, "Report to the Deliberative Democracy Consortium," 1–51.

70. Vincent Price, Joseph N. Cappella, and Lilach Nir, "Does Disagreement Contribute to More Deliberative Opinion?" *Political Communication* 19 (2002): 96.

71. Ibid.," 98.

72. John R. Hibbing and Elizabeth Theiss-Morse, *Stealth Democracy*, 192.

73. Ibid., 193.

74. Ibid., 195.

75. R. Michael Alvarez and John Brehm, *Hard Choices, Easy Answers: Values, Information, and American Public Opinion* (Princeton, NJ: Princeton University Press, 2002); see also John Gastil, "How Balanced Discussion Shapes Knowledge, Public Perceptions, and Attitudes: A Case Study of Deliberation on the Los Alamos National Laboratory," *Journal of Public Deliberation* 2 (2006), http://services.bepress.com/jpd/vol2/iss1/art4 (accessed March 22, 2007).

76. R. Michael Alvarez and John Brehm, *Hard Choices*, 9.

77. Ibid., 123.

78. Philip E. Tetlock, *Expert Political Judgment: How Good Is It? How Can We Know?* (Princeton, NJ: Princeton University Press, 2005).

79. Ibid., 2.

80. John R. Hibbing and Elizabeth Theiss-Morse, *Stealth Democracy*, 5.

81. Ibid., 222.

82. Ibid., 223.

83. Ibid., 6.

84. Alan Wolfe, "What Does New Partisanship Mean?" *Watertown Daily Times*, July 26, 2004, A5.

85. Donald Green, Bradley Palmquist, and Eric Shickler, *Partisan Hearts and Minds: Political Parties and the Social Idenitities of Voters* (New Haven, CT: Yale University Press, 2002), 11.

86. Morris P. Fiorina, with Samuel J. Abrams and Jeremy C. Pope, *Culture War? The Myth of a Polarized America*, 2nd ed. (Upper Saddle River, NJ: Pearson Education, 2006).

87. Andrew Jacobs, "Bush vs. Kerry Ignites Battles over Dinner and the TV," *The New York Times*, July 25, 2004, http://www.nytimes.com (accessed August 22, 2004).

88. "As Political Debate Heats Up at Office, Workers, Bosses Must Tread Lightly," *Watertown Daily Times*, July 25, 2004, E2.

89. Shelby Steele, *A Dream Deferred: The Second Betrayal of Black Freedom in America* (New York: HarperCollins, 1998).

90. Tom De Luca and John Buell, *Liars! Cheaters! Evildoers!: Demonization and the End of Civil Debate in American Politics* (New York: New York University, 2005), 21.

91. Ibid., 27.

92. George Lakoff, *Moral Politics: How Liberals and Conservatives Think*, 2nd ed. (Chicago, IL: University of Chicago Press, 1996).

93. Ibid., 18.

94. Al Gore, *The Assault on Reason* (New York: Penguin, 2007), 259.

95. Ibid., 7.

96. Ibid., 11.

97. Ibid., 9.

98. Ibid., 16.

99. Ibid., 32.

100. Ibid., 29.

101. Ibid., 41.

102. Ibid., 62.

103. Ibid., 10.

104. Ibid., 22.

105. Ibid., 10.

106. Ibid.

107. Ibid., 13.

## Chapter 7: Multiculturalism with Principle

1. Bruce A. Jacobs, *Race Manners: Navigating the Minefield Between Black and White Americans* (New York: Arcade Publishing, 1999), 151.

2. An argument of Mikhail Bakhtin, as summarized by Aileen M. Kelly, *Views from the Other Shore: Essays on Herzen, Chekhov, and Bakhtin* (New Haven, CT: Yale University Press, 1999), 195–196.

3. William E. Connolly, "Drugs, the Nation and Free-Lancing: Decoding the Moral Universe of William Bennett," *Theory & Event* 1(1) (1997), http://muse.jhu.edu/journals/theory_and_event/v001/1.1connolly.html (accessed October 21, 2007).

4. Shelby Steele, *A Dream Deferred: The Second Betrayal of Black Freedom in America* (New York: HarperCollins, 1998).

5. Iris Marion Young, *Justice and the Politics of Difference* (Princeton, NJ: Princeton University Press, 1990).

6. Bruce A. Jacobs, *Race Manners*, 2.

7. Arthur M. Schlesinger, Jr., *The Disuniting of America*, rev. ed. (New York: W. W. Norton, 1992).

8. Ibid., 142.

9. Ibid., 123.

10. Ibid., 142.

11. Philip Tetlock, *Expert Political Judgment: How Good Is It? How Can We Know?* (Princeton, NJ: Princeton University Press, 2005), 3.

12. Bruce, Tammy, *The Death of Right and Wrong: Exposing the Left's Assault on Our Culture and Values* (Roseville, CA: Forum, 2003).

13. William J. Bennett, *The Devaluing of America* (New York: Touchstone, 1992), 22, 59–60.

14. William E. Connolly, "Drugs, the Nation."

15. William J. Bennett, *The Devaluing of America*, 52.

16. Ibid., 26.

17. Ibid., 13.

18. Ibid., 26. Bennett quotes Stanley Rothman, S. Robert Lichter, and Linda Lichter, *Elites in Conflict: Social Change in America Today* (Westport, CT: Praeger, 1992).

19. William J. Bennett, *The Devaluing of America*, 27.

20. Ibid., 28.

21. Ibid., 31.

22. William E.Connolly, "Drugs, the Nation," para. 16.

23. Ibid., para. 29.

24. William E. Connolly, *Pluralism* (Durham, NC: Duke University Press, 2005), 64.

25. John Bodnar, "Introduction: The Attractions of Patriotism," *Bonds of Affection: Americans Define Their Patriotism*, ed. John Bodnar (Princeton, NJ: Princeton University Press, 1996), 7.

26. Ibid., 11.

27. Ibid.

28. Ibid.

29. Arthur M. Schlesinger, Jr., *The Disuniting of America.*

30. Seyla Benhabib, *The Claims of Culture: Equality and Diversity in the Global Era* (Princeton, NJ: Princeton University Press, 2002), ix.

31. Ibid., 18.

32. Bonnie Honig, *Political Theory and the Displacement of Politics* (Ithaca, NY: Cornell University Press, 1993) quoted in Benhabib, *The Claims of Culture: Equality and Diversity in the Global Era* (Princeton, NJ: Princeton University Press, 2002), 258.

33. Seyla Benhabib, *The Claims of Culture*, x.

34. Ibid.

35. Ibid., 102, 106, 131–132.

## Chapter 8: Disagreement Practice

1. Jürgen Habermas, "The Public Sphere," *New German Critique* 3 (1974): 49.

2. Janette Hartz-Karp, "The Case for Deliberative Democracy," in *Insight: Reclaiming Democracy* (Sydney, AU: Centre for Policy Development, November 2007), http://cpd.org.au/insight/reclaiming-democracy (accessed January 3, 2008).

3. Matt Leighninger, *The Next Form of Democracy: How Expert Rule Is Giving Way to Shared Governance—And Why Politics Will Never Be the Same* (Nashville, TN: Vanderbilt University Press, 2006).

4. Francis Moore Lappé, *Democracy's Edge: Choosing to Save Our Country by Bringing Democracy to Life* (Hoboken, NJ: Jossey-Bass, 2006).

5. See http://www.studycircles.org (accessed January 4, 2008).

6. National Coalition on Dialogue and Deliberation, http://www.thataway.org/exchange/search.php?q=study+circles&search=Search (accessed January 3, 2008).

7. Julie Fanselow, *What Democracy Looks Like: Kuna, Idaho, where a Community Pulls Together to Face Growth* (East Hartford, CT: Everyday Democracy, 2004), 2.

8. Ibid.

9. Ibid., 3.

10. Ibid., 4.

11. Ibid.

12. Ibid.

13. Ibid., 5.

14. Ibid., 6.

15. Mark Mazetti, "U.S. Says Iran Ended Atomic Arms Work," *The New York Times*, December 3, 2007, http://www.nytimes.com/2007/12/03/world/middleeast/03cnd-iran.html (accessed January 6, 2008).

16. Dafna Linzer and Joby Warrick, "U.S. Finds That Iran Halted Nuclear Arms Bid in 2003," *The Washington Post*, December 4, 2007, http://www.washingtonpost.com/wp-dyn/content/article/2007/12/03/AR2007120300846.html (accessed on January 17, 2008).

17. National Issues Forums, "About NIF Forums," http://www.nifi.org/forums/about.aspx (accessed January 22, 2008).

18. National Issues Forums, "About Us," http://www.nifi.org/about/index.aspx (accessed 1/22/08).

19. William Molnar, "Dorchester County Growth Forum Report, January 31, 2006," Laboratory for Deliberative Dialogue, Clemson Institute for Economic and Community Development, National Issues Forums, http://www.nifi.org/reports/forums.aspx (accessed January 22, 2008).

20. Ibid., 1.

21. Ibid., 3.

22. Ibid., 5.

23. Ibid., 4.

24. Ibid., 7.

25. Ibid., 4–5.

26. Ibid., 10.

27. Carnegie Foundation for the Advancement of Teaching, "The Political Engagement Project," http://www.carnegiefoundation.org/programs/index.asp?key=25 (accessed January 14, 2008); Anne Colby, Thomas Ehrlich, Elizabeth Beaumont, and Jason Stephens, *Educating Citizens: Preparing America's Undergraduates for Lives of Moral and Civic Responsibility* (San Francisco: Jossey-Bass, 2003).

28. Anne Colby, Thomas Ehrlich, Elizabeth Beaumont, and Jason Stephens, *Educating Citizens*, 11.

29. Ibid., 134.

30. Ibid., 125.

31. Ibid., 225.

32. American Association of Colleges and Universities, Center for Liberal Education and Civic Engagement, "The National Dialogue Project: Institutional Profiles," http://www.aacu.org/civic_engagement/project_descriptions.cfm#StLawrence (accessed January 28, 2008).

33. Ibid.

34. Ibid.

35. Ibid.

36. Anne Colby, Thomas Ehrlich, Elizabeth Beaumont, and Jason Stephens, *Educating Citizens*, 250.

37. Ibid., 54.

38. Ibid., 247.

39. Carnegie Foundation for the Advancement of Teaching, "The Political Engagement Project," http://www.carnegiefoundation.org/programs/sub.asp?key=25&subkey=546&topkey=25 (accessed January 14, 2008).

40. Anne Colby, Thomas Ehrlich, Elizabeth Beaumont, and Jason Stephens, *Educating Citizens*, 158.

41. R. M. Battistoni, "Democracy, Learning, and Power: Reflections from the Margins of Academic Political Science," paper presented at the annual meeting of the American Political Science Association, Washington, DC., 2000, quoted in Anne Colby, Thomas Ehrlich, Elizabeth Beaumont, and Jason Stephens, *Educating Citizens*, 158.

42. Carnegie Foundation for the Advancement of Teaching, "The Political Engagement Project," http://www.carnegiefoundation.org/programs/sub.asp?key=25&subkey=546&topkey=25 (accessed January 14, 2008).

43. Anne Colby, Thomas Ehrlich, Elizabeth Beaumont, and Jason Stephens, *Educating Citizens*, 159.

44. Ibid., 114, citing L. J. Sax, "Citizenship Development and the American College Student," in *Civic Responsibility and Higher Education*, ed. T. Ehrlich (Phoenix, AZ: Oryx Press, 1999), 3–18.

45. Evan Osnos, "Saudi Leaders Seek Reforms to Quiet Extremists," *Watertown Daily Times*, Saturday, November 29, 2003, A4.

46. Inside Cover, *"Groups Protest Ahmadinejad,"* *Newsmax.com, September 23, 2007*, http://www.newsmax.com/insidecover/U.N._Protest_Ahmadinejad/2007/09/23/35060.html (accessed January 7, 2008).

47. Paul Krugman, "A Willful Ignorance," *The New York Times*, October 28, 2003, op-ed, http://query.nytimes.com/gst/fullpage.html?res=9C0DE6DE1E31F93BA15753 C1A9659C8B63&scp=3&sq=Paul+Krugman+%22A+Willful+Ignorance%22&st= nyt (accessed April 13, 2008).

48. Ibid.

49. Mark Juergensmeyer, *Terror in the Mind of God: The Global Rise of Religious Violence* (Berkeley, CA: University of California Press, 2000), xii.

50. Ibid., 12, 190.

51. Ibid., 225.

52. Ibid., 115–116.

53. Ibid., 196.

54. Ibid., 201.

55. See Abdolkarim Soroush's "Official Web Site," http://www.drsoroush.com/English.htm (accessed January 19, 2008).

56. Mark Juergensmeyer, *Terror in the Mind of God*, 236.

57. Ibid., 241.

58. Ibid., 174.

59. Ibid., 184–186; see also 54–55, 115–116.

60. Ibid., 225.

61. Ibid., 139.

62. Ibid., 148.

63. Stephen L. Carter, *God's Name in Vain: The Wrongs and Rights of Religion in Politics* (New York: Basic Books, 2000), 1.

64. Ibid.

65. "We Can Talk It Out: NYU Students Broach Middle East Conflict through Dialogue," *Washington Square News*, February 24, 2003, http://traubman.igc.org/messages/320.htm (accessed January 6, 2008).

66. Jeff Gerritt, "Seeds of Change," *Detroit Free Press*, August 2, 2002, http://www.seedsofpeace.org/node/1957 (accessed January 20, 2008).

67. Ibid.

68. Ibid.

69. "We Can Talk It Out," *Washington Square News*.

70. Ibid.

71. "Constructive Conversations That Reach across Differences," Public Conversations Project, http://www.publicconversations.org/pcp/page.php?id=244&catid=66 (accessed January 6, 2008).

72. *Gallup Poll Social Audit, Black/White Social Relations in the United States: 1997* (Princeton, NJ: The Gallup Organization, 1997); Jennifer L. Hochschild, *Facing Up to the American Dream: Race, Class, and the Soul of the Nation* (Princeton, NJ: Princeton University Press, 1995).

73. Shelby Steele, *A Dream Deferred: The Second Betrayal of Black Freedom in America* (New York: HarperCollins, 1998).

74. Bruce A. Jacobs, *Race Manners: Navigating the Minefield Between Black and White Americans* (New York: Arcade, 1999), 20.

75. Ibid., 173.

76. Ibid., 161.

77. Glenn C. Loury, *The Anatomy of Racial Inequality* (Boston, MA: Harvard University Press, 2002), 29–30.

78. Bruce A. Jacobs, *Race Manners*, 169.

79. Ibid., 75–79.

## Chapter 9: Freedom and Disagreement

1. An argument of Mikhail Bakhtin, as summarized by Aileen M. Kelly, *Views from the Other Shore: Essays on Herzen, Chekhov, and Bakhtin* (New Haven, CT: Yale University Press, 1999), 195–196.

2. Alan Wolfe, *Moral Freedom: The Search for Virtue in a World of Choice* (New York: W. W. Norton, 2001), 195.

3. Michael J. Sandel, "The Politics of Public Identity," *The Hedgehog Review* 2(1) (Spring 2000): 72–88.

4. Nicholas Garnham, "The Media and the Public Sphere," in *Habermas and the Public Sphere*, ed. Craig Calhoun (Cambridge, MA: MIT Press, 1992), 367.

5. Dmitri Nikulin, *On Dialogue* (Lanham, MD: Lexington Books, 2005), xi.

# Bibliography

Ackerman, Bruce, and James S. Fishkin. *Deliberation Day*. New Haven, CT: Yale University Press, 2004.

Ahmed, Akbar, and Brian Forst. *After Terror: Promoting Dialogue Among Civilizations*. Boston: Polity, 2005.

Alvarez, R. Michael, and John Brehm. *Hard Choices, Easy Answers: Values, Information, and American Public Opinion*. Princeton, NJ: Princeton University Press, 2002.

Atlee, Tom. *The Tao of Democracy: Using Co-Intelligence to Create a World That Works for All*. Revised Edition. Cranston, RI: The Writers' Collective, 2003.

Barber, Benjamin R. *A Place for Us: How to Make Society Civil and Democracy Strong*. New York: Hill and Wang, 1998.

Battistoni, Richard, and William E. Hudson, eds. *Experiencing Citizenship: Concepts and Models for Service-Learning in Political Science*. Sterling, VA: Stylus, 1997.

Bellah, Robert N., Richard Madsen, William M. Sullivan, Ann Swidler, and Steven M. Tipton. *Habits of the Heart: Individualism and Commitment in American Life*. Berkeley, CA: University of California Press, 1985.

Benhabib, Seyla. *The Claims of Culture: Equality and Diversity in the Global Era*. Princeton, NJ: Princeton University Press, 2002.

Blattberg, Charles. *From Pluralist to Patriotic Politics*. New York: Oxford University Press, 2000.

Bobo, Lawrence D. "What Do We Think about Race?" In *One America in the 21st Century: The President's Initiative on Race*, 1998. Available at http://clinton2.nara.gov/Initiatives/OneAmerica/bobo.html (accessed August 14, 2007).

Bodnar, John, ed. *Bonds of Affection: Americans Define Their Patriotism*. Princeton, NJ: Princeton University Press, 1996.

Bohm, David. *On Dialogue*. New York: Routledge, 1996.

Bohman, James. *Public Deliberation: Pluralism, Complexity, and Democracy*. Cambridge, MA: MIT Press, 1996.

Bohman, James, and William Rehg, eds. *Deliberative Democracy: Essays on Reason and Politics*. Cambridge, MA: MIT Press, 1997.

Bonilla-Silva, Eduardo. *Racism without Racists: Color-Blind Racism and the Persistence of Racial Inequality in the United States*. Lanham, MD: Rowman & Littlefield, 2006.

Boorstin, Daniel J. *The Americans: The Colonial Experience*. New York: Random House, 1958.

———. *The Americans: The Democratic Experience*. New York: Random House, 1973.

———. *The Americans: The National Experience*. New York: Random House, 1965.

Boyte, Harry C. "The Pragmatic Ends of Popular Politics." In *Habermas and the Public Sphere*, edited by Craig Calhoun. Cambridge, MA: MIT Press, 1992.

Boyte, Harry C., and Sara Margaret Evans. *Free Spaces: The Sources of Democratic Change in America*. Chicago, IL: University of Chicago Press, 1992.

Braestrup, Peter. *Big Story: How the American Press and Television Reported and Interpreted the Crisis of Tet 1968 in Vietnam and Washington*. 2 vols. Boulder, CO, and Washington, DC: Westview/Freedom House, 1977.

Bruce, Tammy. *The Death of Right and Wrong: Exposing the Left's Assault on Our Culture and Values*. Roseville, CA: Forum, 2003.

Campbell, David. "Cold Wars: Securing Identity, Identifying Danger." In *Rhetorical Republic: Governing Representations in American Politics*, edited by Frederick M. Dolan and Thomas L. Dumm. Amherst, MA: University of Massachusetts Press, 1993.

Carroll, James. *House of War: The Pentagon and the Disastrous Rise in American Power*. New York: Houghton Mifflin, 2006.

Carter, Stephen L. *God's Name in Vain: The Wrongs and Rights of Religion in Politics*. New York: Basic Books, 2000.

Center for Liberal Education and Civic Engagement. *National Dialogue Project: Journey Towards Democracy: Power, Voice, and the Public Good*. Association of American Colleges and Universities, 2005. Available at http://www.aacu.org/civic_engagement/ projects.cfm (accessed April 13, 2008).

Cobb, John B., Jr. "Defining Normative Community." In *Rooted in the Land: Essays on Community and Place*, edited by Bill Vitek and Wes Jackson. New Haven, CT, and London, UK: Yale University Press, 1996.

Cohen, Lizabeth. *A Consumers' Republic: The Politics of Mass Consumption in Postwar America*. New York: Alfred A. Knopf, 2003.

Colby, Anne, Thomas Ehrlich, Elizabeth Beaumont, and Jason Stephens. *Educating Citizens: Preparing America's Undergraduates for Lives of Moral and Civic Responsibility*. San Francisco: Jossey-Bass, 2003.

Connolly, William E. "Free-Lancing: Decoding the Moral Universe of William Bennett." *Theory & Event* 1(1) (1997). Available at http://muse.jhu.edu/journals/theory_&_ event (accessed April 13, 2008).

———. *Pluralism*. Durham, NC: Duke University, 2005.

*Constructive Conversations about Challenging Times: A Guide to Community Dialogue*. Version 3.0. Public Conversations Project, 2003. Available at http://www. publicconversations.org/pcp/uploadDocs/CommunityGuide3.0.pdf (accessed April 13, 2008).

Coulter, Ann. *Treason: Liberal Treachery from the Cold War to the War on Terrorism*. New York: Crown Forum, 2003.

Crenson, Matthew A., and Benjamin Ginsberg. *Downsizing Democracy: How America Sidelined Its Citizens and Privatized Its Public*. Baltimore, MD: Johns Hopkins University Press, 2002.

DeLuca, Tom, and John Buell. *Liars! Cheaters! Evildoers!: Demonization and the End of Civil Debate in American Politics.* New York: New York University Press, 2005.

DeMott, Benjamin. *The Trouble With Friendship: Why Americans Can't Think Straight About Race.* New Haven, CT: Yale University Press, 1998.

Dewey, John. *The Public and Its Problems.* Denver, CO: Swallow Press, 1927.

Dionne, E. J., Jr. *Why Americans Hate Politics.* New York: Touchstone, 1991.

Domhoff, G. William. *Who Rules America.* Fifth Edition. New York: McGraw-Hill, 2006.

Dryzeck, John. *Deliberative Democracy and Beyond: Liberals, Critics, Contestations.* New York: Oxford University Press, 2002.

Edsall, Thomas Byrne, with Mary D. Edsall. *Chain Reaction: The Impact of Race, Rights, and Taxes on American Politics.* New York: W. W. Norton & Company, 1992.

Etzioni, Amitai. *Monochrome Society.* Princeton, NJ: Princeton University Press, 2001.

Fanselow, Julie. *What Democracy Looks Like: Kuna, Idaho, Where a Community Pulls Together to Face Growth.* East Hartford, CT: Everyday Democracy, Copyright by The Paul J. Aicher Foundation, 2004.

Farr, James. "Social Capital: A Conceptual History." *Political Theory* 32(1) (February 2004): 6–33.

Fenster, Mark. *Conspiracy Theories: Secrecy and Power in American Culture.* Minneapolis, MN: University of Minnesota Press, 1999.

Fiorina, Morris P., with Samuel J. Abrams and Jeremy C. Pope. *Culture War? The Myth of a Polarized America.* Second edition. Upper Saddle River, NJ: Pearson Education, 2006.

Fraser, Nancy. *Justice Interruptus: Critical Reflections on the "Postsocialist" Condition.* New York, NY: Routledge, 1997.

Fullilove, Mindy Thompson. *Root Shock: How Tearing Up City Neighborhoods Hurts America.* New York, NY: Ballantine, 2004.

Gabler, Neal. *Life the Movie: How Entertainment Conquered Reality.* New York: Vintage Books, 2000.

Garnham, Nicholas. "The Media and the Public Sphere." In *Habermas and the Public Sphere,* edited by Craig Calhoun. Cambridge, MA: MIT Press, 1992.

Gates, Henry Louis, Jr. "Beyond the Culture Wars: Identities in Dialogue." *Profession* 93 (1993): 6–11.

Gentzkow, Matthew Aaron, and Jesse M. Shapiro. "What Drives Media Slant? Evidence from U.S. Daily Newspapers" (November 13, 2006). Available at http://ssrn.com/abstract=947640 (accessed April 13, 2008).

Gibian, Peter. *Oliver Wendell Holmes and the Culture of Conversation.* New York, : Cambridge University Press, 2001.

Goolsbee, Austan. "Lean Left? Lean Right? News Media May Take Their Cues from Customers." *The New York Times* (December 7, 2006). Available at http://www.nytimes.com/2006/12/07/ business/media/07scene.html?_r=1&oref=slogin (accessed April 13, 2008).

Gordon, Mary. *Roots of Empathy: Changing the World, Child by Child.* Markham, ON, Canada: Thomas Allen, 2005.

Gore, Al. *The Assault on Reason.* New York: Penguin, 2007.

Green, Donald, Bradley Palmquist, and Eric Shickler. *Partisan Hearts and Minds: Political Parties and the Social Identities of Voters.* New Haven, CT: Yale University Press, 2002.

Gulick, Luther. *Administrative Reflections from World War II.* Tuscaloosa, AL: University of Alabama Press, 1948.

Gutmann, Amy, and Dennis Thompson. *Why Deliberative Democracy?* Princeton, NJ: Princeton University Press, 2004.

Habermas, Jürgen. *The Structural Transformation of the Public Sphere*, translated by Thomas Burger. Cambridge, MA: Polity Press, 1989.

Harrison, Bennett, and Barry Bluestone. *The Great U-Turn: Corporate Restructuring and the Polarization of America*. New York: Basic Books, 1990.

Hartz-Karp, Janette. "The Case for Deliberative Democracy." In *Insight: Reclaiming Democracy*. November 2007. Available at http://cpd.org.au/insight/reclaiming-democracy (accessed January 3, 2008).

Hayek, Friedrich. "Is Democracy Special?" In *Democracy: Theory and Practice*, edited by John Arthur. Belmont, CA: Wadsworth, 1992.

Herman, Edward S., and Noam Chomsky. *Manufacturing Consent: The Political Economy of the Mass Media*. New York: Pantheon, 1988.

Hibbing, John R., and Elizabeth Theiss-Morse. *Stealth Democracy: Americans' Beliefs about How Government Should Work*. New York: Cambridge University Press, 2002.

Hochschild, Jennifer L. *Facing Up to the American Dream: Race, Class, and the Soul of the Nation*. Princeton, NJ: Princeton University Press, 1995.

Honig, Bonnie. *Political Theory and the Displacement of Politics*. Ithaca, NY: Cornell University Press, 1993.

Howe, Frederic. *The Confessions of a Reformer*. Reprint. New York: Quadrangle Books, 1967.

Hudson, William E. *American Democracy in Peril: Eight Challenges to America's Future*. Washington, DC: CQ Press, 2004.

Huntington, Samuel P. *The Clash of Civilizations*. New York: Free Press, 2002.

———. *Political Order in Changing Societies*. New Haven, CT: Yale University Press, 1969.

Jacobs, Bruce A. *Race Manners: Navigating the Minefield between Black and White Americans*. New York: Arcade, 1999.

Janis, Irving. *Group Think*. Second edition. Boston: Houghton Mifflin, 1982.

Juergensmeyer, Mark. *Terror in the Mind of God: The Global Rise of Religious Violence*. Berkeley, CA: University of California Press, 2000.

Karnow, Stanley. *Vietnam: A History*. New York: Penguin, 1991.

Kinzer, Stephen. *Overthrow: America's Century of Regime Change, from Hawaii to Iraq*. New York: Times Books, 2006.

Lakoff, George. *Moral Politics: How Liberals and Conservatives Think*. Second edition. Chicago, IL: University of Chicago Press, 2002.

Lappé, Francis Moore. *Democracy's Edge: Choosing to Save Our Country by Bringing Democracy to Life*. San Francisco, CA: Jossey-Bass, 2006.

Leib, Ethan J. *Deliberative Democracy in America: A Proposal for a Popular Branch of Government*. University Park, PA: Penn State University Press, 2004.

Leighninger, Matt. *The Next Form of Democracy: How Expert Rule Is Giving Way to Shared Governance—And Why Politics Will Never Be the Same*. Nashville, TN: Vanderbilt University Press, 2006.

Loury, Glenn C. *The Anatomy of Racial Inequality*. Boston: Harvard University Press, 2002.

Lowi, Theodore J. *The End of Liberalism: The Second Republic of the United States*. New York: W. W. Norton & Company, 1979.

Lukes, Steven. "Power: A Radical View." In *Power: A Reader*, edited by Mark Haugaard. Manchester, UK: Manchester University Press, 2002.

Lupia, Arthur, and Mathew D. McCubbins. *The Democratic Dilemma: Can Citizens Learn What They Need to Know?* New York: Cambridge University Press, 1998.

Macedo, Steven. *Democracy at Risk: How Political Choice Undermine Citizen Participation and What We Can Do About It.* Washington, DC: Brookings Institution Press, 2005.

Mattson, Kevin. *Creating a Democratic Republic: The Struggle for Urban Participatory Democracy during the Progressive Era.* University Park, PA: Pennsylvania State University Press, 1998.

McConnell, Grant. *Private Power & American Democracy.* New York: Alfred A. Knopf, 1966.

McGerr, Michael. *A Fierce Discontent: The Rise and Fall of the Progressive Movement in America, 1870–1920.* New York: Free Press, 2003.

Milkis, Sidney M. "Partisan Rancor and Representative Democracy." *The Chronicle of Higher Education* (March 2, 2007): B6.

Muhlberger, Peter. "Stealth Democracy: Authoritarianism, Parochial Citizens and Deliberation." Draft, published in the ACM International Conference Proceedings (2007). Available at http://portal.acm.org/dl.cfm (accessed April 13, 2008).

Navarro, Mireya. "Bricks, Mortar, and Coalition Building." In *How Race Is Lived in America: Pulling Together, Pulling Apart* by correspondents of *The New York Times*, introduction by Joseph Lelyveld. New York: Henry Holt and Company, 2001.

Nikulin, Dmitri. *On Dialogue.* Lanham, MD: Lexington Books, 2005.

Pateman, Carole. *Participation and Democratic Theory.* New York: Cambridge University Press, 1976.

Patterson, Thomas E. *Out of Order.* New York: Alfred A. Knopf, 1993.

Price, Vincent, Joseph N. Cappella, and Lilach Nir. "Does Disagreement Contribute to More Deliberative Opinion? *Political Communication* 19 (2002): 95–112.

Putnam, Robert D. *Bowling Alone: The Collapse and Revival of American Community.* New York, NY: Touchstone, 2000.

Ravitch, Diane. *The Language Police: How Pressure Groups Restrict What Students Learn.* New York: Random House, 2003.

Rosenberg, Shawn W. *The Not So Common Sense: Differences in How People Judge Social and Political Life.* New Haven, CT: Yale University Press, 2002.

Rothman, Stanley, and S. Robert Lichter. "Personality, Ideology and World View: A Comparison of Media and Business Elites." *British Journal of Political Science* 15(1) (January 1985): 29–49.

Rothman, Stanley, S. Robert Lichter, and Linda Lichter. *Elites in Conflict: Social Change in America Today.* Wesport, CT: Praeger, 1992.

Ryan, Mary P. *Civic Wars: Democracy and Public Life in the American City During the Nineteenth Century.* Berkeley, CA: University of California Press, 1998.

———. "Gender and Public Access." In *Habermas and the Public Sphere,* edited by Craig Calhoun. Cambridge, MA: MIT Press, 1992.

Sandel, Michael J. "The Politics of Public Identity," *The Hedgehog Review* 2(1) (Spring 2000): 72–88.

Schlesinger, Arthur M., Jr. *The Disuniting of America.* Revised edition. New York: W. W. Norton, 1992.

———. "Not Right, not Left, but a Vital Center: The Hope of the Future Lies in the Widening and Deepening of the Democratic Middle Ground." *The New York Times Magazine,* April 4, 1948, SM7. Available at http://www.nytimes.com/books/00/11/26/specials/schlesinger-centermag.html (accessed April 13, 2008).

Schudson, Michael. "Was There Ever a Public Sphere?" In *Habermas and the Public Sphere* edited by Craig Calhoun. Cambridge, MA: MIT Press, 1992.

Sennett, Richard. "The New Political Economy and Its Culture," *The Hedgehog Review* 2(1) (Spring 2000): 55–71.

Skocpol, Theda. *Diminished Democracy: From Membership to Management in American Civic Life*. Norman, OK: University of Oklahoma Press, 2003.

Sterngrass, Jon. *First Resorts: Pursuing Pleasure at Saratoga Springs, Newport & Coney Island*. Baltimore, MD: Johns Hopkins University Press, 2001.

Stevens, Edward. "Social Centers, Politics, and Social Efficiency in the Progressive Era." *History of Education Quarterly* 12(1) (Spring 1972): 16–33.

Sugrue, Thomas J. *The Origins of the Urban Crisis: Race and Inequality in Postwar Detroit*. Princeton, NJ: Princeton University Press, 1996.

Sunstein, Cass R. *Why Societies Need Dissent*. Cambridge, MA: Harvard University Press, 2003.

Tannen, Deborah. *The Argument Culture: Stopping America's War of Words*. New York: Ballantine Books, 1998.

Taylor, Charles (au.) and Amy C. Gutmann (ed.). *Multiculturalism and the "Politics of Recognition": An Essay*. Princeton, NJ: Princeton University Press, 1992.

Terkel, Studs. "C. P. Ellis." In *Race, Class, and Gender in the United States: An Integrated Study*, fifth edition, edited by S. Rothenberg. New York: Worth, 2001, 640–648.

Tetlock, Philip E. *Expert Political Judgment: How Good Is It? How Can We Know?* Princeton, NJ: Princeton University Press, 2005.

Warren, Mark. "Democratic Theory and Self-Transformation." *American Political Science Review* 86 (1992): 8–23.

———. "The Self in Discursive Democracy." In *The Cambridge Companion to Habermas* edited by Stephen K. White. New York: Cambridge University Press, 1995.

Watts, Mark D., David Domke, Dhavan V. Shah, and David P. Pan. "Elite Cues and Media Bias in Presidential Campaigns: Explaining Public Perceptions of a Liberal Press." *Communications Research* 26(2) (1999): 144–175.

Wilson, Carter A. *Racism: From Slavery to Advanced Capitalism*. Thousand Oaks, CA: Sage, 1996.

Winerip, Michael. "Why Harlem Drug Cops Don't Discuss Race." In *How Race Is Lived in America: Pulling Together, Pulling Apart* by correspondents of the New York Times, introduction by Joseph Lelyveld. New York: Henry Holt and Company, 2001.

Wolfe, Alan. *One Nation After All*. New York: Viking Press, 1998.

———. *The Transformation of American Religion: How We Actually Live Our Faith*. New York: Free Press, 2003.

Wolin, Sheldon. "Fugitive Democracy." In *Democracy and Difference: Contesting the Boundaries of the Political*, edited by Seyla Benhabib. Princeton, NJ: Princeton University Press, 1996.

———. *Presence of the Past: Essays on the State and the Constitution*. Baltimore, MD: Johns Hopkins University Press, 1989.

Yankelovich, Daniel. *The Magic of Dialogue: Transforming Conflict into Cooperation*. New York: Simon & Schuster, 1999.

Young, Iris Marion. *Inclusion and Democracy*. Oxford, UK: Oxford University Press, 2000.

Zakaria, Fareed. *The Future of Freedom: Illiberal Democracy at Home and Abroad*. New York: W. W. Norton & Company, 2004.

# Index

## About the Author

PHIL NEISSER is professor and chair of the Department of Politics at the State University of New York at Potsdam. He is a coeditor of *Tales of the State: Narrative in Contemporary U.S. Politics and Public Policy* and numerous articles critical of the idealization of centrist politics.